THE MEANING OF
THE DEATH OF GOD

THE MEANING

OF THE DEATH

OF GOD / Protestant,

Jewish and Catholic Scholars

Explore Atheistic Theology

Edited and with an Introduction by

BERNARD MURCHLAND

RANDOM HOUSE / NEW YORK

First Printing

© Copyright, 1967, by Bernard Murchland

All rights reserved under International and Pan-American Copyright Conventions. Published in New York by Random House, Inc., and simultaneously in Toronto, Canada, by Random House of Canada Limited.

Library of Congress Catalog Card Number: 67–12737

Manufactured in the United States of America by H. Wolff, New York. Design by Kenneth Miyamoto

ACKNOWLEDGMENTS

The editor wishes to thank the following for permission to reprint:

The Andover-Newton Quarterly (Newton Centre, Massachusetts: The Andover-Newton Theological School) for "The Future of God" by Roger Hazelton, January 1966;

The Canadian Journal of Theology (Toronto: Knox College) for "Religion *Post Mortem Dei*" by William Fennell, 1963 (9);

The Centennial Review (East Lansing: Michigan State University) for "From Crisis Theology to the Post-Modern World" by John B. Cobb, Jr., Spring 1964;

The Christian Century (The Christian Century Foundation) for "Apocalypse in a Casket" by Warren Moulton, "Deicide, Theothanatasia, or What Do You Mean?" by J. Robert Nelson, "False Prophets in the Secular City" by David Miller, and "Goodbye, Death of God!" by Larry Shiner, all Copyright 1965 by The Christian Century Foundation and reprinted by permission from the November 17, 1965, issue;

Christianity and Crisis (New York: The Union Theological Seminary) for "The Christian and the Atheist" by Michael Novak which appeared in shorter form in the March 21, 1966, issue;

Cross Currents (West Nyack, New York) for "Theology After the Death of God" by W. Richard Comstock, reprinted by permission from the Summer 1966 issue;

Dialog for "The Death of God" by Gabriel Vahanian, published in the Autumn 1962 issue as "Beyond the Death of God: the Need of Cultural Revolution."

The Journal of Bible and Religion (The American Academy of Religion) for "Variations on a Theme" by F. Thomas Trotter, which appeared in the January 1966 issue as "Variations on the 'death of God' Theme in recent Theology," Copyright 1966 by The American Academy of Religion;

Jubilee (New York) for "Is God Dead" by Robert Adolfs, July 1966;

Judaism (New York) for "God-Is-Dead Theology" by Eugene Borowitz, reprinted by permission from the Winter 1966 issue;

The National Catholic Reporter (Kansas City, Missouri) for "The Myth of God's Death" by John Dunne, May 25, 1966;

The Asbury Seminarian, vol. xx, no. 2, June 1966, pp. 40–76.

The Springfielder (Springfield, Illinois: Concordia Theological Seminary) for "A Critique of the Death of God Movement" by John Montgomery which appeared in the Spring 1966 issue as "A Philosophical-Theological Critique of the Death of God Movement";

Theology Today (Princeton, New Jersey) for "Taking the Death of God Seriously" by Emerson Shideler, July 1966; and for "What Does the Slogan Mean?" by Robert McAfee Brown which appeared in the July 1966 issue as a review of "The Gospel of Christian Atheism" by Thomas J. J. Altizer.

Contents

BERNARD MURCHLAND / Editor's Introduction: The Meaning of the Death of God

THE GODS have always suffered the vicissitudes of their creatures. The Judeo-Christian God would seem to share this fate. In an alienated age He becomes the alien God. When death dominates our consciousness, we can meaningfully speak of the death of God. The death of God, as Emerson Shideler argues, is to be taken seriously. The theme has gained wide publicity in our day. It has also, as the essays of this anthology eloquently testify, been the subject of mature cultural and theological reflection.

Clearly the critical mind is onto something important here. But what exactly? What sense are we to make out of the death-of-God theology? What does it tell us about religion, about society, about man himself? I think there is something fallacious in the inference that God is dead. Even as a metaphor it is lacking. But it does alert us to the indisputable fact that many men no longer detect anything of the Divine in their experience. As such the death-of-God movement is related to the phenomenon of contemporary atheism. Will Herberg rightly points out that the death of God theologians are really saying that God has no meaning or relevance for modern man.[1]* In a similar vein, Langdon Gilkey takes the first premise of the new theology to be "the unreality of God for our age; his absence from our current experience; the irrelevance and meaninglessness of all talk about him; the emptiness and actual harmfulness of any so-called relation to him; the impossibility of understanding our experience of evil if we try to believe in him." [2]

Naturally enough there is a good deal of reference to Nietzsche in the following essays. And that is as it should be. He, after all, has bequeathed us the best philosophical analysis and dramatic expression of the death of God. But Nietzsche not only perceived the death of God; he detected the whole crisis of Western culture—the yawning void of nihilism and the frightening necessity of transvaluating all values. For him the "death of God" was a diagnostic formula by means of which he pronounced judgment upon the alienated predicament of Western man. Nietzsche was the philosopher of alienation *par excellence*. Hegel had already diagnosed the malady of his age as "a severance of mind from world, soul from circumstance, human inwardness from external condition" [3] and defined the Alienated Soul as "the consciousness of self as a divided nature, a doubled and merely contradictory being." [4] Similarly, Nietzsche saw the most characteristic quality of modern man to be "the strange contrast between an inner life to which nothing outward corresponds and an outward existence unrelated to what is within." [5]

Consequently, I think we must read the death-of-God movement as a chapter in the larger history of alienation. It is difficult enough to trace the outlines of this history. There are those who believe that man has always been an alienated, divided creature. Tillich, for example, could write that the "state of our whole life is estrangement from others and ourselves, because we are estranged from the ground of our being, be-

* Notes appear at the end of each essay.

cause we are estranged from the origin and aim of our life." [6]
Even if that were the case, which I very much doubt,[7] it remains true that there is something distinct about our experience of alienation today. As Nathan Glazer wrote: "Alienation
expresses a unique facet of the crisis of our times: the widespread belief that there has been a revolutionary change in the
psychological condition of man, reflected in the individual's
feeling of isolation, homelessness, insecurity, restlessness and
anxiety." [8]

Our present state of alienation is widely enough docu-
mented. The difficulty is to determine its origins and development. What intellectual processes lie behind our present
impasse? I am inclined to see the origin of alienation as it is understood and experienced today in the late Middle Ages and
early Renaissance. I say this for three reasons. First of all the
nominalistic concern with singulars introduced a system wherein
the world is no longer seen as continuous but as disparate.[9] An
effort to factualize the world becomes a substitute for the more
comprehensive efforts of a Plato or an Aquinas. There is a connection between the "broken world" (Marcel) of today and
the rise of nominalism. Secondly, the transcendent world receded from the immediate range of men's interests. It became,
as H. Obermann points out in a perceptive essay, a kind of
"dome that shuts out the world of God's non-realized possibilities and provides room on the inside for man's own realm in
which he . . . thinks and acts." [10] This isolation introduces a
large measure of anxiety.[11] It is lonely under the dome.

Consequently, and this is my third reason, man's attention to
singulars is accompanied by an intensified consideration of
himself as an individual. Problems of the self and individuality
begin to emerge in a new way. As Oberman notes, the "autonomy of man—whether expressed as independence from nature,
cosmos, or God—makes of Nominalism and the early Renaissance parallel movements." [12] Cassirer concurs. All the intellectual currents that nourish the Renaissance, he says, flow into
the central problem of self-consciousness.[13] The American introduction to Jacob Burckhardt's *The Civilization of the Renaissance in Italy* offers a succinct summary of these trends:
"Western man has irrevocably been cast out—has cast himself

out—of a childlike world of enchantment and undividedness. Since the days of his exile (or was it withdrawal?) he has been wandering the world. Wherever he goes he is readily recognized since he bears a burden for everyone to see—the burden of selfhood. The ego is at once his sign of Cain and his crown of glory." [14]

The stage is now set for modern man's long, lonely odyssey.[15] Descartes articulated the dynamics of alienation when he introduced his method of doubt. The philosopher can no longer make a vote of confidence in reality. He must begin with the isolated reality of the extramundane Ego—*Cogito ergo sum*. Cartesian dualism marks the birth of modernism. Man is now discontinuous with nature and by the same token with himself. We had to wait until the nineteenth century to label the malady.[16] But that was a tardy diagnosis. The malady had long been present. Erwin Strauss has given us a useful analysis of the implications of Cartesian philosophy.[17] The use of the word *conscientia* in the sense of "consciousness" begins with him. It is cut off from the rest of reality. Since Descartes the soul and nature have had little to do with one another. Sensations do not tell us anything directly about the outside world. Nature belongs exclusively to *res extensa*, to be understood mathematically, abstractly. We know the world only indirectly by inference. We no longer experience the world as directly real (as, for example, a Giotto) or the body as immediate and revelatory of meaning (as, for example, a St. Francis). This, in starkest outline, is the problem we have been wrestling with ever since. In Strauss's own words: "The Cartesian dichotomy therefore not only separates mind from body but severs the experiencing creature from nature, the ego from the world, sensation from motion. It also separates one person from another one, *me* from *you*. The Cartesian ego, looking at the outside world, is in no contact, has no direct communication, with any alter ego. . . . Reality becomes a function of judgment." [18]

Viewed in this context, the death of God theology points ironically to man's lost world and his own consequent death. It is more a commentary upon the present predicament of man than upon God, and that is why the optimism sometimes predicated upon the slogan seems so very shallow.[19] Altizer's dialectical effort to recover the sacred by affirming the secular seems much more constructive. But he, like Cox and others, seems perplexed as to how we make such an affirmation. It will certainly have to be more than an approval of recent fads and fashions.

There is another irony in the death of God theology—its adamant dismissal of any form of transcendence. To be sure, the old supernatural world-view need not be maintained. But the minimal meaning that the doctrines of God and transcendence posit is a whole world, a whole self. To come down categorically on the side of immanence is to preclude the possibility of regaining our human world. It also ignores the projective and intentional nature of human knowledge. Amos Wilder has remarked that if we are to have any transcendence today, even Christian, it must be in and through the secular. That is very true. Transcendence is one of the categories through which we understand the secular, one of the necessary categories, I might add, an ingredient of wholeness. The Hebrews and Greeks knew this very well. The challenge would therefore seem to be to reconstruct the notion rather than abolish it. I consider the Whiteheadean efforts in this direction (Cobb, Hartshorne, etc.) very positive.

It is because we have become alienated from ourselves and our world that we have lost God. It is not likely that we will ever be able to speak of God in the old way. Perhaps, as has been suggested, we can get along without the word. But is it too much to hope that the experience of wholeness will be visited upon us once again?

Notes

1. Will Herberg, "The Death of God Theology," *National Review*, August 9, 1966, p. 771.

2. Langdon Gilkey, "Is God Dead?" *The Voice: Bulletin of Crozer Theological Seminary*, January 1965, p. 7.

3. Cf. Erich Heller, *The Artist's Journey Into the Interior*, p. 103.

4. G. Hegel, *The Phenomenology of Mind*, trans. J. B. Baillie, p. 251.

5. Quoted in Heller, *op. cit.*, p. 103. Other important nineteenth-century diognosticians of alienation would have to include Kierkegaard, Marx, Feuerbach, and, later on, Freud.

6. Paul Tillich, *Shaking the Foundations*, p. 160.

7. I am inclined to agree with Sterling Lamprecht: "The world may well be 'alien' to some purposes and congenial to others. But to speak of the world as 'alien' in some absolute sense is nonsense. . . . The ethical implications of a theory of an 'alien' world are that ideals are *a priori* in origin, that their validity does not depend upon their effectiveness in practice, and hence that they are not really the technique for the guidance of men living the good life" (*Naturalism and the Human Spirit*, p. 19).

8. Nathan Glazer, "The Alienation of Modern Man," *Commentary*, April 1947, p. 378. Cf. C. Wright Mills: "The advent of the alienated man and all the themes which lie behind his advent now affect the whole of our serious intellectual life and cause of immediate intellectual malaise. It is a major theme of the human condition in the contemporary epoch and of all studies worthy of the name"; also Erich Fromm: "Alienation as we find it in modern society is almost total"; and Erich Heller: "One of the distinctive symptoms of modern literature and thought is the consciousness of life's increasing depreciation."

9. A. Pegis, "Some Recent Interpretations of Ocham," *Speculum*, xxiii (1948), pp. 452–463; "Given that being is simple, or, if composite, constituted of really distinct parts; and given that in such a world there are no communities among things either absolutely or in fact—then, failing intuition, knowledge suffers from all the ways in which it does not answer to the pure singularity of things" (*ibid.*, p. 456).

10. H. Obermann, "Some Notes on the Theology of Nominalism with Attention to Its Relation to the Renaissance," *Harvard Theological Review*, LII, 1, January 1960 (53), p. 63.

11. *Ibid.*, p. 68: "In his loneliness Nominalistic man is anxious to keep close to the reality of the world around him, an anxiety quite naturally accompanied by the secularization of his interests . . . his newly won freedom gives him the heavy responsibility of guarding against hallucinations. He can no longer afford to keep his eyes constantly on his ultimate goal as did the Augustinian man, nor to trust his reason to the same extent as did the Thomistic man."

12. *Ibid.*, p. 70.

13. Cf. E. Cassirer, *The Individual and the Cosmos in Renaissance Philosophy*, p. 123.

14. B. Nelson and C. Trinkau, Introduction to *The Civilization of the Renaissance in Italy*.

15. J. S. Miller notes in *The Disappearance of God* that post-medieval literature records the gradual withdrawal of God from the world, and goes on: "Modern times begin when man confronts his isolation, his separation from everything outside himself. Modern thought has been increasingly dominated by the presupposition that each man is locked in the prison of his consciousness. From Montaigne to Descartes and Locke, on down through associationism, idealism, and romanticism to the phenomenology and existentialism of today, the assumption has been that man must start with the inner experience of the isolated self" (p. 187).

    Hannah Arendt makes a similar point in *The Human Condition:* "One of the most persistent trends in modern philosophy since Descartes and perhaps its most original contribution to philosophy has been an exclusive concern with the self, as distinguished from the soul or person or man in general, an attempt to reduce all experiences, with the world as well as with other human beings, to experiences between man and himself."

    Finally, David Bakan uses the term "epistemological loneliness" to describe Western man's experience of isolation from his world. He sees this isolation as stemming from the skepticism which we inherited from the British empiricists Locke, Berkeley, and Hume. He holds the specific error to be conceiving the thinker "as essentially alone rather than a member and participant of a thinking community" (cf. *Existence,* R. May, E. Angel, and H. Ellenberger, eds., p. 57).

16. It seems that the word alienation in its modern sense was first used by Calvin to describe the sinner's estrangement from God.

17. E. Strauss, "Aesthesiology and Hallucinations," in *Existence, op. cit.,* pp. 139–170.

18. *Ibid.,* pp. 141–142.

19. Cf. My review of Harvey Cox's *The Secular City* in *Worldview,* April, 1965.

THE MEANING OF
THE DEATH OF GOD

GABRIEL VAHANIAN / Beyond
the Death of God

The Need of Cultural Revolution

OVER A CENTURY AGO Kierkegaard wrote in *The Sickness Unto Death* that Christianity was "the fundamental misfortune of Christendom." In order to reach a correct diagnosis of the contemporary situation it is necessary to reverse the terms and declare that it is Christendom which is the fundamental misfortune of Christianity. For in the meantime, the transition into the post-Christian era has become an everyday reality, and the "death of God" is the cultural event by which modern man recognizes and admits this change.

The "death of God" is today Western man's "confession" (in the sense of the French "*aveu*"), just as the triune God was once the symbol which inaugurated and sustained the Christian era of Western culture. Certainly, this does not mean that God no longer is, or that one must leave him behind to till the earth or cultivate his garden because now one might take up resi-

(3)

dence on the moon. Nor does this mean simply that the previous era was theologically Christian and that ours is not. For we
all know that—theologically speaking—not even the Christian
era ever quite fully bloomed into a golden age, or else Kierkegaard would not have come to his conclusion.

We must realize, however, that in an earlier period Christianity bodied forth into "the historic reality of Christian culture"
(to borrow the title of the poor book which Professor Dawson
has written on this subject). *Culturally*, therefore, there was a
Christian era. It may not have been perfect, especially from the
theological point of view. It may even have rested on unsound
scientific and philosophical premises. But its culture corre-
sponded with its theology; and more significantly this correspondence, this congruence between theology and culture,
provided man with a key to the understanding of his being and
gave a motif to his existence, to his work, to his art and to his
thinking. He understood in order to believe and he believed in
order to understand. Knowledge was an act of faith and the
business of existing was also an act of faith. Not only from the
theological or philosophical point of view, but even from a cultural perspective the reality of God was taken for granted.

No doubt it will be objected that I am embellishing the past.
Perhaps. It may even be that our theological systems are today
more accurately Biblical than those of scholasticism, whether
Roman Catholic or Protestant. Certainly we have developed a
higher esteem for the dignity of man than was the case formerly. We have grown more refined—in our instruments of
civilization as well as of cruelty. We have domesticated the
earth and we look forward to annexing the moon. But the crux
of the matter lies elsewhere.

Once a no man's land, our world has not become a no God's
land. What this means is that the world has been deprived of its
sacramental significance; human existence has lost its transcendental dimension; and shorn of its *sym-bolic* (*i.e.*, covenantal)
significance, language still performs a duty as a means of communication, but it has been neutralized insofar as communication does not necessarily entail or presuppose communion. In
fact human existence has been neutralized. We live in the latest
fashion of the third person, in the world of the plural, neutral,

anonymous "they" of the crowd. In other words, Christendom (and what else can this term mean today than Western culture?) is the great misfortune of Christianity. The situation would not be quite so ironical were it not that to Christianity itself we owe this Western culture which has changed our world into a no God's land. Post-Christian man is the child of Christian man.

No doubt some definitions are needed here. What does one mean by "Christian man" and by "post-Christian man"? Let us begin with an indirect answer. When the Renaissance humanists revived Greek culture, it evidently represented to them something other than what it actually was, if only because their world-view had been affected by the Christian tradition. Even the Greek tragedies have a different meaning for us, for the simple reason that our sense of the tragic is not undergirded by the same beliefs: We do not believe in the Greek gods. Or, if one prefers, we do not have the same presuppositions, we do not make the same assumptions and we do not enter their world with the same world-view.

Similar observations can be made about our approach to other ancient religions or to contemporary non-Western religions. The point I am trying to make is this: post-Christian man looks at the religion of Christian man in such a way that the former's point of view is radically different from that of the latter. Not that, obviously, Christian man was less in need of God's grace than is post-Christian man. Theologically, there is neither Jew nor Greek, neither Christian man nor post-Christian man. But culturally there is. The "death of God" is the continental divide which separates Christian man from post-Christian man. Needless to say—though one should know why —the "death of God" is a cultural phenomenon. God is not necessary, his reality cannot be taken for granted. Just look at what has happened to apologetics. What role can it play today in confronting the non-Christian? None, if the best we can do is to compare religions. And perhaps this is for the better if it forces theology to become honest again and to content itself simply with being Kerygmatic. But apologetics itself at best helps us to make converts from other Christian denominations. Something then has happened which separates Christian man from post-Christian man and, one must add, something of an entirely different nature from what distinguishes medieval man from modern man, something more like what separates pre-Christian man from Christian man. Indeed, like the early Christian the post-Christian is ushering in a new era, except that the charge of atheism which was leveled at the former is now welcomed by the latter. Post-Christian man even claims it; it is his existential presupposition, the act of his emancipation.

It is important to note that post-Christian man is neither anti-Christian nor non-Christian. For the prefix "post" implies in the last analysis that even the Western man who today has faith in the transcending presence of God's reality as manifested in the Christ-event, that man is post-Christian nonetheless. Or he may be a vestigial Christian by still clinging to superannuated forms of belief expressive of the cultural framework with which they once were congruous, even while otherwise sharing in the post-Christian mentality of his contemporaries.

Be that as it may, the fact is that something has happened in the consciousness of Western man. This event may not have been recorded by theologians. But it has shaken the vision of poets and novelists, of artists and playwrights. On the one hand, the self-invalidation of the Christian tradition has been hailed as at last enabling man both to face his condition and its attendant obligation to greatness and to assume the ambiguities of his self-understanding. On the other hand, the creative imagination has been frustrated or even orphaned by the secularism which has resulted from the expropriation of the Christian tradition. Camus, St. John Perse, and Beckett are examples of the first case. In the second case, one can cite Joyce, Eliot, Faulkner, and Ingmar Bergman. The following lines from T. S. Eliot's "The Rock" quite appropriately describe this situation in general:

> But it seems that something has happened that has never
> happened before: though we know not just when,
> or why, or how, or where.
> Men have left GOD not for other gods, they say, but for
> no god; and this has never happened before.
> That men both deny gods and worship gods, professing
> first Reason,

And then Money, and Power and what they call Life,
    or Race, or Dialectic.
The Church disowned, the tower overthrown, the bells
    upturned, what have we to do
But stand with empty hands and palms turned upwards
In an age which advances progressively backwards?

In some ways the crisis of Western culture is as threatening
and paralyzing as the predicament of the Israelites taken into
exile in Babylon. The passage from "The Rock" is an echo of
the psalmist's lament:

> By the waters of Babylon,
>   there we sat down and wept,
>   when we remembered Zion.
> On the willows there
>   we hung up our lyres
> For there our captors
>   required of us songs,
> And our tormentors, mirth, saying,
>   "Sing us one of the songs of Zion!"
> How shall we sing the LORD'S song
>   in a foreign land:

The Israelites at least had the advantage of being exiles in a
foreign land. We do not. The moment might come when they
will return. But we are exiles in our own land and we cannot
turn the clocks backward; we cannot reverse either time or our
tradition. Our alienation is not only religious, but also cultural.
It has placed us in the same situation as Sartre when he summed
up his judgment of Faulkner's *The Sound and the Fury:* "I like
his art, but I don't believe in his metaphysics." Likewise, we
have severed Western culture from its metaphysical foundations, from its theological roots and from its sacramental significance, although we still like its art and even more its technology (by which we have impressed the whole world from
Ghana to China, including India, for whom Western man must
be synonymous with technological man). Take Florence in
Italy. Who does not love it? We all do, I suspect, slightly because it has become a drive-in museum. But the fate of Western culture and its Christian tradition is not so glorious. It is

that of an average museum, loudly exhibiting this or that piece
to attract the post-Christian tourist.

What I have endeavored to show is that the drive toward
radical immanentism is the sign of our time. Neither a new
reformation nor any kind of religious revival will suffice to
cope with the exigencies imposed by such a context, regardless
of the help—if any—offered by the debilitated institutions
which have survived the radical monotheism of the West. I am
afraid that theologians have not considered this handicap with
sufficient attention and indeed have not even admitted to any
sort of handicap. But today a Christ without culture is just as
much a chimera as a Christ of culture.

In this light the difficulty in communicating the gospel today
does assume the proportions of an insuperable obstacle. That
Bultmann's theology has attempted to solve this problem is itself a sign of the seriousness of the obstacle. Since I have discussed the theological aspects of this problem in my book *The
Death of God*, I should like here to present briefly the cultural
aspect.

No matter how syncretistic the religiosity of the Mediterra-
nean world was in the first century, still it offered certain affinities with the vocabulary of the gospel. One must make this
statement not only in spite of, but precisely because of, the fact
that the gospel was a scandal to the Jew and foolishness to the
Greek. Today, it is neither a scandal nor foolishness.

Those who have seen "*La Dolce Vita*" will remember the
first scenes of that film, where the huge crucifix hanging from
a helicopter hovers incongruously over the utter indifference
of the sunbathers on the roofs. In other words, the Christian
symbols no longer make any claim upon us as they did even
upon those who thought they were scandalous or foolish.

In *The Art of T. S. Eliot* Helen Gardner reports an incident
which eloquently expresses modern man's immunity to the
power of the Christian symbols. She writes: "The most remarkable demonstration I have had of this failure in communication in 'Ash Wednesday' was at a tea-party, when a colleague said that the repetition at the close of Section III always
suggested to him a drunk man coming home late at night and
muttering to himself as he stumbled up the stairs. When some-

one present objected: 'But it is a phrase from the Canon of the Mass,' he replied: 'How am I supposed to know that; it doesn't mean anything to me.' When someone else added: 'But surely you recognize it as coming from the New Testament?,' he answered: 'Well, lots of phrases come out of the Bible ultimately.'" And, as a literary critic, Helen Gardner concludes with this remark: "Even for those who accept the Christian Faith some of the phrases in 'Ash Wednesday' have less than their full effect, for to feel their force one needs to be accustomed to use them in the same context as the poet."

To be sure, it is not merely a question of different beliefs. Nor is it only a question of the substitution of a scientific, technological world-view for a mythological one, although this substitution has had something to do with the transition from radical monotheism to radical immanentism. The malaise lies deeper in the desuetude of the Christian tradition and the consequent revision of the presuppositions on which our self-understanding and our world-view were based. "The trouble of the modern age," writes T. S. Eliot in *On Poetry and Poets*, "is not merely the inability to believe certain things about God and man which our forefathers believed."

Indeed, some of our assumptions are just as preposterous and superstitious, or just as irrational and absurd. But the trouble is "the inability to *feel* towards *God* and man as they did." In other words, the core of the gospel and the Christian symbols are contemporaneous with a definite historical situation. (The Christian way and the Western man's way are synonymous for many an African nationalist.) On the other hand, the inaccessibility of the gospel and the Christian symbols will not diminish if we simply should identify ours with the historical situation into which they were born. (The Lord's Supper thus becomes magic, or merely a "symbol"—in the wrong sense of the term —depending on whether such an identification is intended or not.) One might as well, then, label the Christian tradition as the imaginary and oral museum of Christian antiquities. Just this is what happens in *Waiting for Godot:* "Do you remember the Gospels?" To which is answered: "I remember the maps of the Holy Land. Coloured they were. Very pretty . . . that's where we'll go for our honeymoon."

But if the Christian symbols have thus lost their claim upon man's consciousness and their power to command his mode of being, it is not modern man in his *present* cultural context who will restore these to them. His inaptitude for the reality of God's transcending presence would prevent him from that in the first place. Like Weber, who complained about it occasionally, modern man's soul is *"religiös unmusikalisch."* It is not attuned to the Divine. Sign of progress? . . . or of progressive advance backwards? The same event can present both faces. "The evolution of mankind toward the rationality of positive science was for Comte a distinctly progressive development," writes Eric Voegelin in *The New Science of Politics;* but "for Weber it was a process of disenchantment (*Entzauberung*) and de-divinization (*Entgöttlichung*) of the world." And, recovering from our disenchantment, there is only one thing for us to do—"to recognize that the world has grown godless" (Jaspers).

Now, the significant thing is that this disenchantment is twofold. On the one hand, it has been a disenchantment with religion or the counterfeit of it (as in *The Scarlet Letter*). As Walter Stace has pointed out, modern skepticism was not so much caused by the scientific revolution as by a latent readiness to forsake the Christian tradition. And, on the other hand, there has also been a disenchantment with science (as in *The Birthmark* by Hawthorne). The signs of it are perhaps less obvious, but they become real now and then when the prospects of total annihilation face us threateningly.

The heart of the matter is this. Whether we like it or not, it is not possible to transplant a tropical tree in a northern climate and hope that it will grow—unless nature should change its course. This applies not only to vegetation but also to the Tree of the Cross as well as to all the other symbols of the Christian tradition. The plain fact is that our culture has grown cold to the symbols of the gospel. And in this respect also one can only hope that this culture might change its course.

After all, this has happened before. It was by becoming non-Jewish that the gospel entered the Hellenistic world. And thus Christianity spread from one Greek city to another—thanks to its foothold in Hellenistic culture—until the promulgation of

the Edict of Toleration which ushered in the Constantinian era
and Christianity gradually became the official religion of the
empire.

What is needed, then, is not so much a theological reformation as a cultural revolution.

Every culture is undergirded by a substratum of religiosity.
Although necessary as a cultural accessory, this religiosity is
not essential. What is happening now is that the religiosity of
Western culture is expiring and at last appears as what it truly
is, namely, the paraphernalia of faith in God. These paraphernalia are typically Western and they even more inextricably
show their Western figure in contact with non-Western religi-
osities or in the light of the ambiguous religiosity which is the
lot of every man and on which the triumph of Christianity had
put a damper.

In other words, we have domesticated the universe, or so we
think, but we have lost the cipher of its symbols; we have estranged ourselves from it. We have "desacralized" the world,
forgetting that ultimately culture is a consecration of the
world. Accordingly, a transfiguration of culture is the most
urgent task of the present day. But this is a cultural task; it
cannot be the result of any revival. To this task we are all obli-
gated. It is the cultural obligation of post-Christian man, be he
theologian or not, Christian or not. Indeed, Western culture is
already groping beyond its own devaluation of its symbols for
a new dialect, for a new language. "It is the same epoch,"
writes Paul Ricoeur, "which holds in reserve both the possibility of emptying its language by radically formalizing it and
the possibility of filling it anew by recovering the fullest and
weightiest meanings most closely bound to man by the presence of the sacred." Or, in the words of the psalmist:

> Whither shall I go from thy Spirit?
>   Or wither shall I flee from thy presence?
> If I ascend to heaven, thou art there!
>   If I make my bed in Sheol, thou art there!

To conclude, the Christian era has bequeathed us the "death
of God," but not without teaching us a lesson. God is not necessary. That is to say, he cannot be taken for granted. He can-

not be used merely as a hypothesis, whether epistemological, scientific, or existential, unless we should draw the degrading conclusion that "God is reasons." But if we cannot any longer assume that God is, we may once again realize that he *must* be. God is not necessary, but he is inevitable. He is wholly other and wholly present. Faith in him, the conversion of our human reality culturally and existentially, is the demand he still makes upon us, the choice he confronts us with. "But when the Son of Man comes, will he find faith on earth?"

F. THOMAS TROTTER / Variations on the "Death of God" Theme in Recent Theology

THE EXPRESSION "the death of God" is now well established in the theological vocabulary. Widespread use in publication points to the popularity if not the precise definition of the term. Bishop J. A. T. Robinson's *Honest to God* [1] has brought the theme into the busy pastor's study and even into the mass-media periodicals. As an expression, the "death of God" is very much alive.

In a time of widespread "religiosity," the possibility of serious discussion of the theme is hampered by lack of precision in definition. One observes both panic in the face of "atheism" on the part of defenders of orthodoxy, and uncritical enthusiasm for the expression on the part of dilettanti. Forensic alarms from the former and superficial slogans from the latter serve only to obscure the truly serious issues in the new situation in theology.

(13)

The variations on the theme of the "death of God"—absence, disappearance, silence, withdrawal, eclipse—indicate the particular character of the theological problem but also reveal the difficulty in defining exactly what the Nietzschean expression means in contemporary theological vocabulary. This article will note briefly the historical situation which produced the expression, then indicate three basic variations on the theme in Sartre, Heidegger, and Buber, and finally illustrate how five young American theologians, Vahanian, Altizer, Hamilton, Van Buren, and Cobb, deal with the expression.

I

The striking—and problematic—shape of the term belongs, of course, to Nietzsche, who gave extended expression to the phrase. Contemporary usage is certainly attributable to him, although Buber notes that the term had been employed by Hegel as early as 1802.[2] The content of the "death of God" expression, however, is the religious and philosophical heritage of three hundred years of Western thought from Copernicus to Nietzsche. This period saw the great confessional debates, the rise of rationalism and pietism, and the general erosion of classical doctrinal theology. It has been suggested that Western thought had engaged itself since the seventeenth century in either "out-flanking" or "attacking" God.[3] The former mood reached its fullest expression in the French encyclopedists while the latter found its final shape in Nietzsche.

The debate accelerated and reached its climax in the nineteenth century. The rationalistic atheism of the eighteenth century became the polemical atheism of the nineteenth. Kierkegaard ("faith as subjectivity"), Dostoyevsky ("faith as unbelief"), Feuerbach ("faith as appetite"), and Strauss ("faith as obsolete") all experimented with theological atheism. Melville in America, Browning in England, and Baudelaire in France explored facets of the "death of God" in literary form. J. Hillis Miller, in a useful study, has identified five responses to the theme in nineteenth-century English literature: humanism, perspectivism, nihilism, pious acceptance, and romanticism.[4] The pervasiveness of the problem of unbelief in the nineteenth century is illustrated by Margaret Maison in her study of Victorian religion. "Never has any age in history produced such a detailed literature of lost faith, or so many great men and women of religious temperament standing outside organized religion."[5] Miss Maison is of the opinion that it would be instructive to compile a list of eminent Victorians who lost their faith in the fray, and she does offer a list of those who were destined for careers in the church but renounced them. The list includes Carlyle, Clough, Ruskin, Pater, Hardy, Burne-Jones, Tennyson, Froude, and even Darwin.[6]

Surveying nineteenth-century literature from the vantage point of the mid-twentieth century, one wonders how this inexorable erosion of faith could have progressed so far without widespread notice. Carl Becker, in a fortunate metaphor, suggests that "it was as if a rumor, started no one knew when, had at last become too insistent to be longer disregarded: the rumor that God, having departed secretly in the night, was about to cross the frontiers of the known world and leave mankind in the lurch. What we have to realize is that in those years God was on trial."[7]

If God was on trial, it was Nietzsche who announced that sentence had been passed. "God is dead. God remains dead. And we have killed him. How shall we, the murderers of all murderers, comfort ourselves? What was holiest and most powerful of all that the world has yet owned has bled to death under our knives."[8] This announcement gave vividness to the spiritual crisis of Western thought. The issue was the erosion and bankruptcy of religious sensitivity. Among Nietzsche's powerful images is that of the old saint digging for roots in the forest while Zarathustra brings fire down from the mountain. "Can it be possible? This old Saint in his forest has not yet heard the news that *God* is *dead?*"

Kirillov, in *The Possessed*, suggests that history may be divided into two periods: from the gorilla to the annihilation of God and from the annihilation of God to the transformation of man.[9] Like Dostoyevsky, whose heroes sought a new man-Godhood, Nietzsche also proclaimed a new anthropology. With the death of God, Nietzsche announced that man was freed from superstition and the bonds of slavery to divine tyr-

anny, and would now be able to find joyful release in his human fulfillment. God is an otiose hypothesis, as Laplace was
reported to have explained to Napoleon. God's place will remain empty, man will not be God, but he will be Superman:
"Can you create a god?—Then be silent about all gods! But
you could create the Superman. Perhaps you yourselves cannot, my brothers! But you can recreate yourselves to be the
fathers and forefathers of the Superman: let that be your best
creation!" [10] The Nietzschean proclamation is primarily an announcement of the death of metaphysics or the death of revelation. The Superman functions out of the subjective rather than
the suprasensory realm of divine existence. What has died is
the "reality" of an order of existence that is "other" than self-
perception and subjective appropriation. A new anthropology
is the only possible positive response to the collapse of metaphysics. As Langan notes, "the divine *fiat* has given place to a
new scepter wielded by man: *die Technik*." [11]

Martin Buber, summarizing the impact of Nietzsche, notes
that the "death of God" means "only that man has become
incapable of apprehending a reality absolutely independent of
himself and of having a relation with it—incapable, moreover,
of imaginatively perceiving this reality and representing it in
images, since it eludes direct contemplation." [12] As such, the
crisis of faith in Western culture is indeed deep and decisive
for faith. Philosophy, theology, and the arts in our time remain
Nietzschean in this sense. The problem is one of "digging out
of the Nietzschean ruins," as William Barrett has suggested. [13]

II

To "fill the horizon that has been declared empty" is the way
Buber has defined the task of philosophy and religion since
Nietzsche. Three post-Nietzschean proposals may be viewed as
major types of "death of God" exposition. The theme may be
illustrated by Jean-Paul Sartre ("God is dead"), Martin Heidegger ("God is absent"), and Martin Buber ("God is in
eclipse"). Each illustrates an emphasis latent in Nietzsche but
in a manner somewhat different from the nuances of the

others. Together they illustrate the fact that unity in definition
of the term "death of God" is quite problematic.

1. *"God is dead."* Sartre describes his system as an "attempt
to draw all the consequences of a coherent atheistic position."
The proclamation is to be understood literally. In fact Sartre,
in a rather crude phrase, has suggested that God "spoke to us
and now is silent, all that we touch now is his corpse." [14] It may
be distressing that God does not exist, because all possibility of
finding values in a heaven of ideas disappears along with God.
"Nausea," the vivid symbol of anxiety in the face of awareness
of the collapse of value structures, takes the place of joy and
delight in contemplation of God. With the "death of God," no
longer are there metaphysical or theological supports for moral
action. Man is thrust into his selfhood and loneliness to act responsibly—to be, in short, a man.

2. *"God is absent."* Heidegger rejects the "coherent atheism" of Sartre and remarks that his own thought "can no more
be theistic than it can be atheistic." [15] The "death of God" for
Heidegger is awareness of God's absence from the world. The
question of the possibility of God is simply no longer posed for
man. Unlike Sartre, for whom the existence of God is a matter
of indifference, Heidegger argues from the limitations of human thought. He has demonstrated his profound respect for
the problem of God by insisting that our traditional conceptual
tools are inadequate for the theological task. He turns to the
poet Hölderlin for insight and may be himself identified with
the position he attributes to the poet who stands "in the no-
more of the departed gods and the not-yet of the coming"
God.[16]

James M. Robinson and John B. Cobb, Jr., have introduced
the notion of the "later Heidegger" in a way which suggests
that the philosopher is moving in the direction of a more articulate theistic position. But this "movement" is based fundamentally upon the assumption that theology needs a more adequate
category than metaphysics. To that extent, Heidegger shares
with Sartre the general existentialist posture.

3. *"God is in eclipse."* Martin Buber shows some affinities
with Heidegger's emphases, particularly in his agreeing that

man must practice "openness" and "readiness" to Being. He rejects the notion that one can adequately account for the nihilistic character of our time by observing the changes that have taken place in man's spirit. He also counters Heidegger's skepticism regarding the "suprasensory" world. God is not dead in the literal sense as in Sartre, nor is he absent merely because conceptual tools are inadequate or corroded as in Heidegger. Man cannot unveil the mystery but rather he must submit himself to "the effective reality of transcendence as such." An eclipse, Buber reminds us, is something that occurs between the sun and our eyes, not in the sun itself.[17] For Buber, the "death of God" is an unfortunate phrase, "eclipse" being a more adequate term. However, he agrees with Sartre and Heidegger in the recognition of a "religious need" in modern man. Buber argues that the problem is much deeper than one of dismissing "religious" needs; it lies in the possibility that something is inherent in human existence which cannot be dismissed. The response of Buber is to shift the Sartrian "subject-object" dialectic to the Biblical "I-Thou" relation:

> God can never become an object for me; I can attain no other relation to Him than that of the I to its eternal Thou, that of the Thou to its eternal I. But if man is no longer able to attain this relation, if God is silent toward him and he toward God, then something has taken place, not in human subjectivity but in Being itself. It would be worthier not to explain it to oneself in sensational and incompetent sayings, such as that of the "death" of God, but to endure it as it is and at the same time to move existentially toward a new happening, toward that event in which the word between heaven and earth will again be heard.[18]

III

The impact of the "death of God" philosophy upon twentieth-century literature does not need extensive elaboration. Rainer Maria Rilke, probably the most consistent "Nietzschean" poet, echoes the theme throughout his work. "God is the no longer sayable," writes Rilke, "and his attributes fly back into his Creation." Franz Kafka, Albert Camus, Graham Greene, Marcel Proust, André Gide, William Faulkner, Thomas Mann—all witness to a world in which God is "silent," "absent," "disappeared," or "dead." The attraction of the theme to the novelist is one of the striking features of the whole movement. It is in the mood of the time, the spiritual malaise of the culture, that the most vivid experience of God's absence is apparent.

In this "new situation" has appeared a number of thoughtful works by younger theologians. By and large, these scholars are students of scholars who themselves sought to frame their work within the context of the new cultural situation: Barth, Tillich, Bultmann, Bonhoeffer, Eliade, and Whitehead. Each of the younger scholars, while indebted to the previous generation, represents new and sometimes radical directions. The following are representative of the varieties of recent post-Nietzschean theologizing. Although they certainly do not exhaust the list of outstanding younger theological writers, they represent five fairly distinct reactions to the new situation in theology.

1. *The New Iconoclasm.* Gabriel Vahanian, whose *Death of God: The Culture of Our Post-Christian Era*[19] is an attempt to give systematic expression to the "death of God" idea in contemporary culture, attacks the "idols" of religiosity. "To speak of the death of God means . . . that finally at the end of the Christian phase of Western culture, the reality of the living God is freed from the cultural concepts and other institutions which attempt to objectify and domesticate it. The death of God marks the end of Christian culture and, especially, of its attempt to assimilate *the other God*, the living God of whom our religion as well as our diffuse religiosity is a desperate caricature." [20] Vahanian is an iconoclast in the same sense that Kierkegaard and Nietzsche were attackers of the complacency of the church. Like his mentor, Karl Barth, Vahanian attacks "religiosity," "existentialism," and "immanentalism" and proposes restoration of the Barthian accent upon transcendence.

2. *The New Immanentalism.* Thomas J. J. Altizer is a student of Joachim Wach and Mircea Eliade, the great historians of religion. Altizer emphasizes the dialectical accents of Nietzsche's doctrine of Eternal Recurrence. The proclamation of the death of God is also the announcement of the possibility of human existence. "A No-Saying to God (the transcendence of

Sein) makes possible a Yes-saying to human existence (*Dasein*, total existence in the *here* and *now*). Absolute transcendence is transformed into absolute immanence." [21] Altizer calls for a "genuinely dialectic" theology that refuses to be gnostic because of its affirmation of the present and likewise refuses to be dogmatic because of its negation of the non-dialectical past. "If theology is to transcend itself it must negate itself, for theology can be reborn only through the death of Christendom, which finally means the death of the Christian God, the God who is the transcendence of Being." [22] Altizer argues that Christendom understood the Incarnation as a non-dialectical (or partial) union of flesh and spirit, time and eternity. The result was an autonomous history. This inevitably led to the "death of God" understood as the willing transformation of the sacred into the profane, the non-dialectical separation of man from meaningful existence. The problem for theology, then, is the recovery of a truly dialectical faith in which the sacred and the profane are not separated and in which authentic existence is possible.

3. *The New Ethics.* William Hamilton's debt to Dietrich Bonhoeffer is evident throughout his work. His is a "world come of age" and he takes as his theological task to speak to thoughtful Christians who are "trying to believe in a time of the death of God." The "Augustinian-Reformed" picture of a God of transcendence is problematic to modern man. Not only have the idols or the falsely objectivized idea of God died, in Hamilton's view; there is also the "death in us of any power to affirm the traditional images of God." [23] This strangely poignant and pathetic posture draws from Hamilton a starkly limited theological statement: God "seems to have withdrawn from the world and its sufferings, and this leads us to accuse him of either irrelevance or cruelty. But in another sense, he is experienced as a pressure and a wounding from which we would love to be free. For many of us who call ourselves Christians, therefore, believing in the time of the 'death of God' means that he is there when we do not want him, in ways we do not want him, and he is not there when we do want him." [24] The "pressure" we feel is that which calls us to responsible, humble, neighborly existence in a world come of age. Theology essentially is an acknowledgment of Jesus' lordship over

the world as a lordship of humiliation (our present existence) and a lordship of victory (our hope). The Christian's religious stance is primarily an extension of his sense for the humiliated and victorious Lord who alone survives the death of God.

4. *The New Christology.* Paul van Buren's study, *The Secular Meaning of the Gospel*,[25] also acknowledges the "this-worldly" aspect of the gospel. Like Hamilton, van Buren shares the modern temper which assumes the inadequacy of theological language. Whereas Hamilton seems to return to the barest statement of the meaningful ethic of Jesus, van Buren proposes to attack the problem of theological language by bringing the latter to terms with other modes of contemporary thinking, particularly linguistic analysis. "Linguistic analysis exposes the function of language in just those areas on which modern theology seeks to shed light: the world in which the 'average' Christian finds himself." [26] In effect, van Buren reduces Christian faith to historical and ethical dimensions. To critics who would ask for more, he responds: "What more?" Rejecting both the theological right with its emphasis upon the concrete event in Jesus Christ and the theological left with its emphasis upon analogy, van Buren proposes a theology in which the history of Jesus of Nazareth is the central interpretation and in which the relationship between faith and Jesus must lie in Easter.

5. *The New Metaphysics.* John B. Cobb, Jr., while clearly recognizing the shape of the current situation in theology, rejects the anti-metaphysical trend of most of the "death of God" exposition. He points out that many of the alternatives amidst the passing of crisis theology appear to "return to that relativistic sea from which crisis theology seemed briefly to save us." [27] Noting that much contemporary theology, and indeed contemporary self-consciousness, assumes the problematic character of the objective realm, Cobb correctly reminds us that we do not in fact enjoy even subjective certainty. If we did, the recognition of objective certainty would not be such a serious question. Cobb insists that the serious task before theology is therefore the "question of objective warrant" which "can no longer be pushed aside." [28] He turns to Alfred North Whitehead's "new world": "Whitehead's earlier work reflects

the death of God at least by its silence. But it gradually became clear as his philosophical speculations broadened that the philosophical reasons for the death of God were repudiated by him. Hence once again the questions of being and becoming emerged in his thought in such a way as to cry out for belief in God." [29] Thus Cobb, in distinction from the other thinkers referred to, is seriously in search of a new "Christian natural theology" on Whiteheadian presuppositions. Speaking for himself and a whole generation of younger theologians, Cobb urges serious attention to theological problems: "In our day we must run fast if we would stand still, and faster still if we would catch up. We can only hope that we will be granted both time and courage." [30]

IV

The sense of the "death of God" is a pervasive mood in contemporary thought, and this, inevitably, is the context in which theology exists and works. In the recognition of the seriousness of this spiritual crisis in Western culture lies the hope for Christian thought and experience. To dismiss the problem of the "death of God" as irrelevant or academic would be to fly in the face of the vast secular witness to the withdrawal of the reality of God from contemporary experience. On the other hand, to suggest, as some do, that discussion of this situation obscures the Christian sense of life, is to be equally overzealous in quest of a pattern.

The "death of God" image points to a "style" in contemporary theology and philosophy that is usually anti-metaphysical, earnestly moral, and hopefully secular. The varieties of uses of the term are apparent. But the expression reveals an indisputable fact. What was a powerful metaphor in the hands of Nietzsche has become in our time a rallying slogan for the widespread restlessness regarding traditional ways of speaking about the God who is no longer apprehended in meaningful ways. Truly ours is a world in which truth and reality seem to have collapsed into relativity. The "death of God," despite the speculations of Nietzsche and Dostoyevsky, has ushered in, not the age of man, but rather the age of anxiety, alienation, irrationalism, and boredom. Here is, in truth, the "death of man" as a self-conscious and responsible individual.

Recognition of this crisis of faith has led theologians to use the striking expression of Nietzsche as an announcement of a situation to which they must address themselves. But a proclamation is at best a provisional or propaedeutic gesture. There are signs that the stimulus of the Nietzschean tradition will create a "new breed" of Christian theologian who will heed Cobb's plea "to reach out for a novelty that disdains all appeal to the authority of the past and dares to think creatively and constructively in the present." [31]

Notes

1. J. A. T. Robinson, *Honest to God* (Philadelphia: Westminster Press, 1963).

2. Martin Buber, *Eclipse of God* (New York and Evanston, Ill.: Harper and Row, 1952), p. 20.

3. Cf. Franklin Baumer, *Religion and the Rise of Skepticism* (New York: Harcourt, Brace and World, 1960).

4. J. Hillis Miller, *The Disappearance of God* (Cambridge, Mass.: Harvard University Press, 1964), p. 13.

5. Margaret Maison, *The Victorian Vision* (New York: Sheed and Ward, 1963), p. 209.

6. *Ibid.*, p. 210.

7. Carl Becker, *The Heavenly City of the Eighteenth-Century Philosophers* (New Haven: Yale University Press, 1932), p. 73.

8. Friedrich Nietzsche, "The Gay Science," in *Existentialism from Dostoyevsky to Sartre*, ed. Walter Kaufmann (New York: Meridian, 1956), p. 105.

9. Fyodor Dostoyevsky, *The Possessed* (New York: Dell, 1961), p. 133.

10. Nietzsche, *Thus Spoke Zarathustra* (New York: Henry Regnery, 1957), p. 97.

11. Thomas Langan, *The Meaning of Heidegger* (New York: Columbia University Press, 1959), p. 191.

12. Buber, *op. cit.*, p. 14.

13. Cf. William Barrett, *Irrational Man* (Garden City: Doubleday, 1958), p. 205.

14. Quoted by James Eadie, "The Absence of God," in *Christianity and Existentialism*, ed. John Wild (Evanston, Ill.: Northwestern University Press, 1963), p. 137.

15. *Ibid.*, p. 121.

16. Martin Heidegger, *Erläuterungen zu Hölderlins Dichtung*, 2d ed., p. 44, quoted by James M. Robinson, *The Later Heidegger and Theology* (New York and Evanston, Ill.: Harper and Row, 1963), p. 14.

17. Cf. Buber, *op. cit.*, p. 23.

18. *Ibid.*, p. 68.

19. Gabriel Vahanian, *The Death of God: The Culture of our Post-Christian Era* (New York: George Braziller, 1961).

20. Gabriel Vahanian, "The Future of Christianity in a Post-Christian Era," *The Centennial Review*, VIII, 2 (Spring 1964), 161.

21. Thomas J. J. Altizer, "Theology and the Death of God," *The Centennial Review*, VIII, 2 (Spring 1964), 132.

22. *Ibid.*, p. 145.

23. William Hamilton, *The New Essence of Christianity* (New York: Association Press, 1961), p. 58.

24. *Ibid.*, p. 65.

25. Paul van Buren, *The Secular Meaning of the Gospel* (New York: Macmillan, 1963).

26. *Ibid.*, p. 195.

27. John B. Cobb, Jr., "From Crisis Theology to Post-Modern World," *The Centennial Review*, VIII, 2 (Spring 1964), 178.

28. John B. Cobb, Jr., *Living Options in Protestant Theology* (Philadelphia: Westminster Press, 1962), p. 317.

29. John B. Cobb, Jr., "From Crisis Theology to Post-Modern World," *op. cit.*, p. 183.

30. John B. Cobb, Jr., *Living Options in Protestant Theology, op. cit.*, p. 323.

31. John B. Cobb, Jr., "From Crisis Theology to Post-Modern World," *op. cit.*, p. 181.

JOHN WARWICK MONTGOMERY

A Philosophical-Theological Critique of the Death of God Movement

THE SUBJECT of this lecture is the new theological science of Theothanatology, wherein God's mortal illness or demise serves as the starting point for a radically secular approach to the modern world.[1]

The national publicity lately given to this movement in general periodicals (*Time*, *The New Yorker*, *The New York Times*, etc.)[2] may produce the false impression that here Protestantism has again spawned an unstable lunatic fringe which will disappear before one knows it—or quickly be replaced, as the Beatles edged out Elvis Presley. A closer look, however, reveals that the death-of-God movement is no flash in the theological pan. Stokes, a critical colleague of theothanatologist Altizer at Emory University, has recently and accurately mapped "the nontheistic temper of the modern mind"; the death-of-

* Fred C. Rutz Foundation Lecture, February 3, 1966.

God theologies are consciously relating to this temper.[3] Carl F.
H. Henry, on closely observing the present European theological climate, has noted that, after the relatively brief Barthian
interlude, the cold winds of rationalism are blowing again; in
the death-of-God movement America is beginning to feel these
winds turning icy cold as they are directed through an ideological morgue. *Christian Century's* editor, while varying the temperature, does not minimize the impact of the new theology;
on December 1 he wrote of the so-called "Christian atheism":
"Debate now rages: it looks as if we shall have a long, hot winter." [4] Cold or hot (Altizer would like this conjunction of opposites!), the movement is indeed to be reckoned with. Says
one of its prime spokesmen, William Hamilton: "Members of
this group are in touch with each other; plans are under way
for a major meeting of the group and there is even some talk of
a new journal devoted to the movement." [5]

Protestants in the Reformation tradition should especially
examine this new theology with care, for it is not accidental
that Hamilton regularly appeals to Luther and to motifs of
Reformation theology,[6] or that a critic of the movement has
shrewdly written: "Soon, I predict, Luther will become the
dominant symbol of the God-is-dead theology because he left
the cloister and went into the 'world'—whatever that is." [7]
Even more important, as we shall see, the God-is-dead movement takes its rise from the consistent appropriation and use of
a central theme in Neo-Orthodoxy—the very Neo-Orthodoxy
that many Lutheran and Reformed theologians here and
abroad are naïvely embracing today.[8] Perhaps this lecture will
aid some members of the theological community to check their
tickets more carefully before they board contemporary trains
of thought.

As to the lecture's posture, let it be plainly stated at the outset: in Merrill Tenney's words, "We are not ready to be God's
pallbearers yet";[9] nor are we going to function as pseudosophisticated embalmers of the Infinite. Rather, I find myself at
the presumed death of God in the role of a coroner. My dictionary defines a coroner as "a public officer whose principal
duty is to inquire into any death which there is reason to suppose is not due to natural causes." I have become convinced

that there is some foul play involved in this particular death; and we shall discover, if I am not mistaken, that the death-of-God theology represents a classic case of what mystery writers call "the wrong corpse."

The Morticians in the Case

Five names have become associated, for good or for ill, with the new "Christian atheism." They are: Gabriel Vahanian of Syracuse, a French Calvinist by origin, whose 1961 book *The Death of God* gave the new movement its name; Baptist Harvey Cox of the Harvard Divinity School, rocketed to fame by his paperback, *The Secular City* (1965), which had sold over 135,000 copies at last count; Thomas J. J. Altizer, an Episcopal layman on the faculty at Emory, whose next book will carry the title *The Gospel of Christian Atheism;* William Hamilton of Colgate Rochester, a Baptist, best known for his book *The New Essence of Christianity*, which, however, now represents an earlier, more conservative stage in his development; and Paul M. van Buren, an Episcopal priest teaching in the religion department at Temple University, who took his doctorate under Karl Barth at Basel and whose book *The Secular Meaning of the Gospel* is the most substantial production yet to arise from the death-of-God camp. All of these men are "younger theologians": Cox is thirty-six, Vahanian and Altizer are thirty-eight, and Hamilton and Van Buren are forty-one.

Whether these five theologians actually constitute a "school" is still a matter of debate among them. Cox, speaking in Evanston several weeks ago at the seventh Annual Meeting of the American Society of Christian Ethics, denied the existence of a unified movement (but then observed important common elements among the "Christian atheists");[10] Paul van Buren has remarked: "Langdon Gilkey says we belong to a 'God is dead' movement, but I think Altizer and Bill Hamilton and I are saying different things." [11] Hamilton, on the other hand, has argued cogently for the existence of a definite ideological focus shared at least by Altizer, Van Buren, and himself.[12] Of course the question of a "school" depends on one's definition of the term. The fact that the above five theologians are already

linked in the common mind with the God-is-dead stir requires
that we look at the position of each. Having done so, we can
proceed to note the common elements in their views.

We shall take up the theothanatologists in the order already
employed: Vahanian, Cox, Altizer, Hamilton, and Van Buren.
This order represents, roughly, a continuum from "more conservative" to "more radical," with the caesura between Cox
and Altizer. Such an arrangement takes into account a basic
clarification made both by Cox and by Hamilton: Cox's distinction between the theologians (such as himself) who use the
phrase death-of-God with quotation marks around either or
both of its nouns, and the theologians (such as Van Buren) who
use the phrase with no qualifications, to signify that God is no
longer alive, even if he once existed;[13] and Hamilton's separation of the "soft" radicals ("they have God, but sometimes for
strategic reasons they may decide not to talk about him") from
"hard" radicals such as himself:

> The hard radicals are really not interested in problems of com-
> munication. It is not that the old forms are outmoded or that
> modern man must be served but that the message itself is prob-
> lematic. The hard radicals, however varied may be their lan-
> guage, share first of all a common loss. It is not a loss of the
> idols, or of the God of theism. It is a real loss of real transcend-
> ence. It is a loss of God.[14]

In terms of these typologies, Vahanian and Cox are "soft" radicals who use quotation marks, while Altizer, Hamilton, and
Van Buren, by eschewing qualifications (though admittedly
not always in the most clean-cut fashion) and by endeavoring
to assert the ontological demise of deity, warrant classification
as "hard" radicals.

The five death-of-God theologians may be further distinguished by the way of their academic specializations and tem-
peramental orientations. Thus Vahanian is principally concerned with the relations between literature and theology, and
writes as an urbane littérateur himself; Cox is basically a sociologist of religion,[15] endeavoring to unite Talcott Parsons with
Karl Barth(!);[16] Altizer is "mystical, spiritual, and apocalyptic
. . . all élan, wildness, excessive generalization, brimming
with colorful, flamboyant, and emotive language";[17] Hamilton

is the theologian's theologian, having produced (before his conversion to death-of-God thinking) such standard fare as the *Modern Reader's Guide to the Gospels*, and *The Christian Man* in Westminster Press's Layman's Theological Library; and Van Buren—"ordered, precise, cool" [18] is ever the modern linguistic philosopher: he "has neither wept at God's funeral nor, like Altizer and the dancers at a Hindu procession to the burning ghat, leaped in corybantic exultation. He plays the role of the clinical diagnostician of linguistic maladies." [19] Let us consider in turn the peculiar ideological orientation of each of these thinkers, who, in spite of their wide divergencies, are united in focusing the attention of theology on contemporary secular man rather than on transcendental deity.

Gabriel Vahanian: Mortician-Littérateur. Though Rudolf Bultmann regards Vahanian's *Death of God* as one of the most exciting books he has read in recent years, its author is now considered hopelessly conservative by the advocates of Christian atheism.[20] Why? because he unabashedly uses the expression "death of God" in a metaphorical-literary, not literal, way. The subtitle of his book reveals his major concern: "The Culture of Our Post-Christian Era." "God's death" is evident in the fact that ours is a post-Christian world where (1) "Christianity has sunk into religiosity," (2) "modern culture is gradually losing the marks of that Christianity which brought it into being and shaped it," and (3) "tolerance has become religious syncretism." [21] In his latest book, *Wait Without Idols*, Vahanian explicates: "This does not mean, obviously, that God himself no longer is but that, regardless of whether he is or not, his reality, as the Christian tradition has presented it, has become culturally irrelevant: God is *de trop*, as Sartre would say" [22]—and he illustrates with the opening scenes of the film *La Dolce Vita*, where a huge crucifix suspended from a helicopter hovers incongruously over indifferent sunbathers below.

What is the cause of this "demise of God"? Like Paul Tillich or Christian philosopher of history Eric Voegelin,[23] Vahanian finds the basic issue in "the leveling down of transcendental values to immanental ones," [24] *i.e.*, the worship of the idolatrous gods of cultural religiosity. In a penetrating analysis of Samuel

Beckett's 1952-1953 play *En Attendant Godot* (*Waiting for Godot*), where Godot represents God, Vahanian concludes: "No wonder then that life is lonesomely long, when one lives it out wandering from meaninglessness to meaninglessness, from idol to idol—and not a hope in sight. Modern man's place is the right place; only his religiousness is at the wrong place, addressing itself to the Unknown God." [25]

But Vahanian has an answer for post-Christian man: he must, as his book title says, "Wait without idols." As a Calvinist and as a follower of Barth (he translated and wrote the introduction for Barth's book *The Faith of the Church*), Vahanian believes that secular "immanentism can show that God dies as soon as he becomes a cultural accessory or a human ideal; that the finite cannot comprehend the infinite (*finitum non est capax infiniti*)." [26] What then does modern man wait for? The breaking in of the Wholly Other the transcendent God who can never be "objectified." [27]

> The Christian era has bequeathed us the "death of God," but not without teaching us a lesson. God is not necessary; that is to say, he cannot be taken for granted. He cannot be used merely as a hypothesis, whether epistemological, scientific, or existential, unless we should draw the degrading conclusion that "God is reasons." On the other hand, if we can no longer assume that God is, we may once again realize that he *must* be. God is not necessary, but he is inevitable. He is wholly other and wholly present. Faith in him, the conversion of our human reality, both culturally and existentially, is the demand he still makes upon us.[28]

Harvey Cox: Mortician-Sociologist. Bishop John A. T. Robinson, of *Honest to God* fame, recently commended Cox's *Secular City* as "a major contribution by a brilliant young theologian" and pointed up its major theme: that secularization is "the fruit of the Gospel." [29] For Cox, secularization (as opposed to secularism) is a positive phenomenon, whereby "society and culture are delivered from tutelage to religious control and closed metaphysical world-views." [30] Following Eric Voegelin and Gerhard von Rad, Cox interprets the Genesis account of Creation and the Exodus narratives of the deliverance from Egypt and the Sinai covenant as secularizing-liberating myths—myths of which the secular city becomes a modern counter-part. Urban life, with its anonymity and mobility, can free modern man from bondage to closed, idolatrous value systems, and open him to that which is truly transcendent. He quotes Amos Wilder approvingly: "If we are to have any transcendence today, even Christian, it must be in and through the secular." [31] How will the liberating transcendence manifest itself? Cox suggests art, social change, and what he calls the "I-You partnership" (a teamwork relationship). Through such means the transcendent may eventually reveal to us a new name, for the word "God" has perhaps outlived its usefulness owing to its association with old idolatries. "This may mean that we shall have to stop talking about 'God' for a while, take a moratorium on speech until the new name emerges." [32] But this should not appear strange to us, since "hiddenness stands at the very center of the doctrine of God." [33] Even "in Jesus God does not stop being hidden; rather He meets man as the unavailable 'other.' He does not 'appear' but shows man that He acts, in His hiddenness, in human history." [34] Modern urban-secular life, then, is the vehicle (the "means of grace"!) by which man in our age can be freed from bondage to lesser gods and meet the Transcendent One again.

When Cox revisited his secular city in a conference several weeks ago, he made his position vis-à-vis the "death of God" even more explicit.[35] No, he did not accept the literal demise of deity; as a close admirer of Karl Barth, he firmly believes in a transcendent, wholly other God.[36] Indeed, it is on this basis that his book strikes out against those styles of life that capture and immanentize deity. With Friedrich Gogarten, he is convinced that apart from transcendent reality—an extrinsic point of reference—the world cannot be a world at all. (He illustrated with Muzak: if it were to go on all the time, then music would cease to exist; an anti-environment is necessary for an environment, and the wholly other God is such an anti-environment for our world.) But as to the identification of the Absolute, Cox was no less vague than in his book. There he spoke of atheists and Christians as differing not in their factual orientation but in their "stance"; in his lecture, he employed an aesthetic model for Christian social decisions, and when asked for the criteria whereby one could know that the transcendent is indeed working in a given social change, he optimistically asserted that "the hermeneutical community, with its eyes of faith, discerns 'where the action is.' " Whereupon the questioner shrewdly retorted: "Carl MacIntyre's church or yours?" Cox then readily admitted his enthusiast-anabaptist frame of reference, and noted that Lutherans and Calvinists (mainline Reformation Protestants) had been the chief critics of his *Secular City*.

Thomas J. J. Altizer: Mortician-Mystic. In spite of their radical terminology, Vahanian and Cox are familiar territory to those acquainted with the twentieth-century Protestant thought world. Beginning with Barth's radical transcendence, they condemn the false gods of cultural immanentism and see the collapse of these idols in our day as the entrée to a new appreciation of the Wholly Other. They differ from Barth chiefly in the means by which the Transcendent One will now show himself; for Barth, it is always through the (erring but revelatory) Word of Scripture; for Vahanian and Cox, it is through the pulsating secular life of our time. With Altizer, however, we move into a more distinctively radical radicalism, where God's death is passionately affirmed as a real (though dialectical) event. Altizer's difficult world-view is best comprehended through the influences that have played upon him:

(1) From the great phenomenologist of religion Mircea Eliade, Altizer came to see that modern man has lost his sense of the sacred;[37] but Altizer "refuses to follow Eliade's tempting advice to return to some sort of precosmic primitivism and to recover the sacred in the way archaic religion did." [38] Altizer picks up the principle of the "coincidence of opposites" (*coincidentia oppositorum*) so vital to the thinking of Eliade (and of Carl Gustav Jung), and endeavors to apply it with ruthless consistency: the only way to recover the sacred is to welcome fully the secularization of the modern world.

(2) Altizer's studies in comparative religion, particularly the Eastern religions, provided considerable grist for his mill.[39] He came to identify the basic thrusts of Christianity and atheistic Buddhism;[40] in his judgment both religions seek to liberate man

from all dependence on the phenomenal world (in Buddhism, the negation of Samsara is the only means to Nirvana), yet at the same time there is "a mystical apprehension of the oneness of reality" (Nirvana and Samsara are mystically identified).[41] Here, according to Altizer, is a telling parallel with the Christian Kingdom of God, which is "in the world but not of it."

(3) From modern Protestant theology Altizer has acquired his basic understanding of Christianity. Sören Kierkegaard has contributed the dialectical method: "existence in faith is antithetically related to existence in objective reality; now faith becomes subjective, momentary, and paradoxical." [42] Rudolph Ott[43] and Karl Barth have provided a God who is wholly transcendent—who cannot be adequately represented by any human idea. But Barth, Bultmann, and even Tillich have not carried through the Kierkegaardian dialectic to its consistent end, for they insist on retaining some vestige of affirmation; they do not see that the dialectic requires an unqualified coincidence of opposites. If only Tillich had applied his "Protestant principle" consistently, he could have become the father of a new theonomous age. Wrote Altizer not long before Tillich's death:

> The death of God (which Tillich, who refuses to be fully dialectical, denies) must lead to a repetition of the Resurrection, to a new epiphany of the New Being. Moreover his own principles lead Tillich to the threshold of this position. If Christianity will be a bearer of the religious answer not so long as it breaks through its own particularity, only to the degree in which it negates itself as a religion, then obviously it must negate its Western form. Until Christianity undergoes this negation, it cannot be open to the depths of the ground of being. Nor will Christianity continue to be able to embody the New Being if it remains closed both to non-Western history and to the contemporary historical present. Potentially Tillich could become a new Luther if he would extend his principle of justification by doubt to a theological affirmation of the death of God.[44]

Altizer now clearly sees *himself* in this role.

(4) "If radical dialectical thinking was reborn in Kierkegaard, it was consummated in Friedrich Nietzsche," [45] says Altizer, who sees in Nietzsche's vision of Eternal Recurrence the

ideal myth of the coincidence of opposites, and in his passionate proclamation of God's death—the death of metaphysical
transcendence—the essential key to a new age. For "only when
God is dead, can Being begin in every Now." [46] Therefore, to
turn the wheel of the world we must dare with William Blake
to "name God as Satan," *i.e.*, to "identify the transcendent
Lord as the ultimate source of alienation and repression." [47]
Only then can we affirm "the God beyond the Christian God,
beyond the God of the historic Church, beyond all which
Christendom has known as God." [48]

(5) By a thoroughgoing acceptance of Albert Schweitzer's
eschatological interpretation of Jesus in his *Quest of the Historical Jesus*, Altizer claims Jesus as the prime symbol of his
world-view. "To grasp Jesus as an historical or an objective
phenomenon is to live in unbelief." [49] Jesus is significant because of his single-minded attention to the coming Kingdom
and his sacrifice of himself for it; he thus becomes the Christ
figure—the symbol of a total rejection of the old to achieve the
new—and this "mythical symbol of Christ" is "the substance of
the Christian faith." [50] So Altizer calls on radical Christians to
"rebel against the Christian churches and their traditions" and
to "defy the moral law of the churches, identifying it as a satanic law of repression and heteronomous compulsion." [51] As
"spiritual or apocalyptic" Christians, they must "believe only
in the Jesus of the third age of the Spirit, a Jesus who is not to
be identified with the original historical Jesus, but who rather
is known here in a new and more comprehensive and universal
form, a form actualizing the eschatological promise of Jesus." [52]
The incarnate Word is thus seen to be fully kenotic—capable
of a total new expression in the new age ushered in when dia-
lectically we "accept the death of God as a final and irrevocable
event":

> Neither the Bible nor church history can be accepted as con-
> taining more than a provisional or temporary series of expres-
> sions of the Christian World. . . . Not only does Christianity
> now have a new meaning, it has a new reality, a reality created
> by the epiphany of a fully kenotic Word. Such a reality cannot
> be wholly understood by a word of the past, not even by the
> word "kenosis," for the Christian Word becomes a new reality
> by ceasing to be itself: only by negating and thus transcending

its previous expressions can the Incarnate Word be a forward-moving process.[53]

William Hamilton: Mortician-Theologian. Though Altizer out-barths Barth in his employment of the transcendence principle, thus apparently leaving the "soft" radicals far behind, his affirmation of God's death is, after all, still a dialectic affirmation: from the ashes of God's pyre will rise, like the Phoenix, a "God beyond God." Now let us consider a theothanatologist who has come to reject the dialectic as well.

In a revealing autobiographical article, Hamilton states that he did not attain his present "hard" radical position until 1964, after he had turned forty.[54] This is quite true, and much of the current interpretation of Hamilton falls wide of the mark because it is based on his 1961 book *The New Essence of Christianity*, which explicitly disavows "the non-existence of God" [55] and even affirms Jesus' resurrection "as an ordinary event" (though it is insignificantly relegated to a footnote!).[56] But even at that time, the influence of Barth,[57] Niebuhr, and John Baillie[58] on Hamilton's thought was leading to a more radical position. Thus in the spring of 1963 Hamilton wistfully attempted to save Mozart's Don Giovanni through the employment of Kierkegaard's dialectic of good and evil; Don Giovanni seems to typify the limbo state of the contemporary theologian—neither damned nor saved.[59] Then came Hamilton's first direct attempt to "see if there is anybody out there" [60]—if there were others who shared his growing dissatisfaction with the state of theological life: his essay "Thursday's Child," in which he depicted the theologian of today and tomorrow as "a man without faith, without hope, with only the present and therefore only love to guide them"—"a waiting man and a praying man." [61] When interviewed in 1965 by Mehta, he said: "I am beginning to feel that the time has come for me to put up or shut up, for me to be an in or an out." [62]

The decision to be an "out"—a "hard" radical affirming the literal death of God—was made by Hamilton last year. In his *Christian Century* article previously referred to, he described the breakdown of his "good old world of middle-of-the-road, ecumenical neo-orthodoxy," [63] and outlined his new position in three particulars: (1) God is indeed dead; the Neo-Orthodox "dialectic between the presence and absence of God" has now "collapsed." (2) A free choice is made to follow the man Jesus in obedience—to stand where he stands.[64] (3) A new optimism will "say Yes to the world of rapid change, new technologies, automation and the mass media." The last two points are clarified somewhat in Hamilton's recent analysis of the death-of-God movement, wherein he stakes out his position as compared with the views of Altizer and Van Buren.[65] Christologically, Hamilton, like Altizer, commits himself to a radically hidden, kenotic Jesus: "Jesus may be concealed in the world, in the neighbor, in this struggle for justice, in that struggle for beauty, clarity, order. Jesus is in the world as masked." Moreover, "Become a Christ to your neighbor, as Luther put it." [66]

Yet the theme of the Christian as "both a waiting man and a praying man" still remains. How is this possible if "the breakdown of the religious a priori means that there is no way, ontological, cultural, or psychological, to locate a part of the self or a part of human experience that needs God"—if "there is no God-shaped blank within man?" "Really to travel along this road means that we trust the world, not God, to be our need fulfiller and problem solver, and God, if he is to be for us at all, must come in some other role." [67] Having rejected Augustine's claim that our hearts are restless till they find their rest in God, Hamilton draws in another Augustinian theme: the distinction between *uti* and *frui*—between using God and enjoying Him.

> If God is not needed, if it is to the world and not to God that we repair for our needs and problems, then perhaps we may come to see that He is to be enjoyed and delighted in. . . . Our waiting for God, our godlessness, is partly a search for a language and a style by which we might be enabled to stand before Him once again, delighting in His presence.[68]

In the meantime, modern secular man must grow up—from an Oedipus to an Orestes, from a Hamlet to a Prospero[69]—by moving beyond the anguished quest for salvation from sin to a confident, optimistic, secular stance "in the world, in the city, with both the needy neighbor and the enemy." Thus is the orthodox relation between God and the neighbor "inverted": "we move to our neighbor, to the city and to the world out of a sense of the loss of God." [70] Man, not God, becomes the center of focus while we wait prayerfully for the epiphany of a God of delight.

Paul van Buren: Mortician-Philosopher. Officially, Hamilton rejects a dialectic view of God's existence; yet, remarkably (or paradoxically, in spite of Hamilton's formal break with neo-Protestant paradox!), a *frui* God is hoped for at the death of a *uti* divinity. Prayer is the revealing element in Hamilton's theology: he continues to pray in spite of God's death—thus forcing the conclusion that the dialectic of divine presence-absence that he claims to have rejected has not been rejected at all in practice. Through the contemporary dark night of the soul God *is* in some sense still there, waiting as we wait, the recipient of our prayers. In Paul van Buren, however, this inconsistency is overcome through the cool and rigorous application of linguistic philosophy. Significantly, Van Buren recently admitted: "I don't pray. I just reflect on these things." [71]

Like the other death-of-God theologians, Van Buren began his reflecting as a Barthian. We noted earlier that he took his doctorate under Barth at Basel.[72] Subsequently, however, he came into contact with the *Philosophical Investigations* of the later Wittgenstein and the writings of the so-called linguistic analysis who have followed him.[73] In the process of subjecting his own Neo-Orthodox theology to rigorous analytic and linguistic criticism, he wrote his *Secular Meaning of the Gospel,* a book which, he says, "represented an important step in a personal struggle to overcome my own theological past" [74]—but "what I'm thinking now is a lot more radical even than what I said in my book." [75]

What is Van Buren's current position? It may be represented as a five-point argument, the total importance of which can hardly be overemphasized since it forms the philosophical backbone of consistent "Christian atheism":

(1) Assertions compatible with anything and everything say nothing, and this is precisely the status of Neo-Orthodoxy's affirmation concerning a transcendental, wholly-other God. At

the beginning of *The Secular Meaning of the Gospel*, Van
Buren approvingly quotes the well-known parable by Antony
Flew and John Wisdom, demonstrating the meaningless of
such God-statements:

> Once upon a time two explorers came upon a clearing in the
> jungle. In the clearing were growing many flowers and many
> weeds. One explorer says, "Some gardener must tend this plot."
> The other disagrees, "There is no gardener." So they pitch their
> tents and set a watch. No gardener is ever seen. "But perhaps
> he is an invisible gardener." So they set up a barbed-wire fence.
> They electrify it. They patrol with bloodhounds. (For they
> remember how H. G. Wells' *The Invisible Man* could be both
> smelt and touched though he could not be seen.) But no shrieks
> ever suggest that some intruder has received a shock. No
> movements of the wire ever betray an invisible climber. The
> bloodhounds never give cry. Yet still the Believer is not con-
> vinced. "But there is a gardener, invisible, intangible, insensible
> to electric shocks, a gardener who has no scent and makes no
> sound, a gardener who comes secretly to look after the garden
> which he loves." At last the Sceptic despairs, "But what re-
> mains of your original assertion? Just how does what you call
> an invisible, intangible, eternally elusive gardener differ from
> an imaginary gardener or even from no gardener at all?" [76]

An important section of Van Buren's book is devoted to showing that Bultmann's existential assertions about God do not escape this "death by a thousand qualifications," and that the
same holds true of Schubert Ogden's attempts (God is "experienced non-objective reality," etc.) to stiffen existential affirmations with Whitehead's process-philosophy. God, then, is literally and unqualifiedly dead, and future divine epiphanies
have no more meaning than present-day expressions of God's
existence.

(2) Modern life is irrevocably pluralistic and relativistic, a
market place where a multitude of "language games" are
played, not a Gothic cathedral where a single comprehensive
world-view is possible. The non-cognitive language game of
theology has to be played relativistically in this milieu.[77]

(3) If metaphysical, transcendental God-statements are literally meaningless, what is their "cash value"? The actual worth
of these affirmations of faith can be obtained only by translat-
ing them into human terms, an operation to which the conclud-

ing portion of *The Secular Meaning of the Gospel* is devoted. As Van Buren put it in his recent *New Yorker* interview: "I am trying to argue that it [Christianity] is fundamentally about man, that its language about God is one way—a dated way, among a number of ways—of saying what it is Christianity wants to say about man and human life and human history." [78]

(4) This translation of God-language to man-language must be carried out particularly in reference to the central figure of Christianity, Jesus of Nazareth.

> One of the ways in which the New Testament writers speak about Jesus is in divine and quasi-divine terms—Son of God, and what have you. . . . What I'm trying to do is to understand the Bible on a naturalistic or humanistic level, to find out how the references to the absolute and the supernatural are used in expressing on a human level the understanding and convictions that the New Testament writers had about their world. For by using these large cosmological terms in speaking about this particular happening, this event—the history of Jesus —they were saying the most that they could say about this man. If a man in the first century had wanted to say of a certain person that he had given him an insight into what human life was all about, he would have almost normally said, "That man is divine." [79]

Van Buren claims that his secular translation of the Gospel "stands or falls with our interpretation of the language connected with Easter." [80] What is this interpretation?

> Jesus of Nazareth was a free man in his own life, who attracted followers and created enemies according to the dynamics of personality and in a manner comparable to the effect of other liberated persons in history upon people about them. He died as a result of the threat that such a free man poses for insecure and bound men. His disciples were left no less insecure and frightened. Two days later, Peter, and then other disciples, . . . experienced a discernment situation in which Jesus the free man whom they had known, themselves, and indeed the whole world, were seen in a quite new way. From that moment, the disciples began to possess something of the freedom of Jesus. His freedom began to be "contagious." [81]

(5) Admittedly, theology is here reduced to ethics, but in our secular age we are unable to find any "empirical linguis-

tic anchorage" for the transcendental. After all, "alchemy was 'reduced' to chemistry by the rigorous application of an empirical method." [82] So let us frankly embrace the secular world of which we are a part. Religious thought is "responsible to human society, not to the church. Its orientation is humanistic, not divine. Its norms must lie in the role it performs in human life. . . . Any insights into the 'human situation' which our religious past may provide us, therefore, can be helpful only insofar as we bring them into a dynamic conversation with and allow them to be influenced by our rapidly changing technological culture." [83]

And here *la ronde* is complete, for in his stress on our modern cultural situation Van Buren reminds us of the "soft" radicals, Vahanian and Cox, as much as of his "hard" compatriots, Altizer and Hamilton. Is there then a death-of-God school? Even with the qualifications introduced in our discussion of each of the five theothanatologists, the answer must be Yes. For in all of these thinkers the theological center shifts away from a God whose transcendence causes him to become more and more indistinct, until finally, in Van Buren, he passes into the realm of analytic meaninglessness. And for all of these morticians of the Absolute, God's vague or vacated position on the theological stage is replaced by Man—literary man (Vahanian), urban man (Cox), mystical man (Altizer), social man (Hamilton), ethical man (Van Buren). Correspondingly, the Christ of these "Christian atheists" moves from divine to human status: his kenosis becomes continually more pronounced until finally the divine "hiddenness" in him is absolutized, yielding a humanistic Jesus with whom modern man can truly and optimistically stand in "I-You" partnership in a world of secular challenge and dynamic change.

Efforts at Resuscitation

As the theothanatologists have taken their positions around the divine bier, ready to convey to its final resting place, resuscitator squads of theologians and clergy have rushed to the scene in a frantic effort to show that the Subject of discussion "is not dead but sleepeth." In the five years since the appearance of

Vahanian's *Death of God*, vocal opposition to the movement
has increased not arithmetically but geometrically. The protests have ranged widely in scope and quality—from the revival of the anti-Nietzsche quip ("God is dead!" signed, Nietzsche; "Nietzsche is dead!" signed, God) to Eric Mascall's *The
Secularization of Christianity*, a book-length criticism of the
common theological orientation of Van Buren and J.A.T.
Robinson.[84] In general, it must be said that the attempts to
counter "Christian atheism," though occasionally helpful in
pointing up weaknesses in the theothanatologists' armor, do not
cut decisively to the heart of the issue. In most instances, the
reason for the critical debility lies in the dullness of the theological swords the critics wield. Let us observe several representative efforts to slay the God-is-dead ideology, after which
we will be in a better position to offer our own critique.

Early in this paper we cited Hamilton's colleague Charles M.
Nielsen of Colgate Rochester, who evidently has taken all that
he can bear from Hamilton and his death-of-God confrères.
Nielsen is the best example of the anti-theothanatological critics
who oppose the movement through satire and ridicule. Here is
a delightful sample:

> On the subject of freedom: there is nothing quite like some
> Protestant seminaries. Presumably a medical school would be
> upset if its students became Christian Scientists and wanted to
> practice their new beliefs instead of medicine in the operating
> rooms of the university hospital. And a law school might con-
> sider it unbecoming to admit hordes of Anabaptists who re-
> fused on principle to have anything to do with law courts. But
> almost nothing (including atheism but excluding such vital
> matters as smoking) seems inappropriate in some Protestant
> settings—nothing, that is, except the traditions of Christianity
> and especially of Protestantism. Traditions are regarded as
> "square," supposedly because they are not new. The modern
> theologian spends his time huddled over his teletype machine,
> like a nun breathless with adoration, in the hope that out of the
> latest news flash he can be the first to pronounce the few re-
> maining shreds of the Protestant tradition "irrelevant."
>   So powerful is the thrust toward novelty that a famous Prot-
> estant journal is considering a series of articles by younger the-
> ologians under sixty called "How My Mind Has Changed in
> the Past Five Minutes." The only thing that is holding up the
> project is the problem of getting the journal distributed fast

enough. A great aim of the liberal Protestant seminary is to be so relevant that no one would suspect Protestantism had a past, or at least a worthwhile one. The point is for the seminary to become so pertinent to modern culture that the church has nothing to say to that culture.[85]

Though such passages are great fun and make an important point, they bypass the root question, namely, Are the death-of-God theologians *correct* in what they claim? *Is* God dead? The obvious incongruity in Hamilton's presence on the Colgate Rochester faculty, in Van Buren's retention of Episcopal ordination, etc., pales before the truth question. Nielsen never faces this problem, for he sees the difficulty simply to be a surfeit of "eccentrics" in the church, and pleads for (as the subtitle of his article puts it) "more Benedictines, please!" As a Professor of Historical Theology who highly values the corporate tradition of the historic church, he prays: "Dear Lord, we are grateful for all the individualists and gadflies you have sent us. Hermits *are* interesting, but next time may we please also have a few Benedictines to build, organize and serve the church?" But if the God of the historic church is not dead, then "gratitude" for theothanatological gadflies seems hardly appropriate; and if he is, then Nielsen's Benedictines are a positive menace.

The November 17, 1965 issue of *Christian Century* featured a section titled, "Death-of-God: Four Views," with the following explanation from the editor: "Letters constituting entries in the death-of-God debate . . . continue to crowd the editor's desk. To print them all would be impossible, so as a way out of the dilemma we present four articles which in one or another aspect seem to inculcate most of the views, mainly critical, advanced in the letters." These articles are indeed representative of the general reaction to the movement, and their common theme is the *inconsistency* of the theothanatologists: their impossible attempt to retain love, joyful optimism, the Christian ethic, or Jesus himself while giving up a transcendent God. Warren L. Moulton argues that "without our faith in the reality of God we can know little or nothing about the love which we call "*agape*"; he notes that "for the joy that was set before him Christ endured the cross; with the arrival of 'optimism' and the departure of this particular joy, a central nerve is frayed"; and asks: "Can we stick by Jesus just because we like the toys in his sandbox?" [86] Larry Shiner writes: "To get rid of God and keep a 'Jesus ethic' of involvement with the present human situation is a species of absent-mindedness amazing to behold in a movement that takes its motto from Nietzsche. *He* at least knew better; he never tired of pointing out that Christianity is a whole and that one cannot give up faith in God and keep Christian morality." [87]

But as sound as these criticisms are from the standpoint of the Biblical world-view, they overlook the plain fact that the death-of-God theologians are quite willing to follow Nietzsche, if need be, in a "transvaluation of all values." Altizer, as we have seen, has already called upon radical Christians to "defy the moral law of the churches"; and Van Buren, in his article for *Christian Century*'s "How I Am Making Up My Mind" series, does not mention the name of Jesus once, and defines the task of theology entirely in humanistic terms.[88] It is therefore painfully evident that the charge of inconsistency toward the Christian tradition will not move the theothanatologists to repentance; they are fully prepared to embrace "creative negation" on all fronts. The basic issue remains: Is such negation justified?

The scholarly attempts to meet this fundamental truth question have thus far issued chiefly from the theological camps the "Christian atheists" have endeavored (quite successfully) to demolish: existentialism, Whiteheadian process-philosophy, and Neo-Orthodoxy. The result is a rather painful example of the defense of vested interests. Existential theologian John Macquarrie[89] is willing to admit, with Van Buren, that "our modern scheme of thought affords no place for another being, however exalted, in addition to the beings that we encounter within the world"; but he still sees as a viable alternative the Heidegger-Tillich-Robinson existential-ontological conception of God as Being itself:

> The alternative is to think of God as Being itself—Being which emerges and manifests itself in and with and through every particular being, but which is not itself another such being, which is nothing apart from particular beings, and yet which is more beingful than any particular being, since it is the condi-

tion that there should be any such beings whatsoever. . . . It is Heidegger's merit that he has shown the empirical anchorage of this question in certain moods of our own human existence —moods that light up for us the wider Being within which we live and move and have our own being.[90]

Process-philosophy is made the bulwark of defense against "Christian atheism" by theological advocates of this philosophical school. Stokes claims that a program to counter "the threat of a world view which repudiates the belief in a personal God . . . can best succeed with the aid of personalistic modes of thought which are informed and enriched by some of the insights of Whitehead and Hartshorne." [91] John B. Cobb, Jr., author of the Whitehead-oriented *Living Options in Protestant Theology*[92] (which does not even include orthodox Reformation theology as an option!), informs us that "once one enters the strange new world of Whitehead's vision, God becomes very much alive. . . . Insofar as I come existentially to experience myself in terms of the world to which Whitehead introduces us, I experience myself in God; God as in me; God as law, as love, as grace; and the whole world as grounded in him. . . . If Whitehead's vision should triumph in the years ahead, the death of God's would indeed turn out after all to have been only the 'eclipse of God.' " [93] Bernard Meland argues in terms of process-philosophy and comparative religion that "ultimacy and immediacies traffic together," and that "while notions of the Absolute have dissolved in our modern discourse, the vision of a *More* in experience, as a dimension that is lived rather than thought, is not unavailable." [94]

Even the Neo-Orthodox theology ouf of which the death-of-God theologians have carved their casket for the Infinite is presented as an answer to "Christian atheism." Langdon Gilkey, in his Crozer Lectures on the God-is-dead movement, holds that the theothanatologists are influenced solely by the "negative elements" of Neo-Orthodoxy and "not at all by the balancing positive elements." [95] On the positive side, when one looks deeply into human experience, one finds "a special kind of Void and loss," the character of which is best expressed by such terms as "ultimate," "transcendent," and "unconditioned." Here "there is either no answer at all and so despair,

or, if there be an answer, it comes from beyond the creaturely." At this point revelation puts in its claim: "Revelation
is that definite mode of experience in which an answer to those
ultimate questions is actually experienced, in which, that is, the
reality and truth of language about God is brought home to the
experiencer, in which propositions about God are 'verified.' " [96]
In the Neo-Orthodox spirit, Gilkey quickly adds: "No proof
here is possible; only confession and conviction based on this
experience." In sum: "The 'verification' of all we say about
God occurs, then, in the life of faith lived by the Christian
community, and from that living experience springs the usage
and the reality of its God-language." [97]

The existential-ontological, process-thinking, and Neo-Orthodox arguments against "Christian atheism" ring more and
more hollow as analytical philosophy intensifies its barrage
against these increasingly anachronistic theologies. Theothanatology was built over the wreckage of these positions, and in
itself it has marshaled overwhelming analytical evidence of
their debility. Listen to Van Buren's decimation of such arguments as have just been presented:

> Along comes the knight of faith and speaks of "reality breaking
> in upon us!" Or he speaks to us in the name of "absolute real-
> ity," or, even more confusing, his faith is placed in "an objec-
> tive reality." And here I would suggest that language has gone
> on a wild binge, which I think we should properly call a lost
> weekend.
>
> This knight of faith is presumably speaking English, and so
> we take him to be using words which we have learned how to
> use. Only see what he does with them. "Reality," which is ordi-
> narily used to call our attention once more to our agreements
> about how things are, is used now to refer to what the knight
> of faith must surely want to say is radically the opposite of all
> of our ordinary understandings. Why not better say, "Unreal-
> ity is breaking in upon us"?
>
> I think we can say something about what has gone wrong
> here. There was a time when the Absolute, God, was taken to
> be the cause of a great deal of what we would today call quite
> real phenomena, from rain and hail to death and disease. God
> was part of what people took to be the network of forces and
> factors of everyday existence, as real and as objective as the
> thunderbolts he produced. But today we no longer have the
> same reference for the word "reality." The network of under-

standings to which the word points has undergone important changes. The word "reality" has taken on an empirical coloration which makes it now a bit confusing to speak of "reality breaking in upon us," unless we are referring to, for example, a sudden and unexpected visit from the police or a mother-in-law.[98]

The point Van Buren cleverly makes here applies equally to existential ontologies, process philosophies, and Neo-Orthodox theologies, for all of these positions offer concepts of Deity which, being compatible with anything and everything, say precisely nothing. Macquarrie's "beingful Being" may be nothing but an animistic name for the universe (the existence of which is hardly in dispute!);[99] the God of Whitehead and Hartshorne, as worshipped by Ogden, Cobb, Meland, *et al.*, may likewise be little more than a pantheistic projection of their personalities on an impersonal universe (even William James, whose notion of "the More" Meland appropriates, admitted that it might be only an extension of the subliminal, parapsychological life of man);[100] and Gilkey quite rightly encloses the word "verification" in quotation marks when he uses it, for Neo-Orthodoxy's experience of revelation as filling a "Void" is no more a validation of God's ontological reality than the existentialist's "moods that light up the wider Being within which we live" or the process theologian's experience of non-objective reality." [101] In all of these cases, the source of the experience could be purely psychological, and an appeal to a more-than-human level of explanation totally without warrant.[102]

Some efforts have been made to oppose the God-is-dead ideology from the standpoint of traditional orthodox theology, but these attempts, operating from presuppositionalist or fideist orientations,[103] have had little impact. Paul Holmer of Yale, whose theology falls within the Lutheran spectrum,[104] makes the excellent points that the God-is-dead school has misinterpreted Bonhoeffer, who was no advocate of atheism, and that the theothanatologists have falsely assumed that Christianity can be modified so as to become universally acceptable to modern man while still remaining true to itself. On the latter point he writes: "The Christian idea of God has never been the coin of a very large realm. . . . Theology never did have the allegiance of the intelligentsia in the West, nor did the church's other powers extend over the whole of European social life. . . . The theologian must understand the world and the people in it, not to make Christianity relevant to them as much as to help them become relevant and amenable to Christianity." [105] But when he moves to a positive defense of the Christian view of God, Holmer vitiates his effectiveness by presuppositionally driving a wedge between theology (which, presumably, could remain true no matter what) and secular knowledge (whose development cannot touch theological truth); "Theology was never so much a matter of evidence that it had to change as the evidence advanced." [106]

Robert E. Fitch of the Pacific School of Religion unmercifully castigates the God-is-dead mentality, arguing that "if there is anything worse than bourgeois religiosity, it is egghead religiosity" and that "this is the Age of the Sell-Out, the Age of the Great Betrayal. We are a new Esau who has sold his spiritual birthright for a secular mess of pottage." [107] Particularly telling is Fitch's case for the permanent and culture-transcending impact of Scripture; he tells of the current wave of interest on the part of East Africans in the first published Swahili translation of *Julius Caesar*, and comments:

> Perhaps some cultural relativist would like to explain how an event in ancient Rome could have meaning almost 1,500 years later in Elizabethan England and how it could now, centuries later, be reborn in meaning in east Africa. What is striking is not just the continuity of meaning in the event but the continuity of expression in Plutarch-North-Shakespeare-Nyerere [the Swahili translator]. Our Bible can do as much. Indeed, it always has done so.[108]

But literary impact hardly establishes the cognitive truth of the Bible's claims, and it is the latter that the death-of-God theologians dispute. Moreover, when Fitch opposes existentialistic-experiential thinking with the argument that secular concepts and categories "yield but an erudite darkness until they are illuminated by a vision which sees this world in the light of another world," he does not move beyond the "soft" radical Cox

whom he criticizes.[109] Even if Reinhold Niebuhr, with his transcendental perspective on the human predicament, accomplished
more than secularist John Dewey[110] (a debatable assumption, in
any case), the basic question of the *de facto existence* of the
transcendent still remains. The "world seen in light of another
world" is an argument subject to infinite regress, and the pragmatic effect of belief in Deity can hardly establish the independent existence of Diety. Fitch appears to operate from a presup-
positional orientation which (sound though it may be) leaves
death-of-God thinking basically untouched.

Representing fideistic attacks on the theothanatologists, we
have Episcopal rector David R. Matlack, who speaks eloquently for most Christian believers: "Even if their assumptions were granted and their logic airtight—and this is far from
the case—they would not be touching the real life experiences
I believe I have had of God's grace, and the real life experiences other Christians have had." [111] Here the issue is, of
course, whether Matlack's "real life experiences" and those of
other believers necessarily demand the existence of a transcendent God. Suppose, as philosopher Kai Nielsen has argued
in a paper written from Van Buren's analytical stance, fideistic
claims such as Matlack's "are in reality no claims at all because
key religious words and utterances are without intelligible
factual content"? [112] How does the orthodox believer (any
more than the existentialist) know that his experiential "encounters" require a transcendental explanation? [113] It is the contention of "hard" death-of-God thinking that such "encounters" must be translated into purely human terms to make sense.
Attempts by Christian believers to meet this issue—which lies
at the very heart of the God-is-dead movement—have thus far
fallen wide of the mark.

A Closer Pathological Examination

In endeavoring to strike to the root of the theothanatological
problem, we shall focus attention on the theoretical underpin-
ning which Van Buren has provided for the movement. Our
concern will not center on the metaphorical uses of the God-is-
dead formula as employed by the "soft" radicals, since their

claims that people have difficulty in believing today and that theological language lacks relevance for modern man simply highlight the perpetual need to preach the gospel more vigorously and communicate its eternal truth more effectively. Likewise, we shall spend little time on the positions of the "hard" radicals Altizer and Hamilton, for, as already noted, these thinkers, in spite of the ostensively atheistic character of their affirmations, do in fact allow for the reintroduction of Deity (Altizer's "God beyond God," Hamilton's "God of delight") at the back door even while ejecting him from the front. Cox is right when he says of Altizer, "he will have to be more precise if he's going to be taken seriously," [114] and the recent television discussion in which Oxford philosopher-theologian Ian Ramsey went to work on Hamilton showed clearly that the same charge of confused ambiguity must be leveled at him.[115] The trenchant character of God-is-dead thinking comes not from these basically emotive outcries but from Van Buren's straightforward attempt to show that God-statements are meaningless unless they are translated into Man-statements. What, then, of Van Buren's argument? [116]

First, unlike most theological opponents of the death of God,[117] we readily concede the validity of Van Buren's basic epistemological principle, namely, that assertions compatible with anything and everything say nothing. Contemporary analytical philosophy, in arriving at this principle, has made an inestimable contribution to epistemology, for by way of the principle, vast numbers of apparently sensible truth-claims can be readily identified as unverifiable, and time and energy can thereby be saved for intellectual pursuits capable of yielding testable conclusions. We also agree with Van Buren that this verification principle[118] should be applied in the religious realm as fully as in other areas, and we find the Flew-Wisdom parable of striking value in illustrating the technical meaningless of numerous God-claims made in the history of religions and by many religious believers today, including those Protestants addicted to Neo-Orthodoxy, existentialism, and process-philosophy.[119] The God-is-dead issue, however, depends not upon whether non-Christian religions or contemporary Protestant theologians make meaningless assertions about God's existence, but whether Biblical Christianity is subject to this criticism. Van Buren is thus quite correct to focus attention on the New Testament picture of Jesus, and especially on his Resurrection; but it is exactly here that Van Buren's analysis fails—and, ironically, proves itself to suffer from the very analytical nonsensicality it mistakenly sees in Christianity's continued affirmation of a transcendent God.

The New Testament affirmation of the existence of God (the Divine Gardener in the Flew-Wisdom parable) is not a claim standing outside the realm of empirical testability. Quite the contrary: the Gardener *entered* his garden (the world) in the person of Jesus Christ, showing himself to be such "by many infallible proofs" (Acts 1:3). Mascall illustrates with Jesus' miraculous healing of the blind man in John 9, observing that "one can hardly avoid being struck by the vivid impression of eyewitness reporting and by the extremely convincing characterization of the persons involved." [120] To drive the latter point home, Mascall renders the beggar's remarks into cockney, *e.g.:* "Yesterday I couldn't see a ruddy thing and now I can see orl right. Larf that one orf!" (John 9:25). The Resurrection accounts, as I have argued in detail elsewhere,[121] provide the most decisive evidence of the empirical focus of the Biblical affirmation that "God was in Christ, reconciling the world unto himself." In I Cor. 15 the Apostle, writing in A.D. 56, explicitly states that the Christian God-claim, grounded in the Resurrection of Christ, is not compatible with anything and everything and therefore meaningless: after listing the names of eyewitnesses who had had contact with the resurrected Christ (and noting that five hundred other people had seen him, most of whom were still alive), Paul says: "If Christ has not been raised, then our preaching is in vain and your faith is in vain." The early Christians were quite willing to subject their religious beliefs to concrete, empirical test. Their faith was not blind faith; it was solidly grounded in empirical facticity.[122]

But, argues Van Buren, the New Testament claims only *appear* to be of an empirical nature. When the writers speak of Jesus as God and describe his miracles, "they were saying the most that they could say about this man." The Resurrection accounts are but the final proof of how thoroughly Jesus' liberating personality changed the lives of his disciples; here we see Jesus' followers experiencing what R. M. Hare has called a "blik"—a "discernment situation" in which they place a quite new evaluation on their whole experiential world.

On looking closely at Van Buren's superficially plausible interpretation, we discover that, being compatible with anything and everything, it says nothing! Consider: *any* point of evidence cited from the New Testament documents to refute Van Buren (*e.g.*, the doubting Thomas episode) will be dismissed by him as simply indicating how *powerful* the "discernment" was for the disciples. The peculiar situation therefore arises that *no* amount of evidence (including Peter's direct statement, "we did not follow cleverly devised myths when we made known to you the power and coming of our Lord Jesus Christ, but we were eyewitnesses of his majesty"!—II Pet. 1:16) could dislodge Van Buren from his humanistic reduction of the Biblical narratives.

The meaninglessness of Van Buren's approach will become clearer by the use of analogies drawn from non-religious spheres. Suppose you were to say to me: "Napoleon conquered Europe in a remarkably short time with amazing military resourcefulness, and after suffering defeat and exile, he escaped and came close to overwhelming Europe once again";[123] and I were to reply, "You really are impressed by Napoleon, aren't you?" Obviously irritated, you retort: "Yes, I am impressed by Napoleon, *but* I'm trying to tell you some facts about him, and here are documents to prove what I have just said." Then I would blandly answer: "How wonderful! The very interest you show in marshaling such material shows me how great an impact Napoleon has had on you." Your frustration would be boundless, for no matter what evidence you produced, I could, following Van Buren's approach, dismiss it simply as an empirical code representing a non-empirical "blik" situation.

Or suppose I were to say: "My wife studied art history and enjoys painting"; and you commented: "You really love her, don't you?" "Well, yes," I would say, "but she *does* have artistic interests. Here are her transcripts representing art courses she's taken, here are paintings she's done, and. . . ." At which point you interrupt with a sweep of the hand: "Come, come, no need to bother with that; I can recognize true love when I see it! How commendable!" My composure would be retained with great difficulty, since I would find it impossible under the circumstances to get across a genuinely factual point.

In this way Van Buren endeavors to "larf orf" the empirical claims of Scripture to the existence of God in Jesus Christ; but his endeavor lands him squarely in the abyss of analytical non-sensicality where he mistakenly tries to place the Biblical witness to the supernatural. Indeed, Van Buren is not even being faithful to the Wittgenstein of the *Philosophical Investigations*, whose principles he seeks to follow: for Wittgenstein saw the necessity of respecting the "language game" actually being played and the absurdity of reductionistically trying to say that a given language game really means something else. Wittgenstein asks if it is proper to assert that the sentence "The broom is in the corner" really means "The broomstick is in the corner, and the brush is in the corner, and the broomstick is attached to the brush." He answers:

> If we were to ask anyone if he meant this he would probably say that he had not thought specially of the broomstick or especially of the brush at all. And that would be the *right* answer, for he meant to speak neither of the stick nor of the brush in particular.[124]

By the same token, Van Buren's reductionistic translation of the empirical language game of Biblical incarnation-claims into non-cognitive, ethical language is artificial, unwarranted, and at cross-purposes with the whole thrust of the Biblical narratives. The same is true of the literary, urban, eschatological-mystical, and social reductionisms of scriptural God-assertions carried on respectively by Vahanian, Cox, Altizer, and Hamilton. The God proclaimed by the Bible as having entered the empirical world in Jesus is not dead, though an obvious attempt has been made to murder him using the lethal weapon of reductionistic, humanistic bias. But the murder of God in the interests of Man has always had consequences exactly the opposite of those anticipated, as our Lord indicated when he said, "Whosoever will save his life shall lose it: and whosoever will lose his life for my sake shall find it." It is ironic that the theothanatologists have not learned from the experience of Sartre's Goetz: "J'ai tué Dieu parce qu'il me séparait des hommes et voici que sa mort m'isole encore plus sûrement." [125]

The Case History Yields a Moral

Why have the God-is-dead theologians so easily run into this humanistic dead-end? The answer lies in their starting point, and a sobering moral can be drawn therefrom. As we pointed out through primary and secondary sources employed in the early portion of this paper, every one of the death-of-God thinkers was profoundly influenced by the dialectic orientation of Neo-Orthodoxy. Alasdair McIntyre, in his incisive critique of Robinson's *Honest to God*, draws the connection between Neo-Orthodoxy and "Christian atheism":

> We can see the harsh dilemma of a would-be contemporary theology. The theologians begin from orthodoxy, but the orthodoxy which has learnt from Kierkegaard and Barth becomes too easily a closed circle, in which believer speaks only to believer, in which all human content is concealed. Turning aside from this arid in-group theology, the most perceptive theologians wish to translate what they have to say to an atheistic world. But they are doomed to one of two failures. Either they succeed in their translation: in which case what they find themselves saying has been transformed into the atheism of their hearers. Or they fail in their translation: in which case no one hears what they have to say but themselves.[126]

And why does the Kierkegaardian-Barthian theology operate as a "closed circle"? Because of its basic premise that, as MacIntyre well puts it, "the Word of God cannot be identified with *any* frail human attempt to comprehend it." [127] Since the logical consequences of such a principle are a fallible Scripture and a kenotically limited Jesus, the Bible appears to secular man as no different qualitatively from other human writings, and the Incarnate Christ becomes indistinguishable from other men. The believer thus moves in a closed circle of irrational commitment, which the unbeliever finds impossible to accept. The God of such an irrational faith has no recourse but to become a transcendent Wholly Other, and when analytical

philosophy poses the obvious verification question as to the ontological existence of the transcendent, no answer is possible.
In the Flew-Wisdom parable, the Gardener-God of Neo-Orthodoxy *cannot* be discovered empirically in the garden, for his
transcendence would thereby be profaned;[128] thus the garden
of the world looks as secular to the believer as to the unbeliever, and the latter rightly asks: "Just how does what you call
an invisible, intangible, eternally elusive gardener differ from
an imaginary gardener or even from no gardener at all?" To
this, the "yes-and-no" dialectic of Neo-Orthodoxy can say
nothing whatever; and the obvious result is the death of God.
For contemporary theological thought, the Bible would be no
more erroneous if there were no God; the Resurrection of
Christ in Barth's theology would be no more unverifiable if
God did not exist; and Tillich's "Protestant principle" would
make Jesus no more kenotic if there were no "Ground of all
being." The God-assertions of mainline theology in the twentieth century are compatible with anything and everything, and
therefore can be dispensed with as meaningless. God dies, and
only modern secular man is left.

This appalling situation—what Fitch calls the theological Sell-
Out—is the direct result of a refusal to acknowledge God's
power to reveal himself without qualification here on earth.
The ancient Calvinist aphorism, *finitum non capax infiniti*, has
been allowed to obscure the central Biblical stress on God's
incarnation and on his ability to speak the Word of truth
through human words. The Bible does not present God as Rudolf Otto's transcendent, vague Wholly Other or as Tillich's
indescribable Being, itself, but as the God of Abraham, Isaac,
and Jacob, who through the entire expanse of scriptural revelation speaks inerrant truth to men and who manifestly enters
the garden of this world in Jesus Christ (cf. John 20:15). For
orthodox Christianity, unafraid of a miraculous Saviour or of an
inerrant Scripture, God's existence does make a difference in
the world, for only on the basis of his existence is revelation
explainable. Mainline Protestant theology, having lost its doctrine of revelation and inspiration in the days of liberalism and
never having recovered it, now finds itself incapable of showing why God is necessary at all.

The moral, then, is simply this: Physicians of the soul will inevitably find themselves faced with the corpse of Deity if they lose their confidence in God's special revelation. The final and best evidence of God's existence lies in his Word—in the triple sense of Christ, the gospel he proclaimed, and the Scripture that infallibly conveys it. The historicity of the Resurrection, the facticity of the Biblical miracles, the internal consistency of Holy Writ and its freedom from empirical error: these must be sustained, or the God of Scripture will face away into a misty transcendence for us too, and eventually disappear. Conversely, if we do maintain the doctrine of God's *historische* revelation through an inerrant Bible, we will find that, in an age of almost universal theological debility, we will be able to present a meaningful God to an epoch that desperately needs divine grace. The only living God is the God of the Bible, and for the sake of secular man today we had better not forget it.

Final Autopsy: A Mistaken Identity Revealed

The God-is-dead movement is a reflection and special case of an abnormal preoccupation with Death in our time. On the popular level we have sick comedies such as *The Loved One;* on the sociological level, analyses such as *The American Way of Death;* on the psychological level, the wide acceptance of Freud's theme of the *mortido;* and on the plane of theoretical analysis revealing works such as Feifel's anthology *The Meaning of Death,* containing essays by Jung, Tillich, Kaufmann, and many others.[129]

It is interesting to note other eras when death was an overarching concern. Huizinga, in his classic *The Waning of the Middle Ages* notes how "the vision of death" embraced late medieval man, and how the dance of death, the surrealistic horrors of Hieronymous Bosch's depictions of hell, and the satanic black masses blended into a symbolic projection of a collapsing culture. Fin-de-siècle France is another illustration of the same phenomenon: J.-K. Huysmans' description in his novel *A Rebours* of a "funeral feast" in which the orchestra played dirges while guests, dressed in black, silently ate dark foods served by

negresses was no less based on fact than his accounts of satanic
rites in *La-Bàs;* the Parisian society of the 1880s and 1890s, living in the wake of the Franco-Prussian War, had fallen into
degeneration and corruption, and the preoccupation with
death and hell was the cultural equivalent of psychological sub-
limation.

Today's death-of-God thinking is likewise symbolic. Holy
Scripture speaks of death also, but it is *man's* death upon which
the Bible dwells: "The wages of sin is death, but the gift of God
is eternal life through Jesus Christ our Lord" (Rom. 6:23).
Scripture finds the human race, not God, in the throws of
death. And when God does die, it is on the Cross, as an expi-
ation for man's mortal disease; and God's conquest of the powers of death is evidenced in his Resurrection triumph.[130]

"The sting of death is sin," however, and from Adam on the
sinner has sought above all to hide himself. Thus in our day
men unwilling to face their own mortality have projected their
own deserved demise upon their Maker and Redeemer. As suggested at the beginning of this essay, the theothanatological
movement could provide a mystery writer with a classic case
of the "wrong corpse": for when one examines the body carefully, it turns out to be, not God but *oneself*—"dead in tres-
passes and sins." And *this* corpse (unlike that of Deity) fully
satisfies the empirical test of verifiability, as every cemetery
illustrates.[131]

In romantic literature, the *Doppelgänger* motif (a character
meeting himself) is employed as a device to symbolize the individual's attainment of self-awareness. Let us hope that the
present autopsy, insofar as it brings a sin-sick theology to a realistic confrontation with itself, may contribute to such self-
knowledge.[132] How revealing it is, for example to read William
Hamilton's autobiographical description of his entrée into the
death-of-God sphere at age forty: "Time was getting short and
I saw I needed to make things happen." [133] When we realize the
true identity of the theothanatological corpse, such a remark
fits into place. It is the natural man, the builder of towers of
Babel, who must "make things happen" theologically. For the
essence of the scriptural gospel is that sinful man cannot make
things happen in the spiritual life; the living God has made

them happen in Jesus Christ, and the only true theology endeavors, above all, to remain faithful to the one who "after he had offered one sacrifice for sins for ever, sat down on the right hand of God."

And if, as Christian believers, the silence of God in our age sometimes makes us wonder in the depth of our souls if he still remains with us, let us soberly consider Sir Robert Anderson's profound observation that God's silence is a reminder that the amnesty of the Cross is still available to men: "A silent Heaven gives continuing proof that this great amnesty is still in force, and that the guiltiest of men may turn to God and find forgiveness of sins and eternal life." [134] The task then stands: to work while it is yet day, for the night cometh when no man can work. As for the nature of that work, Henry van Dyke described it well in his touching allegory *The Lost Word;* it is to proclaim to our generation the Word which has been lost through preoccupation with lesser words:

> "My son, you have sinned deeper than you know. The word with which you parted so lightly is the key-word of all life and joy and peace. Without it the world has no meaning, and existence no rest, and death no refuge. It is the word that purifies love, and comforts grief, and keeps hope alive forever. It is the most precious thing that ever ear has heard, or mind has known, or heart has conceived. It is the name of Him who has given us life and breath and all things richly to enjoy; the name of Him who, though we may forget Him, never forgets us; the name of Him who pities us as you pity your suffering child; the name of Him who, though we wander far from Him, seeks us in the wilderness, and sent His Son, even as His Son has sent me this night, to breathe again that forgotten name in the heart that is perishing without it. Listen, my son, listen with all your soul to the blessed name of God our Father." [135]

Notes

1. We prefer the neutral term "Theothanatology" to J. Robert Nelson's "Theothanasia" (implying that the new theologians have put God to death; except for Altizer, who speaks, à la Nietzsche, of "passionately willing God's death," the death-of-

God theologians regard the divine demise as a "natural" phenomenon of our time, over which one has little or no control) or "Theothanatopsis" (which conjures up the shade of William Cullen Bryant, who would have been horror-struck at this whole movement).

2. *Time* initially described the movement in the Religion section of its October 22, 1965, issue; the Easter Cover Story in the April 8, 1966, issue deals with the question of God's existence in light of current death-of-God thinking. For *The New Yorker*'s valuable account of theothanatology in the contemporary theological scene, see note 11 below.

3. Mack B. Stokes, "The Nontheistic Temper of the Modern Mind," *Religion in Life*, XXXIV (Spring 1965), 245–57.

4. "Why This Non-God-Talk? An Editorial," *The Christian Century*, LXXXII (December 1, 1965), 1467.

5. William Hamilton, "The Shape of a Radical Theology," *The Christian Century*, LXXXII (October 6, 1965), 1220. Paul van Buren, however, "expressed astonishment at Hamilton's announcement that there would soon be an organization of death-of-God theologians, with a new journal, etc., etc. Apparently there is less communication within this trinity [Altizer, Hamilton, Van Buren] than is assumed" (J. Robert Nelson, "Decide, Theothanasia, or What Do You Mean?" *The Christian Century*, LXXXII [November 17, 1965], 1415). In a more recent issue of *Christian Century* (LXXXII [February 16, 1966], 223), "Pen-ultimate" provides a satirical application blank for the "God-Is-Dead Club."

6. *E.g.*, in his book, *The New Essence of Christianity* (New York: Association Press, 1961).

7. He continues: "One cannot deny that he left the cloister, had some doubts, stomach aches and a father. At the same time it is equally evident that he was a highly theocentric thinker ('Nothing can be more present . . . than God himself'), and that he was also what Weber and Troeltsch call an ascetic of the 'intramundane' type whose hope was in the world above—which, I take it, is not quite 'the world.' But of course Luther's asceticism and theocentrism should never keep him from being used in Protestantism as a symbol for secular theology and the God-is-dead movement. After all, Protestant theologians have a long and glorious tradition of using history, shall we say, 'freely' " (Charles M. Nielsen, "The Loneliness of Protestantism, or, More Benedictines, Please!" *The Christian Century*, LXXXII [September 15, 1965], 1121).

8. Cf. Montgomery, "Lutheran Hermeneutics and Hermeneutics Today," in *Aspects of Biblical Hermeneutics* ("Concordia Theological Monthly. Occasional Papers," No. 1; St. Louis,

Missouri, 1966), pp. 78–108 (soon to be published also in German translation in *Lutherischer Rundblick*).

9. Quoted in *Time*'s report of the seventeenth Annual Meeting of the Evangelical Theological Society in Nashville, Tennessee, December 27–29, 1965 (*Time* [January 7, 1966], p. 70).

10. Cox's informal paper was titled "Second Thoughts on the Secular Society" and was delivered at the Seabury-Western Theological Seminary on January 22, 1966; further reference to this paper will be made below. I was privileged to attend the Annual Meeting of the American Society of Christian Ethics as Carl F. H. Henry's surrogate; my report of the sessions appears in *Christianity Today*, X (February 18, 1966), 538.

11. Quoted in an interview with Ved Mehta, "The New Theologian. I. Ecce Homo," *The New Yorker*, XLI (November 13, 1965), 144.

12. See especially Hamilton's "The Death of God Theology," *The Christian Scholar*, XLVIII (Spring 1965), 27–48.

13. Cox made this point in his unpublished lecture, "Second Thoughts on the Secular Society"; see note 10, above.

14. Hamilton, "The Shape of a Radical Theology," *loc. cit.* The "hard" radicals have had hard things to say about their "soft" counterparts, *e.g.*: "Dr. Altizer considers Harvey Cox a 'phony masquerading as a member of the avantgarde,' a sociologist in theologian's clothing. Dr. Hamilton of Colgate Rochester describes *The Secular City* as "pop-Barth' . . . 'Dr. Cox will keep neo-orthodoxy alive another six months,' he scoffs" (Lee E. Dirks, "The Ferment in Protestant Thinking," *The National Observer* [January 31, 1966], p. 16).

15. Cf. his article, "Sociology of Religion in a Post-Religious Era," *The Christian Scholar*, XLVIII (Spring 1965), 9–26.

16. So Cox stated in his paper, "Second Thoughts on the Secular Society" (see note 10 above).

17. Hamilton, "The Death of God Theology," pp. 32, 34.

18. *Ibid.* p. 34.

19. Nelson, "Decide, Theothanasia, or What Do You Mean?" *loc. cit.*

20. Mehta, *op. cit.*, p. 138. Gilkey of Chicago, a critic of the movement, is now endeavoring to compile a book of essays on the new Christian Radicalism, but Vahanian was not included among the prospective contributors. Vahanian's relative (neo-Barthian) conservativism is demonstrated in his recent article, "Swallowed Up by Godlessness" (*The Christian Century*, LXXXII [December 8, 1965], 1506), where he argues that the radical death-of-God view "not only surrenders to the secu-

larism of our time but views it as the remedy instead of the sickness"; See G. Vahanian's book, *No Other God* (New York: George Braziller, 1966).

21. Vahanian, *The Death of God: The Culture of Our Post-Christian Era* (New York: George Braziller, 1961), p. 228.

22. Vahanian, *Wait Without Idols* (New York: George Braziller, 1964), pp. 31–32. Several essays in this book have been published in less complete form in journals, *e.g.*, "The Future of Christianity in a Post-Christian Era," *The Centennial Review*, VIII (Spring, 1964), 160–73; "Beyond the Death of God: The Need of Cultural Revolution," *Dialog*, I (Autumn, 1962), 18–21.

23. Tillich described this phenomenon as the substitution of non-ultimate concerns for the only true ultimate concern, Being itself; Voegelin refers to such idolatry as "Metastatic Gnosis" (see Montgomery, *The Shape of the Past: An Introduction to Philosophical Historiography* ["History in Christian Perspective," Vol. 1; Ann Arbor, Michigan: Edward Bros., 1963], pp. 127–38).

24. Vahanian, *Wait Without Idols*, p. 233.

25. Vahanian, "The Empty Cradle," *Theology Today*, XIII (January, 1957), 526.

26. Vahanian, *The Death of God*, p. 231.

27. Vahanian, *Wait Without Idols*, p. 231.

28. *Ibid.*, p. 46.

29. Quoted in Mehta, *loc. cit.*

30. Harvey Cox, *The Secular City: Secularization and Urbanization in Theological Perspective* (New York: Macmillan Paperbacks, 1965), p. 20. In his recent paper at the American Society of Christian Ethics (see note 10 above), Cox stated that a revised, hardbound edition of his book will soon appear, and that this second edition will become the basis of several translations in European languages.

31. *Ibid.*, p. 261. Wilder's statement appears in his essay, "Art and Theological Meaning," *The New Orpheus* (New York: Sheed and Ward, 1964), p. 407.

32. Cox, *The Secular City*, p. 266.

33. *Ibid.*, p. 258.

34. *Ibid.*

35. See note 10 above and corresponding text. Cf. Cox's article, "The Place and Purpose of Theology" (*The Christian Century*, LXXXIII [January 5, 1966], 7), where he hits the "hard" death-of-God Radicals for missing the prophetic challenge of the modern revolutionary polis: "Rather than helping the prophets

greet a religionless, revolutionary tomorrow, some theologians are more interested in dissecting the cadaver of yesterday's pieties."

36. Not so incidentally, Cox approvingly quoted his Harvard acquaintances Krister Stendahl ("you can only have Neo-Orthodoxy after a good long period of liberalism") and Erik Erikson, author of the psychoanalytic study, *Young Man Luther,* whose view of the "identity crisis" makes Stendhal's point in psychological terms.

37. Altizer, *Mircea Eliade and the Dialectic of the Sacred* (Philadelphia: Westminster Press, 1963); the book grew out of an article, "Mircea Eliade and the Recovery of the Sacred," *The Christian Scholar,* XLV (Winter, 1962), 267–89. As Hamilton notes, Altizer's book is a mixture of Eliade's views and Altizer's and therefore is "not structurally satisfactory" ("The Death of God Theology," p. 31).

38. *Ibid.,* p. 32.

39. Altizer, *Oriental Mysticism and Biblical Eschatology* (Philadelphia: Westminster Press, 1961). Some of the material in this book has been incorporated into Altizer's essay, "The Religious Meaning of Myth and Symbol," published in *Truth, Myth, and Symbol,* ed. Altizer, *et al.* (Englewood Cliffs, N. J.: Prentice-Hall, 1962), pp. 87–108.

40. Like Toynbee, Altizer places Christianity and Mahayana Buddhism on the religious pinnacle together. Altizer's dependence on Toynbee would be a subject worth investigating.

41. Altizer, "Nirvana and the Kingdom of God," in *New Theology No. 1,* ed. Martin E. Marty and Dean G. Peerman (New York: Macmillan Paperbacks, 1964), p. 164. This essay first appeared in the University of Chicago's *Journal of Religion,* April 1963.

42. Altizer, "Theology and the Death of God," *The Centennial Review,* VIII, (Spring, 1964), 130. It is interesting to speculate whether Jaroslav Pelikan is fully aware of the consequences of his attempts theologically to baptize Kierkegaard (*From Luther to Kierkegaard*) and Nietzsche (*Fools for Christ*).

43. Cf. Altizer, "Word and History," *Theology Today,* XXII October, 1965), 385. The degree of current popular interest in Altizer's radicalism is indicated by the fact that the *Chicago Daily News* adapted this article for publication in its Panorama section (January 29, 1966, p. 4).

44. Altizer, *Review of Christianity and the Encounter of the World Religions* by Paul Tillich, *The Christian Scholar,* XLVI (Winter 1963), 362.

45. Altizer, "Theology and the Death of God," p. 132.

46. *Ibid.* On Nietzsche vis-à-vis current thought, see the excellent article by Erich Heller, "The Importance of Nietzsche," *Encounter* (London), XXII (April 1964), 59–66.

47. Altizer made this point in a keynote speech at a recent conference at Emory University on "America and the Future of Technology"; it was reported in *Christianity Today*, X (December 17, 1965), 1310.

48. Altizer, "Theology and the Death of God," p. 134.

49. Altizer, "The Religious Meaning of Myth and Symbol," p. 95.

50. *Ibid.*

51. Quoted in a symposium-interview in *Christianity Today*, X (January 7, 1966), 374.

52. *Ibid.* The expression, "third age of the Spirit," comes from the twelfth-century mystic-millennial theologian Joachim of Floris (see Montgomery, *The Shape of the Past*, p. 48). As in Cox, so in Altizer we find a definite tone of anabaptist enthusiasm.

53. Altizer, "Creative Negation in Theology," *Christian Century,* LXXXII (July 7, 1965), 866–67.

54. Hamilton, "The Shape of a Radical Theology," *loc. cit.*, 1219–1220. Apparently Hamilton just made it in time, for Altizer is of the opinion that "the real barrier to this kind of thinking is mainly age, because most of those under 45 do respond to it" (*Chicago Daily News*, January 29, 1966, *loc. cit.*).

55. Hamilton, *The New Essence of Christianity*, p. 55.

56. *Ibid.*, p. 116.

57. *Ibid.*, pp. 93–94.

58. Nelson, "Deicide, Theothanasia, or What Do You Mean?" *loc. cit.*

59. Hamilton, "Daring to Be the Enemy of God," *The Christian Scholar*, XLVI (Spring 1963), 40–54. Barth's lavish appreciation of Mozart is well known.

60. Hamilton, "The Shape of a Radical Theology," p. 1220.

61. Hamilton, "Thursday's Child: The Theologian Today and Tomorrow," *Theology Today*, XX (January 1964), 489, 494.

62. Mehta, *op. cit.*, p. 142.

63. Hamilton, "The Shape of a Radical Theology," p. 1219.

64. Cf. the following lines in "Thursday's Child": "The theologian is sometimes inclined to suspect that Jesus Christ is best understood not as either the object or ground of faith, and not as person, event, or community, but simply as a place to be, a

standpoint. That place is, of course, alongside the neighbor, being for him. This may be the meaning of Jesus' true humanity, and it may even be the meaning of his divinity, and thus of divinity itself" (p. 494).

65. Hamilton, "The Death of God Theology," pp. 27–48. Hamilton is collaborating with Altizer on a soon to be published collection of articles; the book will carry the title *Radical Theology and the Death of God.*

66. Hamilton, "The Death of God Theology," pp. 46–47.

67. *Ibid.*, p. 40.

68. *Ibid.*, p. 41.

69. Interestingly, while Hamilton was still in theological limbo, he wrote an article on Hamlet, finding portrayed there the death of a demonic idea of God: "Hamlet and Providence," *"The Christian Scholar,* XLVII (Fall 1964), 193–207.

70. Hamilton, "The Death of God Theology," p. 46.

71. Quoted in an interview with Mehta, *op. cit.,* p. 150.

72. Van Buren's thesis dealt with Calvin: *Christ in Our Place: The Substitutionary Character of Calvin's Doctrine of Reconciliation* (Grand Rapids, Michigan: Eerdmans, 1957).

73. Van Buren, "Theology in the Context of Culture," *The Christian Century, LXXXII* (April 7, 1965), 429.

74. *Ibid.*

75. Interview with Mehta, *op. cit.,* p. 143.

76. Antony Flew, "Theology and Falsification," in *New Essays in Philosophical Theology,* ed. Flew and MacIntyre (London: SCM Press, 1955), p. 96.

77. Van Buren, "The Dissolution of the Absolute," *Religion in Life,* XXXIV (Summer 1965), 334–42.

78. Interview with Mehta, *op. cit.,* p. 153.

79. *Ibid.*, p. 148.

80. Van Buren, *The Secular Meaning of the Gospel,* p. 200.

81. *Ibid.*, p. 134.

82. *Ibid.*, p. 198. Parenthetically, it is worth noting that Van Buren's argument is no more valid in reference to alchemy than it is in regard to theology; see Montgomery, "Cross, Constellation, and Crucible: Lutheran Astrology and Alchemy in the Age of the Reformation," *Transactions of the Royal Society of Canada,* 4th ser., I (1963), 251–70 (also published in the British periodical *Ambix, the Journal of the Society for the Study of Alchemy*

and Early Chemistry, XI [June 1963], 65–86, and shortly to appear in French in *Revue d'Histoire et de Philosophie Religieuses*).

83. Van Buren, "Theology in the Context of Culture," p. 430.

84. Reference will be made to Mascall's book in the next section of this paper. Any attempt to show the connections between the God-is-dead movement and the popular British radicalism represented by Robinson, Eric Vidler, *et al.* would carry us too far afield; see on the latter my critique of Bishop Pike's theology in the April and May issues of *Sunday School Times*.

85. Nielsen, "The Loneliness of Protestantism," *loc. cit.*

86. Moulton, "Apocalypse in a Casket?" *The Christian Century*, LXXXII (November 17, 1965), 1413.

87. Shiner, "Goodbye, Death-of-God!" *The Christian Century*, LXXXII (November 17, 1965), 1418.

88. Van Buren, "Theology in the Context of Culture," *loc. cit.*

89. Best known for his useful survey, *Twentieth-Century Religious Thought* (London: SCM Press, 1963), which concludes with a treatment of "Existentialism and Ontology" (pp. 351 ff.); Macquarrie explicitly identifies his own position with "those philosophies of existence and being that have been developed by Martin Heidegger and other thinkers" and theologically with "the related work of men like Bultmann and Tillich" (p. 374).

90. Macquarrie, "How Can We Think of God?" *Theology Today*, XXII (July 1965), 200–201.

91. Stokes, "The Nontheistic Temper of the Modern Mind," *op. cit.*, p. 257.

92. Philadelphia: Westminster Press, 1962.

93. Cobb, "From Crisis Theology to the Post-Modern World," *The Centennial Review*, VIII (Spring 1964), 184–85. Cf. Cobb, *A Christian Natural Theology, Based on the Thought of Alfred North Whitehead* (Philadelphia: Westminster Press, 1965), *passim*.

94. Meland, "Alternative to Absolutes," *Religion in Life*, XXXIV (Summer, 1965), 346. For further explications of process thinking in current theology, see Schubert M. Ogden, "Faith and Truth," *The Christian Century*, LXXXII (September 1, 1965), 1057–60; Norman Pittenger, "A Contemporary Trend in North American Theology: Process-Thought and Christian Faith," *Religion in Life*, XXXIV (Autumn, 1965), 500–510; and Gene Reeves, "A Look at Contemporary American Theology," *ibid.*, pp. 511–25 (Reeves employs—with some qualification—the rubric "Christless theology" for process thinking).

95. Gilkey, "Is God Dead?" *The Voice: Bulletin of Crozer Theological Seminary*, LVII (January 1965), 4.

96. Gilkey, "God Is NOT Dead," *ibid.*, pp. 9–10. That Gilkey's approach to revelation is neither that of Reformation orthodoxy (which regard the Bible as God's inerrant word) nor that of classic Neo-Orthodoxy which took Scripture, though regarded as errant, as its theological *point de départ*), becomes clear when he writes: "Our theological analysis must begin with man. If we felt sure that the divine word in Scripture was the truth, then the Bible might be our starting point" (Gilkey, "Dissolution and Reconstruction in Theology," *The Christian Century*, LXXXII [February 3, 1965], 137). But in finding his answers to the human predicament in the revelation of an unconditioned, transcendent God, Gilkey places himself in the general stream of Neo-Orthodoxy.

97. Gilkey, "God Is NOT Dead," p. 11.

98. Van Buren, "The Dissolution of the Absolute," *op. cit.*, pp. 338–39.

99. Cf. Paul Edwards, "Professor Tillich's Confusions," *Mind*, LXXIV (April 1965), 192–214; and note the pertinence of Quine's remarks at the beginning of his essay, "On What There Is": "A curious thing about the ontological problem is its simplicity. It can be put in three Anglo-Saxon monosyllables: 'What is there?' It can be answered, moreover, in a word— 'Everything' [or 'Being itself'!]—and everyone will accept this answer as true. However, this is merely to say that there is what there is. There remains room for disagreement over cases [e.g., the existence of the transcendent God of the Bible!]" (Willard van Orman Quine, *From a Logical Point of View* [2d ed.; New York: Harper Torchbooks, 1963], p. 1). Reference is also in order to the refutations of Hartshorne's ontological argument for God's existence; see *The Ontological Argument*, ed. Alvin Plantinga (Garden City, New York: Doubleday Anchor Books, 1965), especially pp. 123–180.

100. See William James, *The Varieties of Religious Experience*, *passim*; and cf. *William James on Psychical Research*, ed. Gardner Murphy and Robert O. Ballou (New York: Viking Press, 1960), *passim*. Note also my "Critique of William James' *Varieties of Religious Experience*," in my *Shape of the Past: An Introduction to Philosophical Historiography* ("History in Christian Perspective," Vol. 1; Ann Arbor, Michigan: Edwards Brothers, 1963), pp. 312–340.

101. Cf. Brand Blanshard, "Critical Reflections on Karl Barth," in *Faith and the Philosophers*, ed. John Hick (New York: St. Martin's Press, 1964), pp. 159–200 (other papers in this symposium volume are also relevant to the issue); and C. B. Martin, "A Religious Way of Knowing," in *New Essays in Philosophical Theology*, ed. Antony Flew and Alasdair Mac-

Intyre (London: SCM Press, 1955), pp. 76–95.

102. This point is well made by the psychoanalyst in A. N. Prior's clever dialog, "Can Religion Be Discussed?" (*ibid.*, pp. 1–11).

103. I have endeavored to show the fallacies of the presuppositionalist and fideist viewpoints in reference to Christian apologetics; see my articles, "The Place of Reason," *His Magazine of the Inter-Varsity Christian Fellowship*, XXVI (February 1966), 8–12; (March 1966), 13–16, 21.

104. Cf. his book, *Theology and the Scientific Study of Religion* ("The Lutheran Studies Series," Vol. 2; Minneapolis: T. S. Denison, 1961).

105. Holmer, "Contra the New Theologies," *The Christian Century*, LXXXII (March 17, 1965), 330–331.

106. *Ibid.*, p. 332. Note also in this connection Holmer's article, "Atheism and Theism," *Lutheran World*, XIII (1966), 14–25.

107. Fitch, "The Sell-Out, or the Well Acculturated Christian," *The Christian Century*, LXXXIII (February 16, 1966), 202.

108. *Ibid.*, p. 203.

109. See my text at note 36 above.

110. So argues Fitch, *loc. cit.*

111. Quoted in Dirks, *loc. cit.*

112. Nielsen, "Can Faith Validate God-Talk?" in *New Theology No. 1* (*op. cit.*), p. 147. This penetrating essay first appeared in the July 1963 issue of *Theology Today*.

113. Cf. Frederick Ferré, *Language, Logic and God* (New York: Harper & Row, 1961), chap. viii ("The Logic of Encounter"), pp. 94–104.

114. Quoted in Dirks, *loc. cit.* Among the more blatant imprecisions in Altizer's thought are: (1) his highly debatable assumption that negation is the ideal way to fulfillment (does one, for example, create the best society or government by completely destroying the existing order and starting over, or by refining what already exists?); (2) his unbelievably naïve and unrealistic identification of the basic doctrines of Christianity with those of Buddhism (on this, cf. my article, "The Christian Church in McNeill's *Rise of the West:* An Overview and Critique," forthcoming in *The Evangelical Quarterly*); and (3) the utterly unverifiable, indescribable character of his "God beyond God" and of his non-objective, fully kenotic Christ—the "Jesus of the third age of the Spirit" (is he not the Jesus of *Altizer's* spirit? certainly he is not the Biblical Jesus, who is "the same yesterday, today, and forever"!).

115. The discussion took place on Norman Ross's program, "Off

the Cuff," Monday, March 28, beginning at 12:30 A.M. (Channel 7, Chicago).

116. For Van Buren's position, see my text at notes 71–83 above.

117. *E.g.*, M.C. D'Arcy, *No Absent God* ("Religious Perspectives," Vol. 6; New York: Harper & Row, 1962), chap. i, pp. 15–31; and Eric Mascall, *The Secularisation of Christianity: An Analysis and a Critique* (London: Darton, Longman & Todd, 1965), pp. 103–104. Other problems with Mascall's (nonetheless valuable) book are its strongly Anglo-Catholic perspective (stress on natural theology, the visible church introduced as a kind of *deus ex machina* into arguments, and reference to such non-Biblical miracles as the Holy Shroud of Turin!), and a mild incorporation of the *finitum non est capax infiniti* principle (p. 38), which, as we shall emphasize later, is actually one of the ideological roots of the death-of-God error.

118. It will be observed that the principle as here stated is not identical in form with A.J. Ayer's famous verifiability criterion that played a central role in the development of Logical Positivism. Thus the philosophical attempts to break down Ayer's principle are not relevant to the present discussion even if they are held to be successful (which is by no means certain).

119. I have developed this point in reference to Neo-Orthodox and existentialistic views of revelation in my article, "Inspiration and Inerrancy: A New Departure," *Evangelical Theological Society Bulletin*, VIII (Spring 1965), 45–75.

120. Mascall, *op. cit.*, p. 240.

121. Montgomery, "History & Christianity," *His Magazine of the Inter-Varsity Christian Fellowship*, December 1964–March 1965 (available as a His Reprint); and *The Shape of the Past* (*op. cit.*), pp. 138–45, 235–37, and *passim*.

122. Cf. my paper, "The Theologian's Craft: A Discussion of Theory Formation and Theory Testing in Theology," *Concordia Theological Monthly*, XXXVII (February 1966), 67–98 (soon to be published also in the *Journal of the American Scientific Affiliation*).

123. This analogy is suggested by that remarkable apologetic tour de force by Richard Whately, *Historic Doubts Relative to Napoleon Bonaparte* (11th ed.; New York: Robert Carter, 1871).

124. Ludwig Wittgenstein, *Philosophical Investigations*, trans. G.E.M. Anscombe (Oxford: Blackwell, 1953), Pt. I, sect. 60. Cf. George Pitcher, *The Philosophy of Wittgenstein* (Englewood Cliffs, N. J.: Prentice-Hall, 1964), chap. vii, pp. 171–187.

125. Jean-Paul Sartre, *Le Diable et le Bon Dieu* (Paris: Gallimard, 1951), p. 237. Cf. Georges Gusdorf, "The Absence of God in the World Today," *Lutheran World*, XIII (1966), 1–13.

126. Alasdair MacIntyre, "God and the Theologians," *Encounter* (London), XXI (September, 1963), 7. Gilkey in his Crozer Lectures (*op. cit.*) makes the same point. Cf. Robert W. Lunk's comment in his report on the Second Drew University Consultation on Hermeneutics (April 9–11, 1964): "Neo-orthodoxy taught that God is never object but always subject, with the result that third generation neo-orthodox theologians have been forced to wrestle with the non-phenomenal character of God. They are unwilling to settle for God as noumenon (perhaps as a legacy of theologies of history, and perhaps as the result of a radical empiricism), which means that for them God does not 'appear' at all" (*Theology Today*, XXI [October, 1964], 303).

127. MacIntyre, "God and the Theologians," p. 5 (MacIntyre's italics).

128. Cf. Montgomery, "Karl Barth and Contemporary Theology of History," published both in the *Evangelical Theological Society Bulletin*, VI (May 1963), 39–49, and in *The Cresset*, XXVII (November 1963), 8–14.

129. Herman Feifel, ed., *The Meaning of Death* (New York: McGraw-Hill, 1965).

130. Cf. Gustaf Aulén, *Christus Victor*, trans. A.G. Hebert (New York: Macmillan, 1956).

131. The original presentation of this essay in lecture form had to be postponed a week because of the sudden death of my wife's mother. On the day when I was scheduled to lecture on the (unempirical) death of God, I attended the overwhelmingly empirical funeral of a loved one. This was an object lesson worth pondering.

132. Ingmar Bergman's film *The Silence* offers an analogous confrontation: "A silence has befallen us, but it is connected with the cry of the inferno. The men, the women, who have 'freed themselves' from God are not those who are happy and satisfied, who have found themselves. They are the tormented who are shown no mercy, the hungry who are not filled, the separated who cannot get away from one another. . . . Bergman in his film shows 20th century man—who does not cease in his grand technological achievements to sing his own praise and who wants to liberate himself from the tyranny of God—as he is" (Vilmos Vajta, "When God Is Silent," *Lutheran World*, XIII [1966], 60–61).

133. Hamilton, "The Shape of a Radical Theology," *loc. cit.*, 1220.

134. Sir Robert Anderson, *The Silence of God* (8th ed.: London: Hodder and Stoughton, 1907), p. 165.

135. Henry van Dyke, *The Lost Word: A Christmas Legend of Long Ago* (New York: Scribner, 1917), pp. 87–89.

MICHAEL NOVAK

The Christian and the Atheist

LANGDON GILKEY in a recent essay* spoke warmly of the revolution that has overtaken Christian theology in the last five years. He suggested that during the crisis which shook civilization through the twenties, thirties, and forties important weaknesses in the theological revival led by Barth, Niebuhr, Tillich, Bultmann and other giants went unnoticed: "The theological revival of recent decades sought boldly to speak of God in the old terms to a world of modern minds." The boldness succeeded, but after the atmosphere of wars and rumors of wars had been absorbed, harsh questions about neo-orthodoxy began to arise. A generation of younger theologians, who at first saw themselves as "a generation of 'scholastics' whose function would be to work out in greater detail the firm theological

* "Dissolution and Construction in Theology," *Christian Century* (February 3, 1965), 135–139.

principles" they imbibed from their masters, suddenly saw an abyss opening beneath their feet. Neo-orthodoxy had restored the relevance of the mythical language of the Bible. But what, precisely, does mythical language mean? "What did we mean by 'God's mighty acts,' by revelation or by 'an encounter with God'?"

For many generations, Christians had been concerned to distinguish themselves from other men—to show those ways in which Christians had advantages over others in understanding man's destiny. The fact that America was a white Christian nation sheltered American theologians. The newly recovered Biblical categories of neo-orthodoxy were freighted with powerful meaning for the religious world of seminary and pulpit. But after 1960 the style of American politics shifted from that of rural piety to that of crisp urban pragmatism. Secondly, the Negro community began to set revolutionary moral goals for American society; mere resignation gave way to concrete hope and steady accomplishment. Thirdly, American Christianity discovered the secular university. John Dewey was no longer enemy number one; Reinhold Niebuhr, whose great achievement was to puncture naïve liberal optimism before the Cold War pressed it flat, quietly led his followers into Dewey's pragmatism. In the university theologians began reading concrete American sociology, literature, and philosophy rather than traditional German theology. As America became the cultural leader of the world—leader often in ugliness and vulgarity, as well as in openness to the future—Christian theologians discovered and suddenly admired the American pragmatic, empirical temper.

Can Christianity absorb the sudden irrelevance of the categories of European Christendom, and transform its own basic insights and expectations into the language of the American experience? This is the primary question for Christian theology. The secular, urban, pragmatic civilization of the future is being nourished in American supermarkets, air terminals, and explosive slums. Can Christianity make itself heard in the clamor of city streets?

American theologians now identify first with American civilization, even before they identify with a degenerate Christianity; how can they identify with the Christianity of Mississippi rednecks, mellifluous radio preachers, and suburban church organizations in Cicero, Illinois? A deep gap has appeared between the theologians and the ordinary people of America: those good churchgoing people whose Virgin is a tearful, prayerful, white Miss America of unimpeachable mealiness. The God of these good people is, for the theologians, dead. The new theologians believe that they have discovered the reality of America, and the falsity of the American God. They are not sure they can yet speak about the true God. They do not doubt that He lives, but they will not speak of Him since all speech is bound to be falsified by the general piety. And in their self-enforced silence, they are discovering how much in common they have with men who are not Christian, with agnostics, with atheists. For the first time since Clement of Alexandria went to Plato or Aquinas to Aristotle, Christians are faced with a thoroughly worked-out, alternative secular system of values; they are sitting at the feet of atheists to learn.

The achievement of the handful of theologians who, some with forethought and others by accident, made the Death of God an event of mass communications is to have announced the enormous constructive task which lies ahead of every Christian of integrity. Nothing can any longer be taken for granted; not faith, nor the language of faith. The Reverend Billy Graham may know that God exists because he talked to Him last night; but those of pragmatic, empirical temper do not trust feelings in the heart, voices, imaginings, or unanalyzed convictions. How do we know what we mean when we say the word "God"? Sentiments, memories, images, concepts, inherited convictions prove unsatisfactory.

Still, it is too easy merely to announce, seventy years after Nietzsche, that God is dead. It is impossible, moreover, to take refuge in ethics or in the mysterious attractiveness of Jesus. For unless Jesus is God, the mystery of his attractiveness reduces to psychic idiosyncrasy: Why not Camus, or Sartre? Why not the mysterious attractiveness which Goebbels found in Hitler? If Jesus is not God, he does not offer enough to build a life upon. And as for ethics, it seems quite possible to live ethically as well as a man may without Jesus and without God.

For such reasons, I would not count myself among the death of God theologians; the real work, it seems, comes after the proclamation—the proclamation of news which, after all, is new only to pious America. The task before theologians is a constructive task. The time for great syntheses is not at hand; yet ours is, nevertheless, a time to build—or at least to send out explorations seeking materials, and to experiment with designs large and small. The starting place is the opposite of the traditional one; we do not assume that the Christian is different from the atheist, for our experience reveals how similar he is. The difficulty is to state what it is to be a Christian. We must attempt many forays into that no man's land.

What, then, is the difference between a man who is a Christian and a wholly secular man? In the last two generations we have experienced, on a large scale, the positive values involved in atheism. This striking development has unsettled our theories. It is not true that, as Dostoevsky asserted, "if there is no God, everything is permitted." A modest, concerned, effective atheism is now recognized as a viable way of life, not only for individuals but for the whole human community.

"Religion," one might say, has been so successful that even atheists have adopted many of its basic values as their own. Camus has chosen honesty, Walter Kaufmann nobility and creativity, Bertrand Russell compassion, and Alfred North Whitehead scientific conscience, with explicit dependence upon Christian history. There is nothing in a merely scientific view of the world to justify the choice of such values; historically speaking, religion sponsored or nourished them until they ripened sufficiently to be chosen apart from religion.

Quite clearly, Christians *do* certain things that nonbelievers do not—worship, pray, etc. But today few serious Christians are prepared to say that "grace" is operative only in such professedly "religious" acts. Participation in church and sacraments distinguishes Christians in an objective way; but what discernible difference is there inwardly and in action? For most of the moments of every day believers and nonbelievers perform similar acts. We lack a theory to express how, if at all, they differ.

Consequently, the radical problem concerns those human actions that both believers and nonbelievers alike perform: plain, ordinary, nonecclesiastical—in a word, secular—actions. In such actions how does a man of faith in Jesus Christ differ from a man without such faith? Two young men find themselves walking side by side in a march for racial justice in Mississippi; both are equally prepared to accept death as one of the possible consequences of their acts; both are equally willing to lay down their lives for their brothers. Yet one is a Christian, the other an atheist. In what respect do they differ?

One common solution is to point to their different motivations. The Christian acts in imitation of Jesus Christ, but the atheist acts because he believes in justice and equality, and because he has compassion upon those who suffer. However, this solution breaks down. For the Christian may also share the motivations of the atheist; and the atheist may frankly admit that he sees in Christ a model, without accepting "all the other things" about Christ.

Moreover, a "religious" motivation is in itself not discriminating; alone, it seriously weakens the believer's capacity for realistic judgment. Those whose chief motive for action is "the will of God," or the "imitation of Jesus Christ" or even "*agape*" soon find that almost any type of action can be performed, and historically has been performed, in its name. Their version of Christianity will appear to be softheaded and sentimental. The motivations of the nonbeliever will, by comparison, appear to be hardheaded, critical and discerning. A specifically "Christian" motivation, in this view, is mere icing on a cake. Accordingly, only in proportion as the Christian shares the pragmatism and secular discernment of the atheist will he share in the substance of authentic moral action. (In Mississippi, Christian segregationist and freedom worker alike may appeal to the same "Christian" motivation.)

The Pragmatic and the Symbolic

Ineluctably then the realistic Christian appears to be drawn toward the appropriation of hard, profane values and critical, pragmatic methods. Why be a Christian at all?

Our present theoretical impasse appears to have arisen because we do not have adequate conceptual tools for the analysis of human action. Into this vacuum more adequate pragmatic theories rush, but are such theories themselves adequate? Human actions must meet a certain pragmatic standard, it is true; but individual men are not merely instruments of the common good, nor grist for the wheels of progress, nor are they merely problem-solvers.

Thus, the quality of action is not adequately measured by pragmatic standards. Not all the technical adjustments that society still needs will suffice to constitute the moral health or beauty of the human community. To see this, one does not need to minimize the role of pragmatism, technical planning or social reform, but only to note that even the classical exponents of such roles call their theory "instrumentalism." Man does not seem to be merely an instrument. Instrumentalism alone, as Henry David Aiken has been arguing, does not exhaust the capacities of vision, action and development.

In addition to the pragmatic standard, human action must meet other criteria. As we set out to plan the cities in which 90 per cent of the nation will shortly be living, what qualities of human action do we wish most to promote? Having mastered the techniques toward which instrumentalism has so brilliantly directed our attention, and having through these techniques achieved the preconditions of the good life for each and every man, what then shall we do? What kind of life shall we lead? We may wish to live mature, healthy, beautiful lives; and we may wish to know how that is to be done, for the alternatives are many and the time allotted to each of us is brief.

No doubt, each man must answer this question for himself. Each man chooses his own way of life amid the contingencies in which he finds himself. In fact, many do not choose, or do so only imperceptibly; many merely drift. Of our generation, Camus said it would be written, "They fornicated, and they read the papers." There is always, however, an option for each man: to seize some responsibility for the activities of his life. Some men in fact develop their capacities to a higher excellence than others. Consequently a theory of action must account for the differences proper to each individual agent.

But such action is also symbolic. Two men reading the same paper may acquire a similar fund of information, so far as their replies to factual questions may reveal and even so far as their ability to compare and analyze and systematize that information may be tested. But does what they read *mean* the same thing to each? Are their judgments similarly affected, their imaginations stimulated, the trajectories of their subsequent actions altered?

For some persons life is an instance of game theory; it is an endless crossword puzzle, a series of "challenges," delightful so long as boredom is kept at bay. Human action is symbolic, and to many the ultimate symbol is *divertissement;* the ultimate anxiety is tedium.

Thus no single act means only what its pragmatic effect achieves (its "cash value"). Every action also means what the agent intends it to mean, *i.e.*, what he is symbolizing by it. Two men riding the same subway car, working in the same office on similar tasks, may be creating through their lives two entirely different symbolic patterns. Action is like speech: each life utters a unique word.

Thus men strive not only to be effective, to be useful to one another, but also to communicate. Before it is too late they want to make sure their word is heard, their burden expressed, despite their inarticulateness. (When God acted to reveal himself, he spoke a Word.)

The Horizon as a Dynamic Orientation

Each individual agent is unique, because the symbolic value of his actions is his own. Perhaps we may make a common metaphor into a technical term: each action is unique because the "horizon" of each individual is unique. Commonly, a horizon is the limit of what can be seen from a given point. A horizon has two poles, the subject and the range of what the subject can observe. But as I am now using the word, a horizon also indicates a dynamic orientation, for the human subject is not stationary. He moves through many and varied experiences, gains new insights, sometimes is led by experience to shift those criteria of relevance and evidence that guide his judgment, and regularly "tries to do" projects that carry his view into the future.

He is distinctive because he develops in time; his horizon constantly changes both in its subjective pole and in its objective context. His acts of knowing encompass more than enlarged bodies of information. One insight leads to a change in his capacity to understand, and sometimes a whole field of prior insights is rearranged by an overriding insight that throws a new light upon what he knew before. Again, the swiftness and sureness of his judgment in assessing the evidence for his ideas develop as he becomes a master in any given field of inquiry. Finally, what he is "trying to do" with his life undergoes regular revision.

The dynamic concept of horizon has a threefold function:

 • It calls attention to the symbolic dimension of human action (including inquiry). Different men discern different significance in a given action or invest the same acts with different significance.
 • It highlights the fact that the subject and all the objects or persons to whom he is related fall within the same symbolic framework. The dualism of the subject and the object is finally untenable, for objects are known by subjects only insofar as they fall within the horizontal of the subject.
 • It emphasizes that knowing and acting are not exhaustively analyzed into the categories either of classical rationalism or of naturalistic pragmatism. The horizon of a subject is influenced by all the experiences, emotions, memories, tendencies, interests, desires, insights and judgments of the subject. There is no pure isolated ego, no atom of consciousness confronting pure objects "objectively out there now." Nor is the dualism of the emotive and the cognitive tenable.

Finally, the concept of horizon is not Husserlian. It does not attempt to picture two objective spheres "out there," one subsumed within the other. Husserl is Platonist in his epistemology, and consequently his metaphysics includes this world and another world.

But the concept of horizon here adumbrated is not Platonic; it derives from a suggestion by Bernard Lonergan, and its intellectual lineage is anti-Platonic. Its purpose is not to project a metaphysical world out beyond the immediate, tangible world; it denies that there is any metaphysical world out there. Its purpose is to articulate the fact that human deeds in this present concrete, historical world are symbolic of human intentions and not exhaustively translatable into the categories of instrumentalism. Such action does not merely solve problems, control the environment or predict and manipulate effects. It also intends to say something about the character of life; it expresses vision, or lack of it. Action follows from being; what you are speaks through what you do. Your model is reflected in your style.

The Symbolic Content Is Different

Now a Christian who is conscious of what he is (and no one of us fully is, we are only trying to be) is a "new being." He is, according to his belief, sharing in the life of God. But what is God's life? God is not believed to be passive, and hence the best of our inadequate supply of words for speaking of him will surely be gerunds rather than nouns.

God is not truth and love but knowing and loving. To share in God's living is to share in God's knowing and loving. To become a Christian is to begin to "put on the mind of Christ," to begin to enter into a new horizon. It is to start to understand the world, life, history, others, oneself as God understands; and to begin to love as God loves.

Grace is, then, conceived to be a new way of knowing, a new way of loving. For this reason it is said to "build upon" nature; even before the advent of grace men understand and love. It does not destroy intelligence or the capacity to love; it enlarges them beyond limits men could hope to achieve without it. Grace alters the standards of human understanding and loving, and in this sense it "contradicts" nature.

But no one who lives in grace has carte blanche to contemn

intelligence or to denigrate the capacity of men to love. For to do so is to destroy the very operations through which grace acts. If we stifle our drive of inquiry, how can we come to investigate ever more fully the ways of God? If we repress our capacity for love, how can we become agents of the love of God? The capital sin of "the religious age," and of all fundamentalism, is to neglect human intelligence and love, and to construct an artificial, magical world in which "grace" is to operate as if in a vacuum, like some *deus ex machina*.

Nevertheless, a withering critique of "the religious age" can be launched effectively without abandoning the claim that to be a Christian is to be different from a nonbeliever. The differences need not be obvious to every man in the street: a Christian and an atheist sitting in the subway or marching in Mississippi may look alike; they may even be blood brothers. What changed empirically, psychologically, when one became a Christian, or an atheist, was the symbolic meaning of his life. Even if both still take Christ as a model for certain of their actions—sacrificing themselves for others, for example—the way in which they understand this model and relate to it is different.

For the atheist, Christ is a historical figure like Socrates whose life taught a lesson. For the knowledgeable Christian, he is also God who lives yet in the understanding and the knowing of his people.

Christians do not merely *imitate* him; in some further way (how?) he lives in them. Their actions are now not only theirs but his. The significance of what they do may or may not be rewarded with historical, pragmatic efficacy; but because it is also Christ's, their action rescues some of the beauty and the pain of history from going unnoticed and unthanked. Christians are not called to succeed in history, only to labor for success and to care about it. The further standard they hope to meet, beyond pragmatic efficacy, is that of human meaningfulness.

Christians believe that Christ has spoken most adequately of the symbolic content of life in history. A man who consciously lives in Christ and Christ in him seems to live as fully as he can in a given historical context. He experiences its triviality, dignity, joy, emptiness, cruelty, loveliness. God's disclosure of himself in Christ is not yet complete; each Christian discloses something new in new historical contexts.

No doubt there are many men who fail to see in Christ what Christians see, who find in him a narrow, restricting, even degrading view of life. Such men try to symbolize in what they do some other quality of life. What distinguishes Christians is that their actions occur within the unlimited horizon of Christ's understanding and loving. Within that horizon their own present horizon is ever "under judgment." Their judge lives within them, calmly disclosing their insufficiencies. They must gradually "grow up into the stature of Christ."

The Christian in Mississippi or on the subway is conscious that God lives within him, presses upon him, drives him on— not magically but by stimulating his intelligence and discriminating love until they are exercised to their utmost. Grace acts through the secular; there is no other world. But God— through events in our lives, Scripture, life in the church, conscious response to the sacraments—illuminates our understanding of this world and enlarges our capacity to love it, so that we, too, pierced by its beauty, might be willing to die for it.

The atheist, through other events, books, communities, is pierced by the earth's beauty and dies for it without recognizing the significance Christians give it: that it is man's, and we are Christ's and Christ is God's. The difference is not in the external act or in its historical effect but in its symbolic content. Believers and nonbelievers *do* the same things; they interpret their lives differently. Perhaps (as Daniel Callahan has noted) after two or three generations of widespread atheism, the difference between Christian and atheistic symbols will lead to increasingly divergent courses of action.

In any case, to determine which set of symbols is correct is a further question. No one has seen God. Both believer and nonbeliever are in a darkness, searching out what it is to be a man.

ROBERT ADOLFS, o.s.a.

Is God Dead?

THERE IS NOTHING particularly new about the announcement that "God is dead," but since Neitzsche's madman (in *Die Frohliche Wissenschaft*, published in 1882) ran into the market place to shout the death of God, the character of the messengers and the receptivity of their audience have changed considerably. By the end of Nietzsche's prophetic tale it is clear that the fool has not been understood by the people and so he says: "I came too early; my time has not yet come. This dreadful occurrence is still on its way." Perhaps the time has now come and the people are ready to listen. In 1961, an American sociologist of religion, Gabriel Vahanian, in his book *The Death of God*, contended that the Church's understanding of God is the product of a meeting between primitive Christianity and Greek culture. Therefore, the idea of God is an idol. It no longer has any meaning in our profane culture; neutralized by overexposure, it has been done away with. Vahanian concludes that "God is dead and probably shall remain so for the time being." That same year the theme of the death of God was discussed by the American Protestant theologian William Hamilton in his book *The New Essence of Christianity*. Hamilton remarks: "When we speak of the death of God we speak not only of the death of idols or of the falsely objectivized Being in heaven: we also speak of our own vanished capacity to fasten onto any traditional image of God . . . and we wonder if God himself has not vanished." About two years later, another American Protestant, Thomas Altizer, theology professor at Emory University in Atlanta, wrote: "We have to search in our time for a radically new religious understanding. Then we must begin with the honest confession that the God of Christianity is dead. We must admit that the death of God is a historical event: God died in *our* time, in *our* history and in *our* existence."

In 1963, too, Paul van Buren's difficult book *The Secular Meaning of the Gospel* appeared. Van Buren, a theologian and a language analyst, maintains that the *word* God is dead. He says that God is a meaningless word because it deals with something that can in no way be verified and therefore cannot have a function in a language that means something.

What now? Are these theologians crazy or are they perhaps expressing an experience that lives at the very heart of Christendom? Was Neitzsche's madman right after all? Certainly the theme of the death of God appears more or less explicitly in the work of great artists of our time—in the films of Ingmar Bergman, the novels of Albert Camus and in Samuel Beckett's strange play *Waiting for Godot*.

Religious Crisis

A slightly worried Catholic might say at this point that these death-of-God theologians are only muddle-headed Protestants and that contemporary artistic expressions simply mirror the general decadence of Western culture. But that attitude ignores the fact that Christianity is, at this moment, in a serious crisis, a crisis which is manifested in all aspects of the Church.

In the hearts of many Christians, there is uneasiness, uncertainty and sometimes a chilly pessimism, in spite of the "renewal" introduced by the Second Vatican Council, in spite of the changes in the Liturgy, and in spite of the enthusiasm of the followers of Teilhard de Chardin, who believe that a Christian theory of evolution is the key to most problems of faith.

There is a pessimism today which has attacked the roots of all obvious faith. For one thing, many secondary traditional practices, once associated with religious faith, have vanished. For another, some have begun to question important facets of Christianity: morality, the indisputability of dogma, the sacraments, the real presence of Christ in the Eucharist, the Bible as God's word, the Church as an institution, the historical existence of Christ, and now even the existence of God. All this has brought much unrest; one wonders if it does not point to an explosion of unbelief, and if we are not moving toward a God-forsaken era.

Indeed, unbelief seems to be the sign of our time. I do not mean by this primarily the cultural phenomenon of atheistic humanism. Rather, it is a question of disbelief among Christians, and it is not a rebellious disbelief. It is more a quiet indifference, which develops in people who discover that they can be complete human beings without religious faith. Theirs is a kind of positive indifference, which undermines religious faith by a deliberate acceptance of the temporal; they come to realize that work, knowledge, art, politics are worthwhile in themselves, and that one can fill his life with them so that the Church, and even God, become unnecessary. This positive indifference to religion occurs most frequently among the better educated leaders of society. Another kind of indifference, the negative sort, occurs among ordinary citizens, many of whom are not very well educated, and among young people. Here we notice an amazingly large areligious and aspiritual proletariat, whose members have abandoned traditional standards and have tended to become enthusiastic consumers; their values in life reach not much higher than easily earned wages and easily obtainable luxuries.

Is the expression "God is dead" so strange then, when we consider that He is already dead in the hearts of so many? "But we serious Christians still believe," we may say, to reassure ourselves. The little word "still" is significant. We *still* believe, but how much longer? So many honest believers suffer because they detect within themselves uncertainty and fear, as the seemingly firm ground on which they had based their belief since childhood starts crumbling. Is the problem of God, then, the great problem of our time?

The Existence of God

The notion that God is a problem is not an original one. Throughout the eighteenth, nineteenth and early twentieth centuries, the problem of God was the subject of learned discussions among, to name only a few, Kant, Feuerbach, Schleiermacher, Troeltsch, Marx, Nietzsche and Freud. But how much did the average Christian know about that? Within the enclosure of the Churches men felt protected as long as they could be wrapped in an unquestioning abandon to God's word (fundamentalism), or could hide behind an individualistic devotion to Jesus (pietism). Although slight uneasiness existed in clerical circles, simple, God-fearing people calmly continued their pilgrimage, unaware of any danger and therefore vulnerable to the crisis that was bound to come. And then Bishop Robinson's little book, *Honest to God*, broke both a scientific and religious barrier. The problem of God landed in the world press and thereby became the possession of Everyman. Neither theologians nor clerics were prepared to quiet the sudden religious storm which *Honest to God* provoked, nor have the shock waves it produced subsided yet.

Thus, the problem of God in our time has rapidly become a universal problem for all Christians. It is still not said universally that God is dead, but the problematic of God exists for many Christians in precisely this: that all discussions of the existence of God and his real presence in the world are followed by a question mark. In other words, God is no longer self-evident. Almost instantaneously one has become aware of the fact that the areas in which God's existence seemed obviously detectable are shrinking. First it was said: "God is hiding in our time." The hidden nature of God does not in itself denote a religious crisis, however; that is a Biblical notion which appears especially in Isaiah and in the psalms. Furthermore, "hiddenness" is a form of presence. But then one suddenly began to hear of the "absence of God." Last year, for example, Professor Hans Fortmann wrote in an article published in *De Volkskrant*, a Dutch Catholic newspaper: "The absence of God is the problem." Well, that is about the same thought which the previously mentioned theologians tried to express, but in a more pregnant manner, with "God is dead."

The challenge now is how to interpret these disturbing and negative expressions and to see if we can give them a rich and positive meaning. The question is: Why is there now in the Christian world this notion of the death of God? One answer is that people have accepted the secularization of the Western world.

Secularization is a word that needs explaining. The difficulty is that it denotes a phenomenon which is still developing and therefore escapes a complete definition. The word comes from the Latin *Saeculum* which means "*this* world and the expression of *this* time." We might therefore, for the moment, describe secularization as *man's deliverance from all religious, supernatural, mythical and metaphysical manifestations; after which man tries to explain the world and man-in-the-world by examining the laws proper to this world (natural sciences) and by analyzing his own existence (existentialism)*. But that is another mouthful of words which demand further explanation.

Primitive man tried to explain his existence and the mystery of the world surrounding him with mythological stories. In myths, primitive man found the origin of his primitive belief and his moral knowledge. To give a single example: the division of the world in three layers—heaven, earth and the underworld (hell)—comes from mythical thought.

In a later stage, scientific thought emerged and developed into metaphysical thought. Metaphysics appeared because man was not satisfied with the world as it appeared to him in all its immediacy. Early Greek civilization, especially, tried to get past the many manifestations of "this world." What is behind the sensually perceived appearances of our reality? they asked. All realities agree only in that they *are*. And so the metaphysician looks for the deeper meaning of beings, for the *existence* of things. In addition, and from the beginning, metaphysics brought about a separation of two worlds: the world of the sensually perceptible and the extrasensory, or essential world. Plato is, in this case, the classical example. He taught that man finds no meaning in the visible world. "This world," then, refers to the invisible basic forms of a higher "existence," an ideal world which is the real world. Our world is then only a shadow of the higher reality of ideas. This metaphysical explanation of the world and of man, with many variations, has determined the entire philosophical and theological thought of the West.

It is very important to realize that Christianity has been intensely influenced by mythical as well as by metaphysical thought. The Bible originated in a mythically thinking culture. In the third and fourth centuries Christianity came in contact with, and was strongly influenced by, Greek metaphysical thought, and this influence was intensified in the Middle Ages. We may illustrate the combined mythical-metaphysical influence on Christianity with this example from the Nicene Creed: "Who for us men . . . *came down from* heaven" reveals the mythical influence; and "*Of one substance with* the Father" suggests the metaphysical influence.

Now the problematic side of Christian articles of faith and dogma becomes clearer. The Christian declaration of faith is "disguised" with mythical and metaphysical frames of thought. To a secular culture, which rejects the mythical and metaphysical, Christianity and its definitions of God become incomprehensible; belonging to a past phase of culture, they are therefore no longer to be believed.

Freeing Religion

Secularization means, after all, the deliverance of man and society from all teachings of religion and from the religious view of life. Religion and "the religious" are manifestations of a still incompletely adult stage of man's growth. Thus, the religious explanation of the world declares the "unexplainable" to be sacred. For the religious person the world was full of the mysterious "holy," of magic and gods. One may say, however, that

Christianity has purified religion. The sometimes very earthy gods have been returned to one God, and the magical and holy have been adopted and elevated in a sacramental ordinance.

Nevertheless, some theologians now doubt that Christianity is a religion at all; they say that perhaps we ought to leave the religious phase behind us and follow Dietrich Bonhoeffer who spoke of a Christianity without religion. According to Bonhoeffer's way of thinking, Christianity is not a religion but a *belief* (as an existential orientation) in Jesus and the Gospel, in which the final (eschatological) existence of the fullness of time is announced. Christianity must therefore be delivered of its religious character. There are even theologians who say that the excess of religion has its deepest roots in the teaching of the Old Testament and the Gospel.

In this context it becomes clear that one should talk about the death of God in a positive sense. The god of religion, the God of theism (the natural teaching about God) stands outside our verifiable reality, a god both of myth and metaphysics, a god toward whom one is led by the proofs of scholasticism. Nowadays one might say: maybe this god does exist, but he is no longer relevant to our world. Besides, it is possible to doubt, as Van Buren alleges, whether this god is the Father of Jesus Christ and the God of grace. In this sense, one can speak of an atheistic Christianity.

Secularization, then, is the disappearance of the mythical, metaphysical and religious awareness of God. "Then there is nothing left," say some. "That is the end of Christianity." The death-of-God theologians mean, however, precisely the opposite. To them, secularization means a necessary purification and a deliverance of Christianity from the grip of myth, metaphysics and religion.

In fact, for the theologians who have announced the "death of God" the expression means (in the totality of their writings) a deeply believing preoccupation with God. They expect that, in a way as yet unknown, God will once more become relevant to the world of men. They will not say much about it yet, for the manner in which God will reappear will become clear to us only when we have all consummated the death of God. Yet, some already see a light. Altizer thinks that this light

will break when "the holy," the symbolic and the mythical can
be interpreted anew, in such a way that they can become relevant to contemporary sensibility.

Hamilton says that in the realization of God's absence we are
not entirely without hope, because within a truly Christian
"waiting" God will reappear to us. In the meantime, it is our
duty to let ourselves be inspired anew by Jesus and his "way of
life." Our meeting with Jesus will take place in our loving
communion with our spiritually and materially needy fellow
men.

Vahanian looks for the new appearance of God in a reinter-
pretation of the concept of transcendentalism. Transcendentalism means to him not the "other worldly" and the infinitely far
away, but the most imminent possible in historical reality.

Van Buren no longer wants to use the word "God." Perhaps
he is the Father, about whom the man Jesus of Nazareth spoke,
although Jesus himself seems to suggest that we no longer must
look for "the existence of the Father." All we know about him
has been manifested in Jesus, who is the true free man and
from whom a liberating and renewing force emanates. The
Gospel is the good news about a free man, whose freedom is
contagious and leads us to our true humanity.

Finally, now, I will try to give a critical opinion about the
God-is-dead movement. As I noted before, there is a positive
content in the expression "God is dead." It implies a justified
rebellion against the so-called objectivization of God within
the Church's Christianity. God became the object of our
knowledge, the end-product of a metaphysical reasoning. Some
contemporary theologians, in their resistance to objectivism
have ended up with complete subjectivism (under the influence of existentialism: a thinking totally originated from the
human subject). Vahanian has justly noted that "to believe" is
precisely a movement to bring subject (man) and object
(God) together and to reconcile them. In other words: God
and Faith belong together. God has been detached from faith,
however, and subsequently objectivized and hung somewhere
"up there."

Hamilton and Van Buren have not escaped the temptation,
after having rejected this objectivized God, of putting him *en-*

tirely within the sensually perceived world, on a Christ-inspired fellow man basis. However valuable that idea is, it negates an essential dimension (which I discuss below). The death-of-God theologians are right when they banish from their writings any smugness about the existence and being of God. In comparison with the grandiloquent theological treatises on God of later times, Thomas Aquinas was a very humble writer who admitted being a pious agnostic in the following statement (from *De Veritate*): "What God really is remains hidden from us, and this is the best knowledge we can have of God in this life: that we know that he transcends any idea we can have of him."

Should theologians not also take into account the awe and reluctance with which the authors of the Old Testament speak of God? Out of respect they avoided, as much as possible, mentioning the word "Jahweh." The name "Jahweh" was not the name of an objective super-being, but an exclamation, a name to call out, a name to implore and to praise. "Jahweh" did not lay bare his objective being but manifested himself in history, in the historical happenings of a people. The deliverance from slavery in Egypt was a manifestation of Jahweh's love and care for Israel and the initiation of the grace of election. It is on this manifestation of God, which exists in a new perspective of history and therefore also of our own personal lives, that the death-of-God theologians want insistently to dwell. They are convinced that the mythical, metaphysical and religious god has to die first, before we can once more be open to the true manifestation of God.

A Lost Dimension

The great shortcoming of the death-of-God theologians, as I see it, is the overenthusiastic and insufficiently reserved welcome they give to secularization. It is at least questionable whether in the history of man's humanization the mythical, metaphysical and religious manifestation are really stages that definitely belong to the past as vanquished ways of seeing things. Did not something *come to light* in the mythical, metaphysical and religious thought, which has true value for the world in which we live? Bultmann has pointed out that the mythical, in its basically primitive form, is no longer relevant for modern man. Yet he does not want to do away with myths in his demythologizing; rather, he wants to translate them into contemporary (existentialist) terms. And Altizer wishes to reinterpret "the holy."

Modern secular men who hate to minimalize the reality of this world with a "belief" in the supernatural, extrasensory, transcendental and religious, have, through their antipathy, acquired a large blind spot. As a result, they negate a rich accumulation of experience, acquired through preceding generations, and overestimate their own point of view.

Must we not establish that there is in this world a growth of higher awareness of humanity? In spite of the inhumanity of man's wars, his cruelties and egocentricity, still man struggles toward a greater and better humanity. All that is life-renewing and humanizing is greeted and adopted as a true progress. Why is it that in history there has been and is going on a difficult struggle toward a greater humanity, wider opportunities for survival, freedom, goodness, peace and joy in the world? Am I concluding this only from an analysis of my own life? I don't think so. Why should not man just as soon take the road of selfishness, egocentricity and misanthropy? (Indeed, that is a road which he repeatedly takes but he also repeatedly returns from it.) This can only be because man, in some way or other (and here words fail one) is called, spoken to, or—to use an untranslatable German word—"*herausgefordet*." He perceives, as it were, a mysterious "voice" by which he is "called." This is no cheap mysticism, but a life's experience for which there are no adequate words. Man has experienced this "calling" as coming from another dimension than his immediately perceptible world. Mythical man expressed this in his primitive way, the metaphysician spoke of a transcendental truth and the religious man called it "God." And may we suppose that Jesus had this in mind when he referred to "the Father?"

It may be that we can no longer use the word "God" in our situation, but perhaps we should again adopt a listening receptivity toward a mystery that "speaks to us," "calls" and "invites."

The last word about "God is dead" has not been said, but surely we should be able to perceive in this negative expression a prophetic sound from the dark and confused Christian times ahead. It was also dark on Good Friday and a word of God-abandonment was spoken, but to those who held on and did not give up hope the light appeared once again.

EUGENE B. BOROWITZ

God-Is-Dead Theology

IF GOD IS DEAD as Nietzsche said at the turn of the century it is remarkable how alive the discussion of His proper burial remains. Theology in America has been anything but comatose since World War II. What with Barth and the Niebuhrs; Buber, Tillich and Bultmann; explorations of religious existentialism and dialogue with logical analysis, the "gloomy science" has been downright exciting. Now the death-of-God movement is having an impact similar to the unprecedented reception of Bishop Robinson's *Honest to God*. Theology threatens to become popular! It is such news that the scholarly journals cannot keep abreast of the developments. The *New York Times* gives the latest views feature coverage, and, sign of signs, the *New Yorker* devoted extended space in its last three November issues (1965) to an article on Bonhoeffer and his influence.

The characteristic most commonly shared by the death-of-God thinkers is a recognition of radical cultural change. Robert M. Herhold, reporting on "Kirchentag 1965: Call for Reform" (*Christian Century*, September 1, 1965), gives a vivid illustration in the words of Dr. Dorothee Sölle: "Everything that once seemed set—grace before meals, the family attending church together, the authority of the church—can no longer be counted on. . . ." The formal church simply does not speak to modern man. "The church does not ask if a person is a Christian, but is he churchy. It offers a kind of fellowship that no longer interests people. . . . [The church] is introverted, washing its own car every Sunday morning." Or as a British Methodist put it, in his country only about 1 per cent of the population goes to church, many no longer seek even baptism for their children, and in London it is not uncommon to find families who are the third generation of the unchurched.

The fact is that Western culture and society are no longer Christian. The modern world and its citizenry rarely if ever live by their religion even where they maintain contact with an institution. They are, in all the effective levels of their lives, non-religious. Obviously, some significant things are going on in churches and synagogues today. But the most important endeavors on behalf of man take place out of and apart from religious institutions. The Freedom Movement in the United States, to give the most familiar example, may have had some religious leadership and clergy support; but its shock troops were secular, and the critical action has taken place in courthouses, streets, and ghettos, not churches. Religion remains more a hindrance than a spur to the radical social change humanity requires and is seeking. So modern man is secular and happily so. Indeed, with the promise of ever greater abundance coming his way, he is content to be of this world alone. That is why God is dead. People do not really need Him any more; they have outgrown Him. Larry Shiner has argued that there is an intellectual, dialectical thrust to the death of God which is as important a factor in its development as the socio-historical. However, the force of his argument is vitiated by his admission that the dialecticians of doubt and disbelief always overcome them with the ultimate return to faith and affirmation in God

("Toward a Theology of Secularization," *The Journal of Religion*, October 1965, XLV, 4).

The Europeans felt this first since Christianity had always been closely intertwined with their life style, and in many ways spreading prosperity has seemed the only substantial if narcotic answer to the intolerable questions raised by the War. The great contemporary theologies speak only to a handful. Barth's explanation of modern man's failings and hope in what Christ has done for him rests on a radically transcendent sense of God. But contemporary man lives and thinks only in terms of this world, so the vision of a wholly other God Who sends salvation like a stone thrown from heaven does not move him. Nor have the existentialisms of Bultmann or Tillich fared much better. Despite their analyses of the emptiness at the core of man's being and their insistence that only a Christian response can meet its consequent anxiety, modern men increasingly feel, if not self-sufficient, then content with what they can know and do in the every day, without special efforts at belief or faith.

Bonhoeffer anticipated all these tendencies. (See this department, "Bonhoeffer's World Comes of Age," *Judaism*, Winter 1965.) His last letters from prison give the three motifs which recur in the writings of the new movement. For him it was an accepted fact that the world "had come of age" in secularity and would not retreat; that Christianity must therefore assume a "religionless" character, with the word "religion" understood as a need-meeting relationship to God; and this should be the emulation of Christ's "dying to the world" in the sense of forceful ethical response to humanity's most important political and social problems. Bonhoeffer's own heroic stand against Hitler has helped make him the patron saint of the death-of-God theologians. (Yet Steven S. Schwarzschild points out his lack of understanding, even prejudice, with regard to Jewish religious teaching, in a letter to *Commonweal*, 26 November, 1965. The citations given there, it should be realized, are from Bonhoeffer's *Ethics*, which most students of his thought regard as an early stage in the evolution of his mature position.) For himself Bonhoeffer did not believe in anything that might be called, except for the most vulgar public-relations reasons, the death of God. To the very end, he had vigorous faith in the living reality of God and in His undoubted triunity. Bonhoeffer without his firm commitment to Christology is simply unthinkable, as Visser t'Hooft has reminded us ("Dietrich Bonhoeffer, 1945–1965," *The Ecumenical Review*, July 1965, 17, 3).

This paradox, enshrined in the term "death-of-God theology," is undoubtedly titillating the public fancy. How can one say God is dead if one seeks to explicate the *logos* of His existence? How can there be a "science of God" if He is dead? This tension is evident in the institutional polarity of the protagonists of this thesis. The university professors look steadfastly at the world; the seminary professors still have an eye on the Son, and perhaps even the Father.

The first major American exponent of this position was probably Gabriel Vahanian of Syracuse University. In a series of articles published as the 'fifties gave way, he tried to shift religious attention from the criticism of the revival to a recognition that morbidity, not superciality, was the real issue. Perhaps Vahanian pioneered these ideas here because, as a Frenchman, he had some familiarity with what had already become a living issue in Europe. In the same year, 1961, that George Braziller published Vahanian's collection of articles under the title *The Death of God*, the firm also issued Gerhard Szczesny's *The Future of Unbelief*. This avowal of a post-Christian era had been the basis of an agitated public controversy over the future of Christianity in Germany in 1958. Many other examples could be cited.

Vahanian's position then and now was strictly descriptive of a cultural phenomenon. Modern man no longer believes in God, nor feels he needs to. The greatest proof is that he has no desire even to disprove His existence. When atheism and theism are equally boring then indeed God is dead. Vahanian has explored this thesis in several aspects of man's social expression but goes no further than such sociology. This does not prevent him from remaining an incisive critic, and he has indicted some colleagues in this movement with trying secretly to turn atheism into Christ-osophy. Unconsciously, they cannot take the death of God seriously and therefore busy themselves

erecting systems whereby Christianity can speak in secular
terms. That is not religionless Christianity at all but rather a
last-ditch effort to save Christianity as a religion by making it
function in a new way. Vahanian himself seems to believe that
the God of Christianity negates all systems, secular or theological or "religious," but he has not yet indicated why he believes
what he believes, though he too is part of this profane culture;
nor what he thinks its implications ought to be for those whose
faith is like his ("Swallowed up by Godlessness," *Christian
Century*, December 8, 1965).

Vahanian's forthright analyses seem mild in tone when compared to the apocalyptic stance of Thomas J. J. Altizer of
Emory University. He is a thoroughgoing radical when it
comes to God's existence today. The "death of God underlies
every mode of our thought and experience. . . . If God is
dead in the life of faith . . . then the theologian must fully
acknowledge that the Christian God is dead . . . not simply
hidden . . . nor lurking . . . nor will he appear on the next
turn . . . the contemporary Christian must accept the death
of God as a final and irrevocable event" ("Word and History,"
Theology Today, October, 1965, XXII, 3).

Altizer can still consider himself a Christian by redefining
the essence of Christianity. His key terms would seem to be:
eschatology; incarnation; reconciliation. Comparing Christian
religiosity with that of the Far East, Altizer argues that the
unique dimension of Christian piety is its forward-looking
faith. The numinous reality of the universe is not in repose nor
has it yet accomplished its full self-realization. It does so now as
it moves toward the future. That activity is to be found in
history and as part of man's living experience. This was the
burden of Altizer's early book *Oriental Mysticism and Biblical
Eschatology* (Westminster Press, 1961). Thus man is to find
his faith in the becoming he finds in the here and now, not in
another world, in the changing and developing, which is the
very heart of historical reality. In this development the Christian knows that a word (Altizer uses no capital "W") appears
which reconciles man to the dynamic world process in which
he finds himself. Hence Altizer, out of this future-oriented
faith, calls in all prophetic passion for the negation of all the

historical forms of Christian faith and religion. "We no longer know Jesus in the images of the Christian tradition" but only in the word newly unfolding in history. It can only come to us after destroying the dead past, making possible a new and living future. Thus, insofar as Christendom is collapsing on every side that is "a decisive witness to the contemporary presence" of the reconciling word.

What Altizer means becomes more fully apparent when one reads his recent volume, *Mircea Eliade and the Dialectic of the Sacred* (Westminster Press, 1963). Eliade's analysis that much primitive and even some more developed religious experience is based on the ultimate "coincidence of opposites" is used by Altizer as a basis for considering modern man's consciousness of his universe. In about a hundred pages Altizer weighs and rejects the adequacy of Kierkegaard, Dostoevsky, Proust, Sartre, Teilhard, Freud, Marcuse and Brown, after in somewhat similar fashion shaping Kant, Husserl and Heidegger to his purposes—all in order to arrive at the most adequate statement of modern man's condition, Nietzsche's doctrine of the Eternal Recurrence. This Altizer joyously equates with the Biblical Kingdom of God (pp. 196–197). And the last paragraph of his book begins in this appropriate Dionysian fashion: "This terrible 'night' created by the death of God has made incarnate the most awesome nothingness imaginable . . . but Zarathustra [and Altizer: E. B. B.] calls his hearers to affirm this nothing, and to affirm it joyfully, to say Yes to this nightmare of nightmares, this most dreadful of horrors."

Altizer may be right about the cultural situation; Christians competent to speak of their faith will have to say whether faith in a reconciling future is all "the good news"; but what shall a sensitive human being, much less a Jew, say of this boundless affirmation of whatever history brings? How can one not recoil in horror from what twentieth-century history has brought and what with exquisite technical skill it yet threatens to bring if it is simply allowed to pursue a blind course? The past may have had its problems, but, unless there is some transcendent standard by which to guide modern man, how can anyone who has heard of Auschwitz, Hiroshima and the Union of South Africa spurn its ideals for anything the future may bring? And where does a secular man gain unbounded faith in the future? It is difficult to believe that Altizer means what he says theologically since it necessitates a complete suspension if not negation of the ethical. The alternative possibility is that he is unblinkingly naïve about human nature, an unpardonable sin in this half of the century.

Paul van Buren of Temple University does not rest his case on such grandiose judgments about Eastern mysticism, the true if atheistic essence of Christianity and the reliability of the historical process left to its own. His search, prompted by analytic philosophy, is rather for what can still be said that carries meaning. Van Buren does not interpret this in the narrow sense of the earlier analysts, the logical positivists, with their insistence that only the empirically verifiable could be called meaningful, thereby ruling out all discussion of ethics or religion. Rather he operates on the basis of the commonly held sense of reality, so to speak, the common man's implicit metaphysics. This is the framework of meaningful communication with him —and today that is secularity or the death of God. In *The Secular Meaning of the Gospel* (Macmillan, 1963), Van Buren sought to show what happened when one tried to translate the Gospel message into the terms a modern man might understand. Since his sense of reality ruled out a transcendent God and thus an incarnation and a redemption that had anything to do with another world, the Evangel became a sort of enlightened human relations, seeking to make each man more truly a person and society more fully the place of their mutual realization. The book was so effective, Van Buren should be credited with having touched off the first great wave of interest in this new mode of theologizing.

He opened a recent symposium in *Religious Education* magazine ("Linguistic Philosophy and Religious Education," January—February 1965, XL, 1) with a statement, "Christian Education *Post Mortem Dei.*" The pedagogic debate is of less interest here than the fact that many of the symposiasts felt constrained to comment on the religious assumptions underlying Van Buren's article. Notable among the critics was Frederick Ferre, whose own commitment to an analytic philosophy of religion is so profound that he belongs to no church and considers the dogmas of Christianity simply unbelievable. He challenges Van Buren in terms of the intellectual adequacy of his thought (and in a way that few of the men in this movement have yet been challenged). He thoughtfully inquires about the method by which Van Buren has discovered what the characteristic sense of reality of this age is. Can one really find such a thing should it exist, and how in the incredible plurality of belief in our age can one identify "the" prevailing outlook? A similar objection, this time raised to the work of Harvey Cox (see below), was raised on the basis of contrary sociological indications by Father Andrew Greeley in *Commonweal* (12 November 1965). Maurice Friedman's careful dissection of Van Buren's presumptions is also worthy of special attention in the *Religious Education* discussion.

Van Buren's response, that he is simply assaying an experiment in this effort, contrasts poorly with the dogmatic sound of his original formulation. So too, Cox, in his reply, keeps saying that perhaps the fault is his that Greeley has not understood the subtlety of his approach, but his explanations seem more effective on details than on the broad issue. The point is of some importance. Since the death-of-God protagonists pose as the religious affirmers of the clarity and hard-headedness of modern man, why do they not apply these virtues to the fundamental issue on which all rests: is there an intellectual configuration so definite and decisive for the shape of modern culture that religion must adapt to it? If what is being discussed is only one current, perhaps even a minor one, in the swirling flow of modern thought, then why the prophetic announcements about the need for religion radically to adapt itself? One might equally well argue that this anti-religiousness is only the momentary reaction to the revival that brought people back to the church and synagogue or the first enjoyment of affluence. If that is true, what is needed is a momentary strategy for this momentary mood, not the complete sacrifice of the cardinal insight of the Judeo-Christian tradition. If in the name of honesty and clarity religion must undergo a major reconstruction, should there not first be an honest and clear statement of how one can be certain that the secular mood is fundamental, not superficial, permanent and not ephemeral.

Van Buren was challenged on a second issue which must also remain fundamental to any discussion with these thinkers. Insofar as they seek to affirm a secular way of speaking of Christianity, the question must inevitably be raised: "Why bother?" If Christianity can only say what secular culture can hear, that is tantamount to saying that Christianity can say nothing which secular culture already has not heard—if the logic does not require it, the proposals which have been made do. They are quite familiar to any liberal-minded, reasonably well-educated person today. In brief, the new Christianity has nothing to say that the *Saturday Review* isn't already saying to middle-brows, and the *New York Review of Books* to those whose forehead reaches higher. Surely traditional Christianity always said something more than the humanism of its age. Thus to call this an authentic continuation of Christianity seems odd. And what will sustain and continue the Christian traditions should one insist this is Christianity today, was not clear to a number of the respondents in the *Religious Education* discussion. Van Buren's response was buried perhaps in his suggestion that theology may be a "behavioral" science. But if being a Christian is simply a social accident or a choice without reason, that is without any unique content, its value and therefore the hope of its continuity are as good as ended.

Harvey Cox, as we shall see, has a different answer to this problem, and the dimensions of that difference are what classify him with the seminary men as contrasted to those of the university. The latter are in secular institutions precisely because they no longer feel at home in the Church. They can make no room in their systems and consequently in their lives for contemporary religious institutions. (See the remarks by Robert W. Funk on the mood of the "younger theologians" in his "Colloquium on Hermeneutics," *Theology Today*, October 1964, XXI, 3). Undoubtedly much of the interest in graduate study of religion in recent years has been due to this flow of men who love religion but cannot accept its institutional forms, its disciplines, or the responsibilities of being a clergyman. At least they are consistent. They not only do not practice traditional religion, they call upon it to abandon its conventional forms and radically revise its structure to meet the reality of our age. The Jews who hold a similar negative view of God seem to prefer to do so within the synagogue, benefiting from its structure while destroying its religious foundation, enjoying the emoluments of the title "Rabbi" while teaching this is a world where all men should be "Mister."

The seminary professors who must be considered with the death-of-God movement are William Hamilton and, with a different stance, Harvey Cox. For them, though God is dead to the age, there is much that they can positively affirm within the fellowship of the contemporary church. Because the age has so radically changed, the institutional structures of Christianity must be equally reformed. Yet the church remains forever the community of those who are loyal to the Christ though in new and perhaps even currently unpredictable ways. The seminary professors speak from within. Their vocation, though incomparably more difficult than that of previous generations, is the familiar burden of Christian apologetics, speaking from belief to unbelief.

Hamilton affirms far less than does Cox, but it is still much more than the university men can use as the basis of their thought. In his widely discussed article, "Thursday's Child" (*Theology Today*, January 1964, XXI, 1), Hamilton discussed the accessibility of the great Christian virtues faith, hope and love ("charity") to today's theologian.

> . . . One gets the feeling that the American theologian can really live in only one of them at a time, perhaps even only one in a lifetime . . . it may follow that the theologian of today and tomorrow is a man without faith, without hope, with only the present and therefore only one love to guide him. . . . Nor am I inclined to view [this situation] with alarm, for I am convinced that this is something that ought to be, not just a sad inevitability. We should . . . welcome *this* faithlessness.

The positive side of his position is given more clearly, though briefly, in his "The Shape of a Radical Theology" (*Christian Century*, October 6, 1965). ". . . The time of the death of God is also the time of obedience to Jesus." This, of course, is his claim to membership in the church, to the right of the title Christian. But, if he has no accessibility to God the Father, why does he affirm a special relationship to Jesus?

. . . Because there is something there, in his words, his life, his way with others, his death, that I do not find elsewhere. . . . There may be powerful teachings elsewhere, more impressive and moving deaths. Yet I have chosen him and my choice is not arbitrary nor is it anxiously made to avert the atheist label. It is a free choice, freely made.

Hamilton associates this with a high ethical responsibility to one's fellowman. He is determined that the relevance of Christianity be manifested by Christian action in all the tense personal and social situations of this troublesome age. He even goes so far as to call his position theological optimism and one seems to hear in him the echoes of the Social Gospel

Hamilton's Christian liberalism is obviously a far more palatable brew than Altizer's universal solvent or Van Buren's translation games. Were it not for his negations, he would sound not radical but terribly old-fashioned. Only when he insists that God is dead and unavailable for explaining the virtue of Jesus, or that present institutional forms, including "preaching, worship, prayer, ordination, the sacraments," cannot be taken seriously, is his radicalism apparent ("Radicalism and the Death of God," *Christianity and Crisis*, December 13, 1965). When he speaks of what he is for, one might take him for that good old Unitarian type who used Christian symbols to mask his Ethical Culture. If that seems an insulting thing to say about a far-out revolutionary, it should rather be understood as a challenge for Hamilton to give us a statement of his positive theology which is as aggressive and bold as his criticism has been. (Do not look for it in his recently published *The New Essence of Christianity* [Association Press, 1965], as that book was prepared before these thoughts had fully matured. There is a fascinating discussion in the *Christian Century* article of how turning forty precipitated this new position. "Time was getting short and I saw I needed to make things happen.")

Harvey Cox has given us a major positive statement of his position in *The Secular City* (Macmillan, 1965), and not since *Honest to God* has there been such a reaction. (See the four articles in the symposium on the book in *Christianity and Crisis*, July 12, 1965, and the resultant correspondence, October 18, 1965; also Cox's article and the one by Daniel Callahan

in *Commonweal*, 17 September 1965, and the correspondence
of 12 November 1965, which is practically another symposium.) In part this is due to Cox's style. As befits one who
would speak positively of the new technopolis, Cox writes ur-
banely. The language is crisp; the judgments are sharp and unexpected; the examples are everyday but not cliché; the point
of view is different and unembarrassed; there is confidence
enough to meet the trials of a new age, yet tempered sufficiently with openness to other possibilities to keep it from
being overbearing. And there are enough new and unfamiliar
authorities cited, while giving due deference to the traditional
giants and recent peace-makers, to make one envious of the
author's reading rate. Only an utter "square" could fail to ap-
preciate Cox's virtuosity in making form fit content.

And the content itself is continually stimulating. There is no
nagging about the death of God here. Rather Cox puts the situation of modern man in a broad social-historical framework,
relating the change in his general intellectual framework to his
passage from tribal to town to urban culture. The resultant
secularization, with its basic sense of relativism and tentative-
ness, he argues, has its roots in the Bible. More important, religion, instead of constantly complaining about its faults, should
see that it offers new opportunities for religion. Assuming only
that secularity shall not proclaim itself a new absolute, secularism, it may in fact be seen as a liberating process which has
much in common with a Christianity whose essence is the freedom God has given man. His analysis of the religious potential
inherent in the supposed evils of big-city anonymity and mobility, seemed more helpful and insightful than his effort to
evoke the dimensions of secularity by a quick cross-cultural
comparison of the process of secularization.

This new social situation, with its "profanity" and "desacralization" of nature, politics and values, is the social equivalent of
the death of God. To it Cox applies a reformulation of a Christian theology, first of the Kingdom of God, and then of the
Church. The archaic concept "kingdom" gives way to the
more human and ethically responsible image of the secular
city, with its emphasis on man striving to fulfill his humanity
on his own and not relying on other forces to do it for him.

The Church then cannot be thought of in institutional forms alone, particularly those of the past. Cox scores heavily in his insistence that "the Church" seems to mean to most Protestants the old-village type of resident parish, an image which has little or no place in an increasingly metropolitan world and one whose ideals of life are similarly anachronistic. The Church is, in the modern lingo, a task-force or job-team, a group united by function, whose structure should be adapted freely to its ends. It is really the community of those who want to proclaim that God has freed man by making him fully responsible for his world; who seek therefore to reconcile men to one another in all the situations of conflict; and who, in ways Cox cannot yet indicate, show this is their communal relations with one another. There is much useful criticism of present institutional practices and attitudes along the way. The liveliness of theology is well illustrated in every section even as the fulfillment of Bonhoeffer is equally undeniable.

However, the book suffers from its virtues. Because Cox overbrims with the usefulness of his insight he seems unable to avoid overstatement. He regularly compares the best of city culture with the worst of town and village culture. He keeps citing Biblical justification for his ideas in ways that are often fresh but always neglecting to point out that the Bible relativizes nature and society in the name of a living and transcendent God. He sometimes seems to be saying that secularization is an unmitigated blessing for religion, while at other times he asserts merely that it offers significant place for religion to make itself felt. Had Cox said in the volume what a recent letter to *Christianity and Crisis* made clear, that the book "is a kind of tract. Or maybe a manifesto," it would have been read differently (December 13, 1965). And surely the academicism of the documentation invites another type of consideration.

The Jewish reader will be pained by Cox's continual attacks on the two great enemies of proper Christianity, tribalism and legalism. The former is too complex an issue to argue in this context, particularly as much that Cox says about tribalism is in accord with the universalism implicit in Jewish particularism. A word, however, must be said on the subject of legalism because it bears on Cox's implicit optimism. Cox may be anxious to avoid the difficulties of Roman Catholicism, Protestant fundamentalism and proliferating denominations, but where in this world is there, can there be, a city without law? If that sounds too analogical, then what is Cox's doctrine of man that he expects urban relativism and equal openness to all doctrine to lead to greater social peace and harmony than heretofore? If God has indeed freed man and thereby accomplished His fundamental "seizure of power" in this era, then why don't men behave better? And why, as Niebuhr taught us, have religious men, including, let us add, liberals and relativists, been so evil?

What is at stake here is, of course, the ancient argument over the means of salvation. The traditional Christian gave as his alternative to the law, faith in the Christ who by his crucifixion saved mankind. Cox's sociopolitical framework for doing theology will not let him say that. All that Christianity has to say to modern man is that God has given man full freedom; that is what the life of Jesus teaches. That, not answers, is what the Church has to say. Without arguing that Exodus necessarily leads on to Sinai (that freedom inevitably means law) and not to Easter and its alleged freedom, one may raise the inevitable question: "Why bother about Christianity?" The freedom and responsibility message is the wisdom every college professor preaches to his freshman charges, and its social implications are minutely examined in the *New Republic*, the *Nation*, the *Reporter* and their ilk.

Cox has an answer, and with it the wheel has turned full circle, and that is God. Cox believes in God, real, living and transcendent. For 260 pages it is the hidden assumption of all that has gone before; the standard of his judgment; his hope in history; his reason for being a Christian. And when he finally acknowledges it, it seems to me to mock most of what has gone before. Not that Cox claimed to be a member of the death-of-God school, nor that he previously avoided using the word God. No, the problem is rather that if Cox believes that "It is his experience of the transcendent which makes man man," how he can spend the major part of his book glorifying a social situation which has robbed man of his ability to sense the transcendent and whose continuing purpose it is to block him from doing so? Nor will it do simply and quickly now to say that

God meets us in history and politics and that, to take care of Altizer's problem with ethics, He stands before us as a "framework of limitation?" (Is that not law?)

For that, as the book comes to an end, is always what we wanted to know and what secularization has made it so difficult for us to know: where do we find God in the historical process? In the admission of Red China to the UN? In an unconditional cease-fire in Vietnam? In supporting civilian review boards for the police? In busing children to school? If transcendence is so critical to man, why spend so much energy finding a secular style to speak to him within a profane context? Is it not more important to help him recapture the sense of the transcendent? Without it all our secular city talk has no frame of reference. That should have been what this book was about if religion remains the service of a transcendent God in a secular world.

I confess that I do not see much for Judaism to learn from the current Protestant discussions, though a new style for communicating old truths would be useful. It all sounds so familiar. The Haskalah literature is full of the death of God and religion because we have reached the age of science. Our Yiddishists and Hebraists substituted culture for religion; our Zionists and socialists made it politics; Felix Adler tried ethics; and a continuing host try the arts, the university, research, or self-indulgence. Anyone who wants to see what putting religion into secular terms does can come to us for living examples. In the State of Israel we have it at home and in power; in *Commentary* magazine it stamps secular Jewish intellectuality indelibly on American urban culture. Both have their admirable qualities, neither is capable of bringing God's kingdom, nor could they exist in their present virtue except for generations who lived in communal Covenant with God. What their great-grandchildren will be without it is a question which should deeply trouble anyone who believes men worthy as they show themselves possessed of moral passion, applied rationality and self-fulfillment linked to Messianism.

Nor do these strictures make the positive task of Jewish theology any the less vital or immediate. For the Jew is a man of urban culture *par excellence*, and now that his home is in the city itself and not simply in the ghetto he must find a way to speak of his Jewish faith so that he can confirm the devotion of a circumcised heart with the understanding of a secularly trained intellect. Yet if the city be so profane that it have no place for God, then the ever alien Jew must take a stand which may be in the city but not fully of it; which may love the city's tolerance but reject its profanity. That may well turn out to be a minority position. But that is what believing in the Living God has until now made the destiny of the Jewish people.

EMERSON W. SHIDELER / Taking

the Death of God Seriously

> "It must be insisted that this absence or death of God is no mere
> cynicism or loss of faith to be reproved as moral irresponsibility, or
> dismissed as a failure correctly to read the evidence. This is a mood
> of our time to which Christian theology must speak intelligibly. . . .
> It may not represent everybody, but it does represent a large seg-
> ment, of young people in particular, to whom the traditional lan-
> guage and institutional forms of Christianity seem very empty. How-
> ever, this theology is more than a diagnosis. It is also a prescription,
> and a prescription which offers the disease as the cure."

IT IS EASY to dismiss the report that God is dead as another
example of a premature obituary. It is even easier to dismiss the
point of view as un-Christian and intellectually, if not morally,
irresponsible.[1] These dismissals reassure the objectors of their
own orthodoxy, and give comfort to those who feel threatened
by new ideas. However, such dismissals simply confirm the
charge that the whole vocabulary of traditional Christianity, if

not its institutionalized spirituality as well, is wholly empty and dead.

The proclamation that God is dead is not new. It is at least as old as Xenophanes, who said that the Thracians had red-haired gods, and that if the beasts had gods, they would be modeled on their own pattern. Doubtless, some of the Israelites, wandering in the wilderness, looked back at Egypt and said that the Yahweh of Moses now was dead since he had deserted them in this wasteland. More recently, Nietzsche produced the phrase that everyone is now using to identify this point of view. However, Nietzsche raised his cry on behalf of a new and emancipated man who had moved beyond the necessity for the cosmic crutches which measured the steps of ordinary men, while hobbling the feet of the bold and setting blinders on their vision. Nietzsche proclaimed the necessity for a new scale of values, a new measure of worth, to replace, rather than to fulfill, the goals and meaning of the now dead Christian tradition.

Those today who, from within the environment of Christian theology, announce the death of God, put themselves forth as the saviors of the tradition, not its funeral orators. They declare the death of God, not in order to get rid of a religion which stands in the way of man's fulfillment, but in order to release that religious faith and its institutions to do its work. Unlike Caesar's mourners, they have come to bury God, not to praise him, in order to do God's work which, they say, cannot be accomplished so long as men believe that he is still alive. Before those of us who defend the orthodoxy and guard the purity of the covenant community consign these strange voices to the Samaria reserved for those of mixed blood and confused faith, we should pay some attention to what they have to say. It behooves those of us who are not prepared to attend God's funeral to be clearer than we have been about what we mean when we use the divine name.

I

The main claim is clear enough. God is dead, as Thomas Altizer says in each of his articles, and Dietrich Bonhoeffer's notion of a world come of age is invoked as the justification for

the claim. It is less clear, however, which God is dead, and in
what sense the world has come of age. The first question,
therefore, is what is meant by the death of God?

The clearest answer to this question is that given by Bonhoeffer in one of his prison letters:[2]

> So our coming of age forces us to a true recognition of our
> situation *vis à vis* God. God is teaching us that we must live as
> men who can get along very well without him. The God who
> is with us is the God who forsakes us (Mark 15: 34). The God
> who makes us live in this world without using him as a work-
> ing hypothesis is the God before whom we are ever standing.
> Before God and with him we live without God. God allows
> himself to be edged out of the world and on to the cross. . . .
> Man's religiosity makes him look in his distress to the power
> of God in the world; he uses God as a *Deus ex machina*.

There are at least two aspects to Bonhoeffer's insight. One is
the familiar secular quality of science, and the other is the in-
soluble problem of evil, for no appeal to the idea of God re-
lieves the threats of disaster under which we live. It has long
been a commonplace among scientists that God is not to be
invoked as an explanatory principle in any scientific account.
At bottom the reason is simply that scientific explanations shall
be restricted to those quantitative and impersonal factors
which can be studied, tested, experimented with, because they
are intrinsic components of the situation to be explained. By
definition, whatever God is or however he acts within or upon
the situation, he is beyond the reach of any experimental prob-
ing. As Paul van Buren puts it, speaking of Paul's statement in

II Corinthians 5: 19:

> "God . . . did not count men's trespasses against them and en-
> trusted to the disciples the word of reconciliation." What can
> this mean? It cannot be a straightforward empirical assertion,
> for who can say how the world would be different if men had
> not been pardoned? [3]

Since we have no alternative world to serve as a control, statements which drag God in are simply meaningless. They leave
the situation exactly as it was before, and identify no differences in our empirical experience. How would things be differ-

ent if the whole notion of God were to be abandoned? And the
answer for science must be that there would be no change at
all. The description of empirical events would remain precisely
what it was before, because the description is confined to those
factors which belong intrinsically to the process being described. What lies outside that process or beneath it or prior to
it or above it cannot be specified in any fashion which makes
any difference to the account of the process.

Our world has come of age in the sense that now we do have
fully adequate patterns of explanation for all the events of our
natural and social lives without appealing to any forces or entities outside the circle of empirical events. We now think in
terms of a self-sustaining world, operating according to its own
inherent patterns of relationship. Whether it is a world of inexorable "natural law" or a world with a built-in randomness is
beside the point, for either way its pattern belongs to and is
revealed in the course of events themselves. No appeal to any
external power is necessary or helpful in elucidating the pattern of events. In short, in order to know what to do we con-
sult nature rather than God. Some among us may still endow
masses for the repose of men's souls, but the practical-minded
endow medical research for the repose of living bodies. The
future may be as closed to us as to those ancients who deci-
phered the entrails of sacrificial animals, but we look in a
different place for clues as to what the future might be.

II

Our personal lives have taken on the same this-worldly character, in order to relieve, if we cannot prevent, the evils surrounding us. We buy life insurance to provide for our families
in the certain event of death; the only imponderable is the date.
We employ the most extraordinary technological virtuosity to
prolong physiological processes, and it is subtly hinted that if
we contribute to the heart fund or the cancer drive we will not
die. Our lives are no longer in the hand of God, but in the
hands of medical technologists and the research specialists who
are seeking cures for these fatal diseases which still take us off.

It is true that this shift in the ground of our existence makes us no more secure personally or emotionally than our fathers were when they lived in dependence upon the will and acts of a God whom they could only petition but not control. Our own sense of security and power, which comes from the hope that our technology will succeed in conquering both the physiological and the social ills that threaten our lives, has pretty well evaporated under the pressure of events that are too large and complex for us to control. Our national involvement in Southeast Asia is a case in point. None of the alternative courses of action open to the United States is congenial, and no explanation of how we got involved, or declaration of the goals we seek, established a secure and comfortable course of action for us to pursue from here on. Most of us now earn our livings in circumstances which give us very little control over the size of our salaries, and not much power to determine whether we shall have jobs or not. These decisions are made by faceless beings beyond our reach. Young people feel even more insecure in this world of natural and social forces. For them it is no idle joke to say, "Eat, drink, and be merry, for tomorrow we are drafted." All planning of their lives revolves around military service, for most job opportunities require that one has already satisfied his military obligation. But that service itself carries the imponderable risks of survival, about which no meaningful predictions can be made.

We are finally forced to say that God has departed from our world in two ways. We not only find him unnecessary, indeed otiose, in explaining what goes on, we also realize that the kind of security for both the present and the future which traditionally has been associated with God is also gone. The impersonal, self-sustaining natural world around us gives us no confidence, either in ourselves or in our fellows. Talk about God seems to refer to some other world, which probably never was, certainly does not now exist, and has a hollow ring for young people who know how precarious their lives really are. We have not only pushed God out of our world; he has abandoned us in our world so that we must go it alone.

It must be insisted that this absence or death of God is no mere cynicism or loss of faith to be reproved as moral irresponsibility, or dismissed as a failure correctly to read the evidence.

This is a mood of our time to which Christian theology must speak intelligibly.

It is at just this point that the God-is-dead theology raises its most difficult problem. Insofar as this theology describes an audience to which the Gospel must be declared, we can take it with complete seriousness. It may not represent everybody, but it does represent a large segment, of young people in particular, to whom the traditional language and institutional forms of Christianity seem very empty. However, his theology is more than a diagnosis. It is also a prescription, and a prescription which offers the disease as the cure: it is not only necessary for Christian theology to recognize the absence of God, it is necessary and desirable to abandon him, for the essence of the business has no place for him any more. The business of Christianity is with the concrete world of practical events in which men live. In other words, what is demanded is a secular Gospel for a secular world.

III

What is a secular Gospel? What is the secular meaning of the Gospel? This is the question that Paul van Buren addresses himself to in his notable—in some views, notorious—book, *The Secular Meaning of the Gospel*. Van Buren discusses many things in his book, including linguistic philosophy, Bultmannian existentialism and demythologizing the Gospel, as well as the classic creeds, particularly Chalcedon, and patristic theology. All these themes revolve around the central topic, namely the empirical content of the Gospel that remains when it is divorced from its irrelevant and objectionable supernaturalism. Linguistic analysis, specifically the verification criterion of meaning, provides the tool to be used to separate the empirical essence from the supernatural excrescences in religious langauge. Application of these techniques shows—to Van Buren's satisfaction—that the empirical content of the Gospel is not to be identified with Bultmann's existentialism, but rather with the extraordinary freedom of Jesus, and the correlative freedom he released within and for those who came into relationship with him. The source of this freedom in Jesus is not explained, and how it comes to be the possession of his followers is explained only by reference to the Easter event as the occasion when they acquired it. Nothing can be explained by appealing to the concept of God,[4] because this word, ostensibly a proper name, does not behave as proper names do. The meaning of the Gospel must instead be stated in directly empirical terms which make no appeal to factors beyond the reach of empirical investigation.

One can sympathize with this endeavor. It attempts to do what Christians have long said was necessary, namely, make the Gospel relevant to ordinary life by connecting its statements and claims with the concerns, problems, and experiences of daily existence. Moreover, this is the same task that existential interpretations of the Gospel undertake, by showing that the experiences of estrangement and anxiety, and the burden of guilt, are the universal human experiences to which the Gospel spoke in the first century and now. However, Van Buren's translation comes out somewhat differently from the existentialist one. All that we can or need to know of God we find in the man Jesus of Nazareth. Van Buren says:

> To what extent do Biblical-christological statements and our interpretation's statements about Jesus and Easter function in the same way? . . . Since there is no "Father" to be found apart from him, and since his "Father" can only be found in him, the New Testament (and this passage specifically) gives its answer to the question about "God" by pointing to the man Jesus. Whatever men were looking for in looking for "God" is to be found by finding Jesus of Nazareth.[5]

The reason for confining all knowledge of God to Jesus of Nazareth is that in him we have verifiable empirical data. For "God" we have no such data which would enable us to get behind the actual events of the first century. Van Buren continues:

> We have no idea what would count for or against the assertion that in seeing Jesus one had seen the Father. Unless we know already the meaning of the word "Father," how could we verify or falsify this claim? . . . Undoubtedly Jesus believed he was obeying some "one," whom he called "Father,"

but the Gospel of John, as well as the logic of language, forces
us to silence before all questions concerning that "one." We
can only follow the recommendation of the evangelist to look
at Jesus himself; questions about "God" will receive their only
useful answer in the form of the history of that man.[6]

The proposal that it is the intention of the New Testament
writers and the apostolic community to foreclose inquiry
about God by pointing instead to Jesus is simply fantastic, because it ignores the nature of the intellectual problems the
writers confronted. Their problem was to demonstrate the
identity between Jesus and God, so that in worshipping Jesus
they could show that they were worshipping God. They were
not claiming that Jesus of Nazareth gives us all the empirical
information about God that we need.

IV

The secular Gospel is two things at once. On the one hand it is
the familiar challenge to translate the content of the Gospel
into terms which are relevant to the world of scientific thought
and action in which the audience lives. But on the other hand,
in Van Buren's hands, the secular Gospel is also the insistence
that the authentic content of the Gospel is identical with a
translation confined to non-metaphysical, empirical terms.[7]

Recent philosophical investigation has shown that metaphysical assertions, and world views in general, are not verifiable in
the fashion that statements about experience are verified. But
many philosophers, including Van Buren, have jumped from
this springboard to the conclusion that statements about empirical experience are validated in some direct fashion independ-
ently of any metaphysical assumptions. This epistemological
position rests upon an implicit and unrecognized metaphysic
which assigns a self-subsistent character to a "physical" world
independent of man who is merely an observer of this world.
At this point the methodological separation between observer
and phenomenon required by scientific work has become a
conclusion about the nature of the world itself. This metaphysical commitment is clearly revealed in the following statement
from Van Buren:

When an ordinary situation becomes an occasion of discernment for a man, the change lies in the viewing, in what now
becomes clear, in the light breaking; it is not an empirical
change in the situation. All the physical facts remain the same,
even if they can never seem quite the same to him again. This is
not a metaphysical paradox; it is the expression of a change in a
way of seeing.[8]

There can be no empirical foundation for the assertion that,
"All physical facts remain the same, even if they can never
seem quite the same to him again," as Van Buren himself recognized in his Introduction when he said that no speaker, ". . .
least of all the author, may claim to have found a neutral
ground from which to describe 'the way things are.' " [9] On
empirical grounds one is forced to say that since the physical
facts (what does the term "physical fact" mean?) can no
longer seem the same, they have changed. Unless one is prepared to be a pure phenomenalist, which Van Buren is not, an
empirical test of truth always rests upon the smuggled metaphysical assumption that the observed world remains constant
in character despite the change in experienced phenomena. For
this assumption there can be no empirical demonstration, or
verification. Of course we assume this to be the case, and we
conclude accordingly that the change has occurred within ourselves. But when we so assume, we are no longer the kind of
empiricist that Van Buren wants to be, or the kind to which he
wants to reduce the content of the Gospel. The assumption
that the meaning of the world is to be found in the purposes
and activity of God is no more metaphysical than the assumption that we are confronted with a constant, external "physical" world in which our experience is rooted, and to which it is
confined.

In this empirical, secular Gospel, an epistemological premise
has become a metaphysical principle, despite the disavowal of
metaphysics in Van Buren's book. His epistemological premise
attempts to express Wittgenstein's familiar closing aphorism in
his *Tractatus*, "Whereof one cannot speak, thereof one must
be silent." [10] But he violates that dictum by assigning ultimacy
to the world given in sense experience on the assumption that
only empirical statements are verifiable and therefore meaning-

ful. Statements that are not empirically verifiable are meaningless, and since metaphysical statements and much Christian talk
are of this kind, such talk must be eschewed.

V

Metaphysics serves a different function from the one traditionally asserted, or the one being attacked by the empiricists of
the stripe of Van Buren. They are correct in saying that a metaphysics as the basis of a deductive construction of the world
and experiences cannot be sustained. They are correct in rejecting metaphysics as a set of necessary presuppositions one
must affirm before rational analysis of experience can begin, as
both idealism and Thomism have asserted. But metaphysics
does a different job. Metaphysics spells out the key assumptions
in terms of which we structure experience. It formulates the
pattern or principles in terms of which we understand ourselves and our world of experiences. It is the picture, the model
if you will, of the world which we use to fit experiences together, to direct our attention, and to suggest interpretive clues
by which to tie new experiences into a total flow of events.
Metaphysics, in the phrase of Dorothy Emmet, is a grand hypothesis which gives order and meaning to the separate events
of our lives. It is itself undemonstrable because it is the basis of
demonstration of lesser things. By its terms we give meaning to
individual events because it is the proclamation of the meaning
by which we live.

   Under the impact of a conversion, of falling in love, of the
Beatrician vision, we may shift to a new pattern of interpretation, a new metaphysic, a new model for meaning by which to
live, and now by the terms of the new view the old one is false
and illusory, a blind guide. The status of being a believer is to
be possessed by some meaning for one's life. It is to stand
within some recognized structure of relationships. It is to
affirm a metaphysic by whose terms one interprets himself and
his experience. Accordingly there is no basis, except in a careless use of words, for identifying believers with those who
affirm the Christian faith and the non-believers with those who
reject it.[11] There is a distinction between beliefs, for not all of

us understand the world in the same way, and what to some of us seems illusory and undependable, seems to others of us the very substance of reality itself.

Van Buren himself recognizes and affirms this distinction between beliefs.[12] In his preface he says, "The question to which this book is addressed is a frankly autobiographical one and will have wider interest to the extent that others stand at or near the place from which it is asked." [13] And the last sentence of his book says, "The way which we have followed is admittedly conditioned by the particular attitudes with which we began this investigation." [14] He makes considerable use of R. M. Hare's unhappy notion of "blik" to express the recognition that the believer stands someplace and understands his experience from that place. It is worth noting that Hare seriously weakens his own argument by inserting the distinction between the insane blik of his lunatic, and the sane blik that the rest of us have about Oxford dons. On Hare's own terms, however important it may be to have the right blik, there is no way to choose between bliks in terms of truth and error. The blik within which one operates is an arbitrary choice, which, once made, then governs our understanding of all experience, but which no experience can contradict or even cause us to change.[15] Van Buren does not wish to make Christianity this arbitrary,[16] because there is always the reference to the historical Jesus who stands as an external fact, an empirical datum which is presumably identical for all persons, and about which one must make a decision. The argument that Van Buren makes for his own statement of the Gospel in secular terms is that this is the only way of speaking which does make sense to a significant portion of the contemporary world. And just here the importance of Van Buren's implicit metaphysic becomes clear.

He expresses a view which is widely shared in our scientific, technological culture, namely, the view which thinks in terms of an absolute distinction between person and world. It is a world whose parts are externally related to each other so that the "facts" about the world and our interpretation of them stand wholly independent of each other.[17] The essential principle is that empirical experience is identical for all people, except as their own sense receptors differ, because the person is not part of the event. Knowledge consists of the communications which have been received from this external world, and these can be compared between persons because the world which provided them is identical for all persons. It is also a world whose events are fixed absolutely in space and time. This is the presupposition which causes Van Buren to say of the crucifixion of Jesus:

> Whatever else may be said about the cross, it was two pieces of wood joined together and used for the execution of Jesus of Nazareth at a certain place and time, most definitely in the past. It cannot, for many obvious reasons, become present at all, least of all in words, unless the madness of metaphysics is truly upon us in considering this problem.[18]

By perpetuating what Whitehead has called the fallacy of simple location,[19] this world-view fails to do justice either to scientific methodology, or to the phenomena under investigation. We are now aware that the observer is part of the system he describes, his participation is part of the phenomenon. Scientific methodology recognizes that observation affects the phenomenon in ways we cannot precisely predict or control; therefore, we cannot recover the unaffected event in itself. What a thing is known to be depends upon how we stand in relationship to it.

Put in very simple human terms, it is the difference between sight and touch. From all casual observation, our seeing something leaves it unaffected, while touching it obviously affects it even at the level of gross sensory events. Moreover, we can look at it without ourselves becoming directly involved. But we cannot touch it without becoming a part of the event. We have always known that this was true in our relations with other human beings, but only recently have scientists come seriously to consider the same consequence in dealing with events of subatomic size. Here our illuminating photons approach the size of the objects to be observed, and the model shifts from seeing at a distance to touching at first hand. If the only way to find a billiard ball on a table were to touch it with the cue, we would be aware of our own participation in the event.

In short, Van Buren, speaking for many people today, wants both a world and a religion in which man is present as the same kind of impersonal and interchangeable unit as the other components of a dead world. In such a world, man is no longer a responsible participant, but acts only from the impact of external forces, except when he becomes a detached observer of these impacts upon other persons. In such a world God also is dead, precisely because only a dead God conforms to these conditions. When this view seeks God among the other causal forces to be identified in empirical events, it not only repeats Moses' request to see God's glory;[20] it tells God where and how to stand as we pass by.

VI

However, having in so many words dismissed this point of view as a modern form of idolatry, a nagging question remains. Our culture is so completely committed to the general scientific and empirical point of view represented by the God-is-dead group that one is forced to ask what can be said to those who think this way. Van Buren has exhibited the content—or at least one statement of the content—of the Gospel in what he claims to be exclusively empirical terms, and he has failed to show that this is more than remotely Christian. What is left is not what Christians are concerned to say. Or to put it differently, if this is all that Christians can say in the name of the Gospel, then the Gospel is gone. The Christian message cannot be grounded on a non-theistic, humanistic base. The content of the Gospel cannot be confined to what humanists are willing to say. Granting the empirical premises for this kind of secular gospel, the given content follows. But must one grant the premises? The God-is-dead school says yes, that this is the world in which we live, that in fact this is the world in which men have always lived without recognizing it or being able to articulate its premises and conditions. Indeed this is the natural and ultimately appropriate way to understand ourselves and our experience of the external world.

But it is interesting that at the very time that theologians are proclaiming the death of God and the necessity for an imper-

sonal and empirical Christianity, students riot in protest against
precisely this kind of educational environment in which they
are treated as interchangeable units in a vast mechanism. Mass
production industry, and apparently mass production education, depends upon complete interchangeability of parts. We
can and do deal with human beings, with ourselves, in these
terms, but when we do so, do we still have human beings? In
other words, is this way of construing ourselves and our relationship to our experience adequate to accept the full range of
phenomena? Rather than escaping from metaphysics, this point
of view has substituted a peculiarly flat earth view for the rich-
ness and variety of the Biblical view of man and his world.
What is needed is not the supposed absence of metaphysics,
but an adequate metaphysics.

Supernaturalism and transcendental categories are an attempt
to broaden the range of our perceptiveness and responsiveness.
This model of another world beyond our directly experienced
one may not be the most effective way to say it. But there is no
doubt that we want and need to say more about our experience
than we can say in terms of the carefully bounded world of
direct empirical language. Our lives are indeed circumscribed
and they are supported by something beyond their perceived
limits. Instead of reducing our appropriation of the possibilities
of experience to the confines of strictly empirical speech, we
should be enlarging our perceptiveness and imaginative responsiveness to include an ever increasing range of relationships and
participation.

When a larger range of interactions enters into the account
and thus becomes a part of the total event, such a statement as
Paul's, "it is no longer I that live, but Christ that liveth in
me," [21] becomes both plausible and comprehensible. For he is
saying something that cannot be expressed in terms of the notion of his own new freedom, and the nature of the "Christ"
that now "lives" in him cannot be stated in any customary empirical terms at all. What precisely he is saying can be announced and received only by one who himself participates in,
indeed is constituted by, the same web of interrelationships.

VII

The God-is-dead theology presents us with the classic problem of Christian theology, namely the Incarnation. It has been the central claim of Christianity that God became flesh in Jesus Christ and men have always had difficulty believing it. In traditional form, the issue of the Incarnation is how two utterly unlike substances, one divine and the other human, could be combined in such a way that one does not obliterate the other. The problem was finally resolved by asserting that the two substances—in the Chalcedonian formula, the two natures— were combined without either one obliterating or qualifying the nature of the other, and this ambiguous formula has stood ever since as the answer. But it bequeathed a dualistic structure to the problem which has continued to dominate western Christian thought in the form of a contrast between spirit and matter, sacred and secular.

The tendency sharply to distinguish the secular and the sacred led in St. Augustine to the City of God in contrast to the City of Man, and made the church the mediator between them. And it led also in Protestant thought to the functional separation of church and state, so that two realms of action and relationship were clearly distinguished. Meanwhile the concrete world of direct experience has become increasingly important with the growth of science and the expansion of a technological culture. Our own pluralistic society has accentuated the fading of the spiritual realm, because the traditional assumption that our society was identical with a Protestant free church ethos has collapsed under the pressure of a wide variety of alternative and competing religious groups with differing notions about dominant values.[22] In the presence of this clamor of voices, religion has been retired to a private and internal realm where it has little connection with practical affairs. Attempts, therefore, to assert or retain the authenticity of a "spiritual" realm in addition to the secular seem to be proclaiming something irrelevant to the main concern.

Here Western Christianity has something to learn from Eastern Orthodoxy with its sacramental view of life, a position strongly resisted by Harvey Cox in his *Secular City*.[23] This sac-

ramental view sees this world as the bearer of the Spirit, rather
than something antagonistic to the Spirit. In an introductory
essay to *The Orthodox Ethos,* Walter E. Wiest, who is himself
not Orthodox, says (quoting Zernov) that for Orthodoxy:

> "Spirit and matter are two manifestations of the same reality,
> and when they are sanctified and made the temple of indwell-
> ing Grace, then the past, present and future join together, and
> time stops its flow as it merges with the ocean of eternal life
> and light." [24]

Wiest adds the comment:

> The material is meant to bear the stamp of divine glory, and
> this fact is an additional part of the meaning of what happens in
> the Eucharist.[25]

In contrast to this Orthodox view of the unity of life and the
participation of spirit and matter in each other, we see in the
God-is-dead theology the dead end of the western tendency to
cut the material and spiritual apart by rejecting the possibility
of the Incarnation. A sacramental view of the world is open to
perversion, not the least of which is an ecclesiastical totalitarianism masquerading as a divinely instituted theocracy. It can
also become a sentimental estheticism expressing itself in the
nature mysticism of Kahlil Gibran and summer conference
vespers which worship sunsets in lieu of God, or which attempts to "enrich" free church worship with alien elements
borrowed from other traditions. It can be constructed to a
pious preoccupation with certain specific sacramental acts in
which the divine substance is mediated through material vehicles. But a sacramental view can also open windows through
which something of the outer reaches of the relationships in
which we live can be discerned. This world can become a
channel through which we see and appropriate what lies beyond immediate perception.

Instead of magnifying the importance of the secular world
by denying any relationship with a transcendent realm, the
God-is-dead theology succeeds only in denying that there are
any possibilities of experience and relationship beyond those
which are immediately perceived by the senses. The result is
not a larger and more comprehensive view of the world to re-

place a divided, if not schizophrenic view, but is instead a disastrously constricted one.[26]

VIII

At this point we confront the fundamental problem, and it is a problem not so much between the God-is-dead theologians and those of us who wish to talk some other way. It is much more a problem within ourselves, for we wish to stand off from any such involvement as a sacramental view of the world implies, in order to have its precise rules of procedure and relationship spelled out before we enter the game. We want to know what it means for Christ to live in us, what it means for us no longer ourselves to live but to have a new center and source of life beyond ourselves taking control and ruling and supporting our existence. We want the security of precise definitions, clear distinctions, definite boundaries between ourselves and other beings and relationships. And this is just what we cannot have if our understanding and our language are to be competent to embrace what we fully are as human beings.

In short, the problem is what kind of reason is to reign. It is true that what Christianity has to say is unwelcome and alien to the kind of mind represented by the God-is-dead theology. From this fact two alternative implications follow. One is that the thought forms and basic understanding in Christianity must be revised to fit the needs and moods of modern men who think in another way. This is the implication drawn by the God-is-dead theology, and the result is that Christianity is gone down the drain. The other implication is announced in the familiar words of Paul in I Corinthians 1: 22–25:

> For Jews demand signs and Greeks seek wisdom, but we preach Christ crucified, a stumbling block to Jews and folly to Gentiles, but to those who are called, both Jews and Greeks, Christ the power of God and the wisdom of God. For the foolishness of God is wiser than men, and the weakness of God is stronger than men.

Christianity does demand a choice, for men must be reborn and the old man replaced by a new. Between the Kingdom of

God (a term which does not occur in the index of Van Buren's book) and the world there is enmity, strangeness, distance. And we are in the dilemma that we live simultaneously in both worlds: we are at once pagans and Christian. Therefore the demand for a decision to go one way or the other runs through our own living and speaking. The God-is-dead theology has resolved this dilemma by grasping one horn and has lost the Christian faith. Others who call themselves Christian resolve the dilemma by grasping the other horn and rejecting the world entirely, some in a physical sense by actually withdrawing into separated communities which participate as little as possible in the commerce of relationships enfolding the rest of us who continue in the world. Others have withdrawn conceptually by focusing the content and the intent of Christianity upon another world than this one, the world that will come in heaven or at the end of time, while this one is to be borne as something ultimately irrelevant and without value. Still others simply avoid the problem neither facing nor solving it, by reaffirming the traditional vocabulary of words, ideas, formulas, and perhaps also the three-story world-view, which they have received through the tradition.

The problem rests directly and heavily upon those of us who are concerned to be both Christian and relevant. For us the God-is-dead theology represents a problem which we must answer, but a form of answer we cannot accept, for we cannot simply seize one horn of the dilemma. And so we live in a continual tension, desiring on the one hand to speak clearly and directly, concretely and empirically, and on the other hand, speaking in such a way that our words convey the full dimension of the relationships and responses within which we live.

One desire continually frustrates the other. And so in both our thought and our speech we take refuge in the forms of myth which image that which we have perceived and shared but cannot fully encompass or comprehend. When we speak religiously, when we speak Christianly, we are not trying to escape from the concrete world of daily necessities. We are trying instead to show how that world is sustained within the larger web of relationship and response created by the will and action of God.

Of course God is a myth; so also is his death. But myths are true in the only meaningful sense the term "true" has, namely, that they express adequately and comprehensively the full dimension of meaning by which we live. Sometimes myths die— that is, they no longer represent a community of faith; they no longer convey the meanings by which men live. For some people apparently, God is a dead myth. If God is dead it is because some lesser myth has come to be adequate to sustain and to create a smaller kind of human life than that which is declared and given in the resurrection of Jesus Christ. Of course the resurrection is a myth; but how else can we proclaim the new life given by God in Christ, through whom he reconciles the world to himself?

Notes

1. Cf. Charles Boleyn, "God is not Dead!" *Christianity Today*, X 6 (December 17, 1965), 7–8, and an editorial, "Shadows of the Antichrist in the Decline of Western Theism," same issue, pp. 21–23, and Ilion T. Jones, "Is Protestant Christianity Being Sabotaged from Within?" *ibid.*, X 7 (January 7, 1966), 3–6.

2. July 16, 1944.

3. Paul van Buren, *The Secular Meaning of the Gospel* (New York: Macmillan, 1963), p. 150.

4. Cf. *ibid.*, p. 145.

5. *Ibid.*, pp. 146–147.

6. *Ibid.*, pp. 147–148.

7. Cf. *ibid.*, pp. xiv, 20, 71, 198.

8. *Ibid.*, p. 167.

9. *Ibid.*, p. 20.

10. Ludwig Wittgenstein, *Tractatus Logicus-Philosophicus*, 7.

11. Van Buren, *op. cit.*, p. 167.

12. *Ibid.*, p. 20.

13. *Ibid.*, p. xiv.

14. *Ibid.*, p. 200.

15. Cf. Antony Flew and Alasdair Macintyre, eds., *New Essays in Philosophical Theology* (London: SCM Press, 1955), pp. 99–103.

16. Cf. Van Buren, *op. cit.*, p. 200.

17. *Ibid.*, p. 167.

18. *Ibid.*, p. 71.

19. Alfred North Whitehead, *Science and the Modern World* (New York: New American Library 1953), p. 50.

20. Exodus 32:18.

21. Galatians 2:20.

22. Cf. Franklin H. Littell, *From State Church to Pluralism* (New York: Doubleday, 1962).

23. Harvey Cox, *The Secular City* (New York: Macmillan, 1965).

24. William H. Wiest, "An Appreciation," in A. J. Philippou, ed., *The Orthodox Ethos* (Oxford: The Holywell Press, 1964), p. 10, quoting Nicholas Zernov, *Orthodox Encounter* (London, 1961), p. 55.

25. Wiest in *ibid.*, p. 11.

26. Cf. Van Buren, *op. cit.*, p. 198.

ROGER HAZELTON

The Future of God

MY TITLE, I suppose, requires some few preliminary words of self-defense. My interest is not that of calling in question the classical prerogatives of God—his eternity and aseity for example, by which he was thought to be above change and time. Actually I am more concerned in this address with the future of my own professional work as a theologian; but I strongly suspect that it is to be closely bound up with the radically changing patterns and models by which Christian faith in God is conveyed and comprehended. The wrench is so great with respect to the neo-orthodox modes of thought which held the field until very recently, and so much strain is being put upon our accustomed manner of speaking and thinking about God, that it is fair to ask whether the God recognized by revelational, kerygmatic theology has any future at all as a mode of faith's understanding of itself.

(128)

It was almost half a century ago that Alfred North Whitehead remarked that there was then only one question in debate: "What do you mean by God?" Now, much later, and far
later than most Christian people think, the question has become: "Can anything be meant by the word God at all?"
Strange that this stage of theological desperation should have
followed hard upon massive efforts of systematic and Biblical
theologians to give scope and density to the word God, now
called by novelist John Updike "the ominous hollow noun." It
is as if so much talking about God had only weakened our confidence in all such talk, simply darkening and deepening the
very question to which theology vainly tried to proclaim the
answer. Nevertheless, that is our present situation, and we shall
have to face and cope with it as best we can.

Does God as the explicit object of concern and interpretation for Christian theology have a future? Or do we have to
agree with those of our contemporaries who insist that God
must be either dismissed or reduced—dismissed as an archaism
and an irrelevance, or else reduced to understandably human,
natural terms? This of course brings into view the problem of
the task and method of theology itself; but this problem is most
properly and fruitfully raised with reference to theology's
own reason for being, which has been immemorially called
God. If God does not exist, then certainly theology has no justification either. It is not a matter merely of having to change
our conceptions of him, or of needing to update our language.
If God is dead and we have killed him, as Nietzsche declared
and Sartre has repeated, then theology had better recognize
that it is done for and dissipate its remaining energies in other
directions.

Indeed, there are some who suppose that such a declaration
of theological bankruptcy is already overdue. In their opinion
the influence of Bultmann and Bonhoeffer has been no blessing
at all to theology, but a disintegrating force; and when we add
to it the critical work of logical and semantic analysts, psychol-
ogists, and sociologists, we may well wonder if they have left
theology anything of its own to think and talk about.

Those theologians who have been most sympathetic to these
influences have also been most ready to abandon much of the

classical outlook and objectives of theology itself and in particular the assurance that God can be said to exist or that he can be characterized in any referentially meaningful way. Hence it is being widely asked whether theologians ought not to close up shop altogether, or let others take over and mind the store.

As one of an evidently dwindling number of theologians who protest this conclusion, I feel impelled to state my conviction that God is still, and is bound to remain, the proper object of my speech and thought. Of course I cannot expect to justify my protest fully in the space of a single lecture; it is not possible to do more than sketch a few of the issues which seem to me crucial for the future of Christian theology, and in suggestive fashion at that. I shall only recognize and make response to the effect of two influences that are gathering strength in contemporary theology: the death-of-God movement, and the trend toward a Christological humanism.

Death-of-God Psychology

The representatives of this first movement speak very clearly for themselves. In the words of William Hamilton:

> We are not talking about the absence of the experience of God, but about the experience of the absence of God . . . the death of God must be affirmed; the confidence with which we thought we could speak of God is gone, and our faith, belief, experience of Him are very poor things indeed. . . . There really is a sense of not having, of not believing, of having lost, not just the idols or the gods of religion but God Himself. And this is an experience that is not peculiar to a neurotic few, nor is it private or inward. Death of God is a public event in our history, we are saying.[1]

What is taking place in this movement is that atheism—belief in the non-existence of God—is being *welcomed* into the perspective of theology itself. These men wish to be known and judged as Christians and Protestants; they are searching for a new theological idiom that is realistic, up-to-the-minute, and above all "honest"; but they are convinced that God as a point of reference, about whom the theological statements may properly be made, is simply not available to us any longer.

There is, beyond doubt, a large measure of truth expressed in the Nietzschean myth of the death of God; it is indispensable for Christian thinking in our own particular kind of world. If it is not a Christian truth in some narrowly dogmatic, doctrinal sense, it is at any rate a human truth not to be disregarded by Christian reflection, and even at some points thoroughly congenial to it. What Hamilton calls "the experience of the absence of God" is simply a fact of Christian, of churchly, life in our own time. What teachers and preachers have to contend with, therefore, is not atheism as an ideological enemy to be fought against by taking a stronger party line, but atheism as a human fact which conditions every Christian utterance and informs each Christian action in a "world come of age."

Moreover, the accompanying themes of religionlessness, of waiting in the dark, of worldliness, of deprivation of God as need-fulfiller and problem-solver, are to be hearkened to and accepted as telling symbols of the milieu and matrix of present-day theology. This means, for one thing, that the day of theological system-building is surely past, although the ever distant goals of generality and finality in theological statement will not cease to beckon us, as they must always do. For another, this means that the well-worn distinction between the dogmatic and the apologetic functions of theology is no longer either accurate or useful. As Claude Welch says, "Theologically, nothing is required for the address to the 'unbeliever' that is not necessary for the Christian community's own understanding of its faith," [2] and it may be added, required for the theologian's own self-understanding as well. It means, again, that the whole attempt of neo-orthodox theology (which only yesterday seemed so impressive) to pinpoint God in history or to locate him with reference to his "mighty acts" is to be given up in understanding our theological present. God *means* absence, not presence. He is known, if he is known at all, by where he is not and by what he does not do. That is the rather obvious consequence of "taking seriously" the myth of the death of God in theology.

Let me now venture some criticisms of the movement I have been describing, though with genuine appreciation for much that I am learning from it. First, I am perhaps unduly impressed by the fact that these men seem unwilling to treat God as the dead fact they say he is. They would like to discover evidence of his continuing activity, for example, in the civil rights movement, or in the contemporary arts, or in urbaniza- tion and technology. They look for God in unexpected places, to be sure, but they do not give up looking. One might suppose that a dead God could be decently buried and forgotten; but this God's death, it seems, is never completed; His absence, in fact, seems to be only a particularly striking mode of presence. The death of God theologians are obviously reluctant to let God stay dead, and insofar as this is true, their own position is a questionable one.

Second, I am troubled by the rapid transition which these thinkers make from an experience of God's absence to an as- sumption of his death. Evidently a stronger word than absence is here required to explicate the sense of absence; this is more than God's not being there, more than withdrawal merely, more even than continued separation from God; it must be rendered by the symbol of death, and moreover a death which is a murder, for we killed God, according to the way the story runs. I believe this movement of thought to be entirely correct in thus indicating what Father John Courtney Murray calls "the will to atheism," [3] the free choice of existence without God. But has not faith in God, and the theology based upon it, always recognized man's responsible role in the experience of God's absence? Is Sartre any more bereft of God, forsaken by him, than was Jeremiah, Job or Jesus? There is even a sense in which only the living God can be thought of as being absent, though I should not want to make cheap apologetic use of the truism (which is also true) that absence is a mode of presence. I am, however, not persuaded that the myth of the death of God is the best, or only, way of presenting the widespread ex- perience of God's absence as "a public event in our history."

My third comment has to do with this movement's unhesitat- ing acceptance of the secular world as able to fill the vacuum left by the God of religion. When Hamilton writes, "we do not ask God to do for us what the world is qualified to do . . . we trust the world, not God, to be our need fulfiller and prob- lem solver," [4] I am not at all sure what he intends to assert. One can scarcely draw a meaningful contrast between God and the world if then the world is to be thought of as catching up wholly within itself the values formerly ascribed to God. That is, we do not seem to be given a choice that is either significant or fraught with genuine risk. Also, it should be pointed out that belief in God may be quite as productive of "world-affirmation" as is disbelief. The alternatives "God" and "world" are simply unreal as possibilities for choice or as options for belief. A refusal to turn to God for the sort of help which the world can give, moreover, is not confined to those who are persuaded that God is not available or approachable. Such refusal is fully consonant with the liveliest faith in the divine presence and power. I am afraid I just do not see what this movement's preference for the secular and the contemporary, which I find admirable, really has to contribute to the argument that God is dead.

These comments have perhaps more the character of hesitations than of outright criticisms. That is because I find the death of God a most suggestive, though not entirely compelling, symbol for rendering the temper and tendency of the religious situation that is peculiarly our own. We *are* without God in the world, to a degree unknown in many generations. "Something serious has happened," as Karl Jaspers says. However, it is at the point where this pathos becomes a kind of program that I must refuse to go further. One cannot, after all, simply embrace "the world without God" in this wide-open, almost Whitmanesque manner. The world can no more be an object of devotion, a focus of loyalty, than the "God up there" who is regarded as dead. It is good and right to become alert and alive, to be a man of one's own time and place, whatever one's religious preferences or antipathies. But this is not and should not be the same as hailing the world, any kind of world, as a God-substitute.

Christological Humanism

The second tendency in contemporary theology to which I wish to pay my disrespects in this lecture is a difficult one to define. I call it "Christological humanism" because that term seems best suited to suggest some of its leading motifs. The view I am describing holds that although we cannot any longer speak significantly of God as object, as transcendant reality, we may still find positive meaning in Jesus as the Christ, if only we identify him with ourselves "in the midst of life" by coming to understand and live out "the secular meaning of the Gospel." There is a radically ethical orientation to this view which is impatient with all purely speculative considerations and sits very loosely to dogmatic points of reference in the major theological traditions. Yet it also makes striking, frequent use of Christological doctrine for illuminating and invigorating "life in the world." It is Christ as man, as revelation of the depths of human being in grandeur and misery, that claims our attention in this view.

It is as if we were told, "You cannot be sure of God, but you can know and follow Christ. If your prayers have no real object, at least your actions can have genuine motivation. If Christ as God means nothing to you, then consider Christ as man—as present in the neighbor and the brother, waiting to be served and believed in." In this view it is declared that "Jesus is in the world as masked, and the work of the Christian is to strip off the masks of the world to find him, and finding him, to stay with him and to do his work." [5]

This point of view deserves to be called Christological, since it is more than a pietistic or moralistic patterning of Christian behavior on the reported actions of the earthly Jesus; in fact, it is not such a patterning at all. The ethical note struck here is anything but normative or prescriptive; instead it is drastically situational and at some points even antinomian. Jesus is in the world, by the power of the incarnation, not to tell us how but to show us why to live. And he shows us, not by giving us a model demonstration, but by waiting for us to catch up with him, by allowing us to read our world in terms of his own concealment in it—a concealment which to faith becomes a disclosure. The doctrines of the incarnation and the atonement, although lying always in the background of this view, are nonetheless prominent, which justifies us in calling it Christological in character.

Now a brief word in explanation of the term "humanism."

First, this view insists upon a high and generous estimate of man, like all humanistic thought. By way of example, note its distaste for anything resembling a doctrine of original sin. Here is H.A. Williams of Cambridge University, in what I regard as the best book of sermons published since that of David Roberts a decade ago: ". . . in our assumption of our unworthiness . . . there lies a common distrust of what God has made . . . Behind such confessions there lies, hidden and unseen, a vote of no confidence in the Creator." [6] On the contrary, positive and glowing appreciation of whatever is truly human is the very signature of the tendency I am delineating here. Listen to Dean Williams again: ". . . being human is not a shabby thing to be ashamed of. For us human beings being human is God's gift of Himself, the way in which His charity operates." [7] Thus we see how closely this way of thinking is allied with humanistic affirmations which appear in other respects quite unlike those of Christian theology.

There are those who regard Christological humanism as a movement from faith to love, from correct believing to right doing. This is indeed one of its characteristic stresses, but there are some real difficulties in the way it is presented—difficulties which are not solely theological, but moral too. I am to love my neighbor as if he were Christ. Does this mean that I love Christ in the neighbor, or the neighbor in Christ? And I am to love Christ only in the neighbor. But does this mean utter identification with the neighbor's need and radical openness to his reality, or is the neighbor simply the place and opportunity for service in the name of Christ? What does it mean to hold that Christ is incognito in the neighbor? Has the mystery of presence, of incarnate love serving men, been fully or fairly faced in this perspective? Is my love my own, or God's love working in and through me? These and many similar questions are posed and await clarification in this way of putting Christian responsibility and obedience.

I am convinced that this reduction of God to purely human dimensions in Christ leaves a great deal to be desired. Rather than settling once for all the problem of Christ's relationship to God, Christological humanism only raises this problem in its acutest form. Do I see more than neighbor when I see Christ in

him? And if I do not see more, how do I come to recognize
Christ's claim upon me given in the neighbor? It is plain that
we must still find the problem of God at the center of any
living or thinking that deserves to be called Christian. He who
says Christ in faith says "God" as well as "man"; or else he does
not even say "man" clearly enough, compellingly enough. The
mystery of a life hid with Christ in God is not dissolved by
any humanism that is Christological only by intention, and not
by determination.

The effort to reduce God is as inconclusive and as unillumi-
nating as the attempt to dismiss God altogether. We cannot eat
our Christian cake and have it too. That is the lesson to be
learned from these recent and admittedly exciting essays in
theological restatement. I do not deny that the absence of God
is a fact of life for us, both public and private. Nor do I refuse
to face the disturbing implications of his presence in the struggle for justice and peace which mightily engages us. I only
protest that neither the experience of the one nor the effort
toward the other can provide sufficient standing ground for
Christians in our moment of history, unless we call to our aid as
well what T. S. Eliot termed "the backing of the dead."

Recently I have been reading, with much profit, Professor
Helmut Gollwitzer's book, *The Existence of God as Confessed
by Faith*. In speaking about Bultmann, for instance, Gollwitzer
points out how an advance interest in human self-determination and "authentic existence" drastically shapes and distorts
both the range and depth of faith in God. He writes: "This
pragmatic way of thinking that sets out from man's interests
leaves no room for the importance of the question of God's
own interest, of God's own reality 'in himself' . . . it arranges
a priori what faith has to be interested in, instead of leaving
that to faith itself as it hears the Word." [8] I think this is precisely what is taking place also in the movements of thought
which I have been considering with you today. Let us learn all
we can from them and feel our way into their picturing of our
condition and our Christian future as deeply as we can. But let
us also be warned by what Martin Luther said once about the
Swiss thinkers of his time: "They define the Word not in
terms of the God who speaks it but in terms of the man who

receives it." [9] Let us, at all costs to our pretension or our despair in our theologizing, avoid this temptation, and we shall not need to worry about whether God has a future.

Notes

1. "The Death of God Theology," *The Christian Scholar*, Spring 1965, 31, 41, 45.

2. "Theology as Risk," *Christian Century*, June 2, 1965, 708.

3. See his *The Problem of God* (New Haven: Yale University Press, 1964), p. 85.

4. Hamilton, *loc. cit.*, p. 40.

5. *Ibid.*, p. 46.

6. *The True Wilderness* (London: Constable, 1965), pp. 132–133.

7. *Ibid.*, p. 105.

8. Gollwitzer, *op. cit.*, p. 33.

9. Quoted in *ibid.*, p. 122.

JOHN B. COBB, JR. / From Crisis Theology to the Post-Modern World

AFTER THE THUNDER of a great generation of theologians in the twenties and thirties of our century, the theological horizons of the sixties are painfully silent. Even the voices of the great old men are quieter now, and in any case they cannot answer the questions of a new generation. There exists a vacuum in which even the splash of a small pebble attracts widespread attention. Theologians console themselves that the time for great systems is past and the time of the essay has come. Yet the essays for the most part are trivial.

The silence of our time is especially surprising since there is no lack of highly trained and intelligent men keenly interested in constructive theological work. Why are we so inarticulate? Why must so much of our energy be devoted to studying or interpreting our past? And why are the few efforts toward dealing with our own problems so provisional?

(138)

I would suggest that the disappearance of crisis theology has led to a situation so difficult for the theologian that he is likely to exhaust himself in taking his bearings. I will attempt in what follows to focus the problem in terms of the renewed openness of theology to culture and of the problem of historical relativism. I will then indicate in a highly personal way a response to this crisis and a possible way ahead.

I

Roughly we may characterize the theology of the nineteenth century as one which sought a synthesis between faith and culture. Culture was positively appraised, and pride was taken in the success of faith in christianizing it. Further victories were hoped for and worked for. Dissenting voices vigorously protested that faith lost itself in this synthesis, that Christendom is a fraud, and that only by rejecting culture can faith be true to itself. But these voices were not heard until World War I had proved them prophetic.

Crisis theology undertook to distinguish sharply between faith and culture. Culture is human; faith, of God. Faith seeks no sustenance in culture and makes no special claims to benefit culture. It belongs to another sphere which radically transcends culture and is even, essentially, indifferent to it. In fact, of course, the crisis theologians were far from indifferent to the events of history and took an active and creative part in molding them. It was they and not the remnants of nineteenth-century liberalism who gave effective leadership to resistance against Hitler. Within their own thought, the separation of faith and culture gave way, although the insistence on the duality remained. The legacy of crisis theology is therefore a new openness to culture, an awareness of its importance. It is *this* world in which we are called to faith, and though the faith to which we are called is not simply the culmination of culture, still it must learn to provide an authentic witness within it.

In this formal statement, the new recognition of the inescapability of taking culture seriously seems relatively innocuous. The problem, however, is that the culture we are called to take seriously is one increasingly devoid of Christian form and sub-

stance. It is a post-Christian culture, a culture for which God is
dead. What does it mean for Christian theology to take this
culture seriously?

For some, it means that we are to look in the culture for
authentic expressions of man's humanity, and to see in them
new forms of unconscious and unintended expression of the
Christian faith. However, this will not do. We can, of course,
as historians point out that the influence of Christianity is not
dead even where it is denied, but if we are to take our world
seriously we must acknowledge that the existence in which it
seeks a new authenticity is not that of its Christian past.

For others, it means that we are to see in modern culture the
direction in which man must inevitably fall when he turns
away from faith. But this will not do either. That much in the
modern world does indeed express just this is beyond question.
But this approach presupposes that there is an island of security
in the modern world from which it is possible to view it from
without and thus take warning not to follow that course. This
is precisely *not* to take seriously the modern world. This is to
assume that the modern world is optional, that we choose to
live in it or out of it as we choose unbelief or belief.

A third alternative is to understand the modern world as asking questions which it cannot answer, questions which can be
answered only by faith. But this approach also fails. The modern world does not in fact seem to be asking those questions to
which the Christian gospel provides an answer. To achieve a
correlation of question and answer we seem forced to destroy
the integrity both of the world and of the gospel.

A fourth alternative is to take from the modern world only a
new conceptuality in which faith can express itself. Surely this
is acceptable and commendable as far as it goes, but it does not
deal frontally with the problem of faith and culture. What is to
be expressed in the conceptuality taken from the culture? Is it
something which challenges the culture, which roots itself outside the culture and claims autonomy from it? Then again the
modern world is not being taken with full seriousness, for the
modern world denies every transcendent perspective. Then
again one presupposes an island of refuge from which one may

decide how and in what way to be a part of the modern world
and how and in what way to transcend it.

We seem to be confronted finally by only two choices. We
may really take the modern world seriously, acknowledge that
it is the only world we know, accept it, affirm it, and live it. To
do so is to accept and live the death of God. On the other hand,
we may refuse the modern world, distance ourselves from it,
fence in our world of traditional faith, and seek to preserve it
from the corrosion of the world outside. Both expedients are
desperate ones. It is no wonder that theologians find it difficult
to speak relevantly in such a time.

The problem for contemporary theology is acutely compounded by historical self-consciousness. Since we are accustomed and compelled to think historically, we are accustomed
and compelled to think in terms of the variety of ways in
which men seek understanding and fulfillment. We see that
Christian faith is one among these ways, that it arose in particular circumstances in conjunction with particular beliefs and
expectations, that it spread in some directions and not in others,
and that it is fundamentally an historical accident that we happen to be Christians rather than, for example, Moslems.

We may, of course, argue that the historical origins of a belief have nothing to do with the responsible judgment of its
truth or falsity. But if so, we must at least assume that we do
have some criteria for judging. When our suggestions of such
criteria in their turn are found to be products of a peculiar history, we begin to feel the ground sinking beneath our feet. We
seem plunged into an infinite regress in which every possibility
of normative thinking is destroyed.

If we argue that we must believe something, and then by a
leap of faith choose to be Christian, we find ourselves still confronted by the most bewildering diversity. Faith does not seem
to mean the same thing for Eastern Orthodoxy, for Roman
Catholicism, and for Protestantism. Even within Protestantism
the variety is great. Having leapt into Christianity, are we to
leap into one or another form of Christianity as well? And
what attitude are we to take toward those who leap in another
way? Having leapt in our particular way, are we given to

know that they have leapt wrongly? Or do we simply confess
our own commitment and accept other commitments as equally
valid?

It is clear that one of the reasons for the power of crisis
theology was that it placed faith radically outside this relativism. For it faith is the gift of God and is validated in its giving.
It does not have to claim superiority over unfaith or over competing religions in any other way. Nevertheless, this solution
above all sounds like special pleading. Are we really prepared
to say that God has given faith overwhelmingly to Westerners
and that all the religious attainments of the East are to be seen
as so much vain human striving? Is not our belief that this is so
clearly a function of our historical conditioning? Can we really
claim that this belief is given with the gift of faith so that it too
is validated by the act of God? Or if we affirm that God has
given faith to all men, what can faith mean any longer? And
what happens to the Biblical distinction between believers and
unbelievers?

That these difficulties can be multiplied indefinitely goes
without saying, and with the passing of crisis theology they
have come very much to the fore. The Christian must now
recognize that his faith is one among many and that it cannot
be set over against all other human phenomena as that one
point at which God has acted. Yet the alternative seems to be
to return to that relativistic sea from which crisis theology
seemed briefly to save us.

II

In the above I have called attention to the two features of the
contemporary situation which seem to be most critical for the
theologian. Our culture, the culture in which we do and must
live, is characterized by the death of God. We cannot but understand ourselves and our beliefs historically and hence relativistically.

These two problems are intimately interconnected. The
death of God is caused in part by the historicizing of all our
thinking. Since we understand an idea by understanding how it
arises and develops, we can no longer view the idea as having a

one-to-one correlation with reality. We can talk seriously about ideas of God but are not able to speak directly of God. More broadly, we can enter imaginatively into many ways of perceiving reality, but just for that reason we cannot affirm any of them as true. Indeed, the word "true" we are forced to place in quotes, not knowing any longer what we can mean by it.

It is also the case that the death of God is a *cause* of relativism. As long as God's reality remained a fixed pole for thought, the relativity of human experience and belief could be understood as reflecting varying ways of grasping one ultimate reality. Truth was found in God's knowledge, and even though we might not claim any final criteria for identifying the content of truth, that there existed a final truth about all things was clear. With the death of God, however, truth and reality are alike relativized. They exist nowhere.

This world in which God is dead and truth and reality are without meaning is indeed our world. Yet it is not our total world. If it were, no such statement about it could be understood. If God were wholly and unequivocally dead for us, the statement that it is so would not be made. Indeed, all discourse would be at an end. Every statement assumes that it somehow transcends total relativism, that it points to some kind of reality, that it participates in some kind of truth. We do still live in a world formed by a past that remains alive even in its decay.

I do not mean to seize the point that total relativism is self-contradictory as a basis for setting relativism aside. The *affirmation* of total relativism is self-contradictory, but there is a sense in which relativism can be lived unspoken. The complete relativist would never apply the term relativism to his own thought, for he would not think in such universals. It is the reality of lived relativism, not its philosophical defense that seems to lie ahead for our world.

I do mean to say, however, that the reality of the death of God and of the concomitant relativism does not exhaust our contemporary world. If we take seriously the historical consciousness which we have already seen to play such havoc with traditional forms of faith and theology, we must also see that the death of God and the concomitant relativism are likewise a function of time and place, one way of being among others, in themselves neither absolute nor final. History shows us that just at that point at which a *Zeitgeist* seems to have swept all before it, it may already be giving way in the minds of the most creative and authentic persons to something quite different, something that certainly will not repeat the past, but something which may yet recover out of the past just what seemed in greatest danger of being destroyed. Perhaps even today at the point at which all rational structure and all human meaning seems to be evaporating, new structures and new meanings may be emerging.

If this is so, and I earnestly hope that it is so, then we may escape the desperate choice indicated above between affirming the modern world and reacting against it defensively. We may refuse the modern world not by defending the past but in the name on the new world which *may* be born. We cannot of course know that it will be born. We cannot even know whether our decision for it may help it to be born. But we can affirm it, and in doing so we can repudiate the modern world in the name of the world we will to be the post-modern world.

The picture I am proposing may be sketched as follows. The *Zeitgeist* of our world is one in which God is dead and all truth and reality have collasped in relativity. That *Zeitgeist* is working its way into ever more consistent expression in thought, art, and existence. It leads to the death of man in the sense of self-conscious, responsible, historical, individual man. Its chief obstacle to total victory is the vast deposit of centuries of Christian thought, art, and existence which, partly consciously but more largely unconsciously, is expressing itself in a still powerful humanism. This is our contemporary post-Christian situation.

If this were the total situation, I have argued above, then the theologian could only decide between throwing his lot with the new and reacting defensively against it by appealing to the authority of the past. He has learned, as many of his colleagues have not, that there is no resting place in the midway point of rationalistic or romantic humanism. But I am suggesting now that this is not the total situation. In addition to the remnants of Christendom and to the demonic powers released by the death

of God, there are other thrusts here and there, thrusts which
are as authentically modern as any nihilism, but which refuse
nihilism in the name of truth.

These emergent claims upon the future are endlessly varied,
and there is no place to stand from which one may judge the
likelihood of the success of one or another. Nor is there a place
to stand from which one may safely baptize one or another
such thrust as Christian. Yet I believe that, ignoring the question of success and risking the danger of apostasy, the Christian
thinker today must reach out for a novelty that disdains all
appeal to the authority of the past and dares to think creatively
and constructively in the present.

Teilhard de Chardin is a recent figure who represents such
daring. The world he knew, however strange, was surely authentic, genuinely contemporary. He discounted nothing of
the magnificent intellectual achievements of science. He did
not appeal to the authority of the past. He took the risk of
apostasy. Whether in the end his vision is durable we cannot
yet know, but that it struck a responsive chord in the minds of
many is clear. That it *could* point to a new world, the beginnings of a new *Zeitgeist*, cannot be denied. For my part I
would far rather live in that world than in the world being
fashioned by dominant modernity.

The work of Teilhard is instructive in that though it fundamentally eschews the authority of the past it affirms Jesus
Christ as the center of reality. Skeptics will understandably regard this as a nostalgic remnant of inherited faith or as a con-
cession aimed at placating the church. But I do not believe this.
Whether by historic accident or by supernatural purpose,
there is an absoluteness in Jesus Christ which can speak not
only through the continuity of Christendom but also across the
gulf of centuries and cultures. To refuse the authority of the
past need not mean to ignore its truth and reality.

I mention the work of Teilhard de Chardin not to hold it up
as the one great hope for the future or for the theologian. On
the contrary, I find it often vague, confusing, and unsatisfactory. But it represents a mood which challenges the predomi-
nant *Zeitgeist* on its own terms, defending nothing on the
ground that "it is written" or that "it is Christian," avidly open

to all truth—yet still *believing*. This mood is one with which I can identify myself as theologian, as Christian, as man.

My own effort to share in the work to which this mood gives rise is directed toward thinking into the new world opened up in the philosophy of Alfred North Whitehead. To enter Whitehead's world is to experience a psychic revolution as great or greater than the Cartesian and Kantian revolutions. To experience that revolution is to enter into possibilities of thought and self-understanding at which Whitehead himself barely hinted. I believe that from within this new Whiteheadian world one can appropriate also the world of Teilhard de Chardin—as of other revolutionary thinkers of our day—with greater clarity than they themselves could achieve.

III

Although any serious exposition of Whitehead's thought is beyond the scope of this paper, it is appropriate that some indication be given of the aspects of his thought which seem relevant to this context. Whitehead himself speaks of his speculative philosophy as like a poem, mutely appealing for understanding. One cannot begin with terms and objects as defined within some other vision of reality and then state unambiguously that which Whitehead intends. This procedure is impossible wherever there is genuine novelty of sensibility and vision. Hence, all the more, a few brief paragraphs on his thought can hardly hope to be intelligible. Yet, one must try.

Whitehead alters the locus of concreteness as over against modern common sense. Especially with the decay of idealism, modernity has identified concreteness either with things presented to us in sense experience or with the sense data themselves. Whitehead declares this to be "the fallacy of misplaced concreteness." What is concrete is experience as such, just as it occurs in each particularized moment. Whitehead's "actual occasion of experience" has close affinities with the "shining present" of Brightman and the "*Dasein*" of Heidegger. To this extent, what I have called the psychic revolution demanded by Whitehead is seconded by personalistic idealism and by existentialism.

However, Brightman and Heidegger alike, although in quite different ways, limit this revolution to human (or at least animal) reality. Brightman sees the "shining present" in the context of the "illuminating absent." Heidegger sees "*Dasein*" in the midst of other "*Seiende*." For both of them, the physical world, the world of objects, remains something fundamentally other than the experience to which they rightly direct us as the starting point. Whitehead, in contrast, sees the whole physical world as itself also composed of "actual occasions of experience" and of societies of such occasions. There is and can be no object which is not itself a subject or a society of subjects. The physical is one dimension of all experiences including the human, but it is not at all the name of a realm over against that of experience. Whitehead also differs from both Brightman and Heidegger in perceiving experience as a momentary becoming and perishing rather than as a continuum of becoming.

The profoundly distinctive character of Whitehead's vision is apparent in his understanding of relations. All real relations are the re-enactment in new experiences of elements of old experiences. All causality is to be understood in this way. Through its causal efficacy the past always profoundly affects the becoming present but never determines exactly how it will become. Causal influence and free self-determination alike characterize every entity in the world.

In terms of these briefly identified principles almost all the traditional problems of thought receive new answers or new versions of old answers. Furthermore, light is shed upon the special problems of modern mathematics and physics that relates these disciplines to human existence in a quite new way. In this context, however, we can note only the relevance of Whitehead's thought for the two acute problems previously discussed—the death of God and universal relativism.

Whitehead's earlier work reflects the death of God at least by its silence. But it gradually became clear as his philosophical speculations broadened that the philosophical reasons for the death of God were repudiated by him. Hence once again the questions of being and becoming emerged in his thought in such a way as to cry out for belief in God. It is fascinating to watch the uncompleted process whereby step by step—

reluctantly, it seems at times—Whitehead unfolded a doctrine of God.

Whitehead's doctrine of God has many points of contact with traditional Christian thought—more, I think, than either he or his critics generally recognize. Nevertheless, it is profoundly new. It has been transformed by modern science and mathematics, on the one hand, and by the revolutionary vision of the world as a society of societies of occasions of experiences, on the other. The understanding of God's relation to the world is further transformed by the new understanding of space-time and of relation as re-enaction and by Whitehead's special doctrine of God's providing each momentary occasion with its ideal aim. After generations in which theologians and religious philosophers have struggled to defend some one relation in which God's importance for the world can be argued, we are confronted with a new world of thought in which all manner of modes of relatedness to God are affirmed. Within the Whiteheadian context we can understand both the Person-to-person encounter of modern Protestantism and the mysticisms of both East and West. We can agree with those who have seen the relation of man to God in the ethical dimension and with those who have reasoned to God from the order and directionality of nature. We can see both the reality and the all-determinativeness of grace and also the freedom and responsibility of man. But we see all this in a frame of reference that to some degree transforms the meanings of all the traditional terms and problems.

The point of the above is not to explain Whitehead's doctrine of God—that again would be impossible in a few paragraphs—but simply to stress that once one enters the strange new world of Whitehead's vision, God becomes very much alive. The understanding of the world begins and ends with him to a far greater extent than Whitehead himself made explicit in his writings. Insofar as I come existentially to experience myself in terms of the world to which Whitehead introduces us, I experience myself in God; God as in me; God as law, as love, as grace; and the whole world as grounded in him. And I experience this not as in some separation from or tension with what I know of myself physiologically and psychologi-

cally, but precisely as illuminative of the fragmentary knowledge afforded by these and all other disciplines. If Whitehead's
vision should triumph in the years ahead, the "death of God"
would indeed turn out after all to have been only the "eclipse
of God."

The problem of the relation of Whitehead's vision to the
encompassing relativism of our time is still more complex. Obviously his vision is one among many, conditioned by time,
place, and circumstance, subject to interpretation biographi-
cally, psychologically, and historically. Unlike most philosophers, Whitehead's philosophy articulates itself as just such a
relative undertaking and achievement. One cannot *prove* its
truth; one can only display its extraordinary coherence, relevance, and adequacy. And of course, even the acceptance of
such criteria is also conditioned and relative. There is and can
be no escape from the circularity of all thinking.

Yet if we take seriously also the conditionedness and relativity of relativism, we will cease to see in the relativity of a position a reason for its rejection. Furthermore, within the position
we may find an explanation of how relativism is transcended
that seems to account both for relativism and its transcendence
more satisfactorily than can be done while one remains, or tries
to remain, at the merely relativistic level. Just this is the
achievement of Whitehead's thought.

For Whitehead there is no reality that is not relational. For
example, one cannot talk first of what occurred at a given time
and then separately of what was experienced or perceived.
What occurred was just these experiences and perceptions. If
we ask "what really happened," we should always be asking
"what was really experienced." And all such experience was
that of one subject or another. The question of what happened
in general is ultimately meaningless. In this sense, the relativity
of truth is absolute.

However, this relativity is limited in two ways. First, it is
objectively true that such-and-such experiences occurred.
Whether they occurred is not relative to *our* opinion, available
evidence, or taste. The experiences of the past are objectively
immortal. Also, what occurred was not limited to the human
experiences. There were electronic, atomic, and cellular ex-

periences as well, and the reality of their occurrence does not depend on human knowledge of them.

Hence there is a reality to which our opinions and experiences as a whole correspond more or less well. Truth is an important relation in experience, although certainly not the only important one. Reality as known to us is a function of our interests and our instruments, but reality as it experiences itself is relative only to its own interests. We live in a very real and determinate world, a world in which all things are relative, but determinately relative.

From this perspective, we may indeed understand how human experience and belief are functions of the everchanging situation. Certainly the genesis of ideas helps us to understand them, and appropriately so. The complexity of the reality which confronts us is so vast that our ideas can never have a one-to-one relation with it. Yet our ideas do emerge out of reality in a positive relation with it. The most diverse and even apparently contradictory ideas can have some correspondence to that reality, and the ideal of a greater, more inclusive truth-relation is by no means illusory.

Furthermore, when we combine the Whiteheadian doctrine of God with his triumph over nihilistic relativism, we can see that the truth we seek is already real. There is a perspective which shares all perspectives and relates them all truthfully to each other. And that perspective is already effective for us despite the exceedingly distorted and fragmentary character of our own participation in truth.

IV

One may well object that the effort to explore a new world of thought beyond the dominant modern world is not "theology" but "philosophy." How then can one whose passion drives him in this direction characterize himself as a theologian? The answer to this returns us yet again to the problem of relativism. I know that when I most totally reject the word of the past as authority for my thinking or respond most affirmatively to ideas suggested to me by Whitehead, I am expressing the vision that has become mine as my very selfhood has been formed by my past. When I realize and acknowledge to myself the conditionedness of my being and my stance, there does emerge some degree of transcendence over that conditioning. I can affirm it or I can reject it. Even if I reject it, it still continues to operate in me, but its power over me is nevertheless broken in principle and incipiently in fact as well. If I accept it, what had operated as a blind force becomes now my own will.

I know that the selfhood I experience is formed in the church, in Christian history. What I see in others and in the world, I see through eyes given vision by a Christian past. Knowing this, I am free also to reject it. I might reject it because there are anguish and estrangement given with the Christian vision, a burden of responsibility for a world that denies Christian truth. I might reject it because I see that it is indeed an historical accident that I am grasped by this vision, that I can show no ultimate rational justification for retaining it. Or I might reject it because so much of the reality I perceive through that vision enters into me as destructive of it and as denying its authenticity.

But I do not reject it; I affirm it. It may seem that in this act I contradict all I have said about refusing the authority of the past. This would be true except that the grounds of affirmation can only be that the Christian vision forecloses nothing, conceals nothing, refuses all self-defense. It is particular, but not exclusive. The belief that this is so is itself, of course, a function of the vision. This circularity cannot be avoided. One can only seek in complete openness to expand the circle indefinitely.

Because I know that my quest for a new world is motivated by my Christian selfhood and that the new world I see is seen through Christian eyes, I must acknowledge that all my thinking is Christian thinking, whether or not it is acceptable to other Christians. I cannot claim, as philosophy seems often to want to claim, that any intelligent person should be able to see the truth of my premises and the validity of my arguments.

But why "theology?" If Christian philosophy is the open quest for truth of a self who affirms the Christianness of the vision which is his, then theology is thinking that reflects upon the giver of that selfhood. Christian selfhood experiences itself as a gift in two modes. Historically, it is a gift of a community of faith grounded in Jesus Christ. Existentially, it experiences itself as a gift of God. Theological reflection must seek to understand how these two modes of giving are connected with each other, and in the process it must reflect on such traditional topics as Jesus Christ, the Holy Spirit, the church, the Bible, as well as God. Furthermore, even if such reflection in our day is prompted by our concern for our selfhood, the reflection itself must turn away from that selfhood toward its source in such a way as to bring that selfhood also under most radical judgment.

But this specific theological reflection upon the gift of Christian selfhood is never separable from the Christian philosophical reflection upon reality as a whole and in its parts. The theological must both illustrate and illuminate the categories of philosophical reflection. Each must act as criterion for the other, and each criterion in turn is modified and reshaped by the total reflection. At every point the decision to affirm rather than to reject the starting point in Christian selfhood and vision is open for reconsideration as reflection modifies its self-understanding or casts doubt upon its adequacy.

In this approach, theology is a part of the total reflective process and is *totally vulnerable*. There is no built-in safeguard to insure that in the end there will be any place in one's world for God, or Jesus Christ, or Christian selfhood. Because I believe God *is*, and that in Jesus Christ we find what it means to know God as he is, I also believe that reflection must ultimately lead us toward rather than away from these truths. But I know also that my belief may be shattered in the process, and I cannot appeal to some protected ground of confidence when all else fails.

WILLIAM O. FENNELL / Religion

Post Mortem Dei

ONLY THE PERSON who has not been reading widely in the
fields of religious and secular literature in the postwar years will
find anything startling in the title of this review article. References abound to our time as a cultural period which can be
spoken of not only as post-Christian but also as *post mortem
Dei*. For the point is not simply that the Christian religion no
longer in any vital sense forms and informs the general culture
of our day. It is religion as such, in any traditional sense of the
term, with its belief in some kind of transcendent divine being
who is related meaningfully and purposively to the world of
nature and to human history, which has lost credence today in
the countries of the West. All four of the books under review
here state this as a fact, attempt to show its causes and consequences, and in one way or another raise the question of the
future prospects of religion in Western culture.

Of course, the death of God does not necessarily have as its consequence the demise of religion. Indeed the time of the death of God can be a time of religious revival, such as that of the 1950s on the North American continent, according to Dr. Gabriel Vahanian. The fact that churches are well attended, that religious books can head the best-seller list, that the language of religion permeates the culture, is not in itself a sign that God has not died or that religion has survived. It may simply be the case that, with God's death, religion is tranformed into religiosity in which all sorts of substitutes for God give some kind of meaning and encouragement to lives that have not the strength of mind and heart to admit God's death.

The first part of Vahanian's *The Death of God* (New York: George Braziller, 1961) is entitled "The Religious Agony of Christianity," the second party "The Cultural Agony of Christianity." In the former he attempts, with abundant reference to religious and secular literature, to show the transformation that has taken place in our day of Christian faith into religiosity. The chief characteristic of religiosity as compared with traditional Christian believing is the immanental rather than transcendental "object" of religious experience and belief. Religiosity is marked by the following traits: a faith in faith which substitutes for faith in God; a desire for "togetherness" instead of genuine "community"; an amorphous mixture of Christianity, secularism, and secularity; a narcissistic, hedonistic, man-centered religion, marked by a faith so inflated that it has lost all its value. It was not true religion which experienced a revival in the 1950s but rather the upsurge of this sentimental, man-centered cult of reassurance and success which bears incontrovertible witness to the fact that God is dead. The religious agony of Christianity in which God dies ends, not in the death of religion, but in the birth of a god "who reflects the image of man all too faithfully."

Dr. Vahanian begins his analysis of the "Cultural Agony of Christianity" by noting that "theologically speaking, every age is post-Christian." He means by this statement that there is no period in human history that does not stand under the judgment of God. (This is the Kierkegaardian insight that no man can speak of himself as *being* a Christian but only as *becoming*

Christian applied to man's cultural history as a whole.) But the
uniqueness of our age is that it is *culturally* post-Christian. This
means not only that Christianity has ceased to have any significant relevance for modern man but also that "the fundamentals
of our culture—those things that govern our self-understanding
—make us impervious to the conception of Christianity, so that
our culture makes it impossible for us to become Christian." As
already noted, the world-view of Christianity is transcendental; the world-view of our culture is radically immanental.
Since the context of our self-understanding is the reality of the
world in all its immediacy and immanence, it is easier for us to
understand ourselves without God, than with him. The world-
view of our time makes God irrelevant. His existence is no
longer called into question intellectually, as it was in an earlier
anti-Christian period. Even the *question* about God's existence
has ceased to be relevant in our time. God has ceased in any
real sense to inform life and therefore must be presumed to be
dead.

Those who want their expositions of such serious themes
neat and tidy will not be satisfied with this book. There is a
lack of precision in the use of terms which gets in the way of
understanding. Paul Ramsey in a helpful introduction under-
lines as one of the main points of the book that it is Christianity
itself which is responsible for the loss of God today. But one
finishes the book with no very clear impression of the way in
which this has been so. Moreover, one is never quite sure what
is meant by "Christianity" in the author's use of the term. At
times it is used as a synonym for Biblical faith, or Biblical religion, or ecclesiastical history, or modern Christian thought,
and at times it is difficult to infer just which of these meanings
is intended. In its impressionistic way, *The Death of God* does
lead to insight into the spiritual condition of ourselves and our
contemporaries and into the implications of that condition for
anyone concerned about the Christian faith. It raises very
sharply, but does not answer, the question: What essentially is
the relation between Christianity as faith and Christianity as
religion? And the subsequent question: What is the relation
between the Christian faith and the cultural enterprise of man?
The chapter "Christianity, Secularity and Secularism" seems to

point in the direction of an answer to such questions when the author suggests, without developing the thesis, that "secularity is a Christian obligation" and shows that "secularism" is the fate that befalls Christianity itself when it degenerates into religiosity. Even a Christian of sound faith can today make some sense out of speech about God's death when it implies an experience of God's absence and especially when it indicates the passing of a religious world-view. But it is difficult to know what a Christian is to make of the author's contention that post-Christian culture is such as to make it *impossible* for modern man to become a Christian through faith in a transcendent God. For it would indeed be a sure indication, not merely of God's death through absence, but that he never lived except through poetic fiction, if he, the living God, self-revealed in Jesus Christ through the Holy Spirit, could not bring it to pass that men are sustained or recreated in faith even in the midst of a culture that gives every indication that he is dead.

Whereas Dr. Vahanian has given us a suggestive account of the popular religion that has survived the death of God in Western culture, Dr. Franklin Baumer in his book *Religion and the Rise of Scepticism* (New York: Harcourt, Brace, 1960) presents a carefully structured, historical account of the rise and development of the skeptical tradition and its effect upon the religious beliefs of the educated man. With respect to the latter, he too is led to speak of the religious situation of today as a time of the death of God, "The Death of God" being the title of his third chapter.

Dr. Baumer discovers four main types of skepticism, each marking a principal phase in its development. There is the Enlightenment type of the eighteenth century, with its anti-dogmatic, anti-clerical, anti-Christian, but not necessarily anti-religious, attitudes and ideas. This period was preceded and prepared for by the attack in the seventeenth century on the teleological view of nature under the providential ordering of God from the side of the mechanistic views of nature and the empirical views of knowledge that had their origin in the new science of the day. Accompanying this intellectual attack on traditional Christian views of nature in its relation to God were the skeptical attitudes that resulted from increased travel, which brought the educated person into contact with cultures whose religious or secular foundations differed from those of the West; from the proliferation of Protestant sects, each with its own claim to authoritative and absolute knowledge, the general effect of which was the relativizing of all such claims; and from the revival of interest in antiquity, which also tended towards the relativization of Western man's attitude towards his own particular cultural tradition. Eighteenth-century skepticism developed into the peculiar type of the nineteenth century, which found its most pointed expression in Nietzsche's proclamation of the death of God and Feuerbach's less funereal but equally serious contention that theology is virtually anthropology. What Nietzsche and Feuerbach shared in common was the assertion that man is the *fons et origo* of the notion of God and that for his own freedom and development he must consciously set himself the task of becoming the God he confesses. Such views as these gave rise to a new set of gods, replacing the God of traditional Christian believing, whose names were variously Humanity, Society, Science, History, and Culture. The skepticism of this age seemed to be accompanied by a sense of expansive freedom, as men cast off what was felt to be the yoke of Christian tradition and gave themselves to the nurture of their manmade gods. But today, in the middle of the twentieth century, this optimistic skepticism of the nineteenth century has yielded to an anxious skepticism of which the literature of our day speaks. For Dr. Baumer it is best characterized by Arthur Koestler's novel *The Age of Longing*. The main characters of this book show no sense of freedom in their failure to believe. They have lost all confidence in manmade gods. Skepticism has become a burden to them. They have an acute sense of longing for the birth of a new god who, like the old, would possess the quality of transcendence but who would not make the demands against intelligence that Christian believing makes. In this day of the death of God, marked by a skepticism combined with longing, three alternatives confront the intellectual: nihilism, the revival of the God of Christian origin, or the painful waiting for the birth of a new god that will satisfy both man's longing and the requirement of intellectual honesty. In the concluding section

of the book, Dr. Baumer asks whether the latter hope and possibility will give rise to a "Layman's Religion" which will creatively combine skepticism and religious aspiration. Such a religion will be marked by a multivariety of forms of religious
expression, a renouncing of all vanity of dogmatism, and a recognition that all religious language is symbolical and mythical,
not literal, in function and meaning. These marks, if taken seriously, will make impossible a revival of the Christian faith with
its archaistic thought-forms and language and the gross presumption of its claim to finality of revelation in Jesus Christ.

While reading this book the reviewer was made aware of the
large degree to which his own Christian thinking had developed in more or less conscious dialogue with the skeptical tradition of doubt of which Dr. Baumer speaks. Therefore, he could
not but regret the implicit contention of the author, explicitly
attributed to others, that anyone holding to Christian beliefs
and attitudes must fall short of thoroughgoing intellectual honesty. For an ordained theologian, the offense is compounded by
the suggestion that only a "Layman's Religion" could satisfy
the demands of religious longing and rigorous thought. Surely
Christian apologetic belongs in any comprehensive history of
religion in relation to the skeptical tradition, especially when
such a history concludes with a discussion of religious possibilities in the face of skeptical doubt. No attempt to give contemporary Christian answers to questions of doubt is made in this
book. One can therefore be excused for continuing to believe
that there is more promise for man's longing in a renewal of
Christian believing than there is in the vague outline (with
which the book ends) of a religion that satisfies longing only to
the extent that it is bereft of intellectual content. Baumer seems
to be groping for the solution to the demands of the age already arrived at by some, not least by W. T. Stace in the book
next to be reviewed. This solution is mysticism. But the god of
the mystic is a very old god indeed.

In Dr. Stace's book, *Religion and the Modern Mind* (Philadelphia and New York: Lippincott, 1960), one finds what a
modern intellectual who well knows the skeptical tradition still
thinks it possible to affirm about religious belief and experience. As suggested above, he is not one of the vanguard of the

Lay Founders of a new religion about whom Dr. Baumer
speaks, for there is nothing new about the religion of which he
speaks. Even in this modern scientific age the essence of all
valid religious belief and experience remains inviolate from any
strictly logical, rational point of view. It is true that the history
of modern thought, as reflected in the art, literature, or philosophy of the modern period, has been the history of the conflict
between two radically opposed views of the world, the religious and the scientific. But it is Dr. Stace's conviction, the
grounds for which he is intent to show in this book, that the
conflict between the two world-views has been rooted in logical fallacy. Its origins lie in psychological impressions, not in
rational thought.

The authors of the two previous books drew heavily on the
literature of the modern period as source and illustration of
the points they wished to make. Perhaps because he is a philosopher, it is Dr. Stace's view that "[an age's] philosophy is perhaps a better key for unlocking the secrets of its *Weltanschauung* than either its art or literature." He therefore traces
the rise and development of the scientific world-view, and the
skeptical tradition to which it gave birth, in the history of
modern philosophy. But first he gives an account of the "medieval world-picture," pointing in it to the three affirmations
basic to any religious view of the world: (a) the divine government of the world; (b) the teleological or purposive nature
of the world; (c) the world as a moral order. The author then
shows how in the development of the scientific world-view
into a thoroughgoing naturalism it was thought necessary to
call into question these basic religious affirmations. But this (he
argues) is a false conclusion originating in a logical muddle. In
the third and final section of the book, entitled "Present Problems," the author seeks to show what a modern man concerned
about intellectual integrity may in all honesty affirm about religious truth and reality. He must assert, as Dr. Baumer has
insisted, that the language of religion is metaphorical and mythical, that the religious Object is a mystical reality which is
neither objective nor subjective but transcends the split between the object and the subject, and therefore that continual
openness to the possibilities of mystical experience is the re-

ligious way of life. It may be affirmed, Dr. Stace believes, that
there are two worlds, or two dimensions of the one world, each
of which looks to the other like an illusion. "That God is an
illusion is the standpoint of naturalism. That the world is an
illusion is the standpoint of the eternal." Kant saw clearly the
truth about these two orders of the one world, that naturalism
is the sole truth about the natural order, and religion the sole
truth about the eternal order. Kant's only mistake was his failure to recognize that man can have a direct experience of the
eternal order in the mystical vision.

As a contribution to the intellectual history of modern man's
dialogue with doubt the Christian scholar will find Dr. Stace's
book interesting. But because of the author's insistence on sub-
suming Christian understanding under the general category of
religion, without any attempt to show how Biblical or catholic
Christian tradition fits the application, his book is not instructive for the Christian who wishes to carry on *his* dialogue with
doubt. The latter may indeed accept all that Dr. Stace wishes
to affirm about the mystical as well as naturalistic dimensions of
human experience, without believing that in either he has encountered the living God self-disclosed for him in Jesus Christ.
It is again interesting to note that Dr. Stace makes no mention
of the significance of modern *theological* revivals in both Protestant and Roman Catholic quarters for any account of "Religion and the Modern Mind" today, though he does note that
Neo-Thomism as a religious philosophy is failing to make any
serious impact on the modern skeptical mind. Moreover, considered from within the limits of the author's own presuppositions, it is difficult to see how the understanding of religion
with which he ends satisfies the requirements necessary for a
valid religious world-view which the author himself sets down
earlier in the book. Rather than asserting the divine government of the world, the purposive nature of the world, and the
world as an objective moral order, does not the mystical approach to religion inevitably deprive the world of any ultimate
purpose and meaning, as the author himself states when he says
that, looked at from the viewpoint of the eternal, the natural
world appears as an illusion? And surely the man in whom the
naturalistic and mystical orders of the world meet must be a

terribly split personality when each of these orders is necessarily experienced as an illusion from the standpoint of the other. It is precisely to the healing of this split that the Christian understanding of salvation could address itself. For both the reality of God and the reality of the world are affirmed in the gospel of the Word made flesh, in a reconciling act which makes it possible for man to love God and world together as they meet in Jesus Christ.

With William Hamilton's book *The New Essence of Christianity* (New York: Association Press, 1961) we return again to the theme of what it is possible for a man to believe in the time of the death of God. Dr. Hamilton is concerned to say what he believes it possible for a Christian to assert with a sense of reality and honesty in this time of skeptical doubt. He is concerned equally with the question of the way in which the Christian ought to go about stating his convictions. The style of life of the Christian is as important as the content of his Christian believing. The author implies that his contemporary "theological betters" have been guilty of attempting to say too much in the way of Christian affirmation and that they have certainly said it with a kind of aggressive assurance that is lacking to him. Should not the Christian, like the admirable secular man, Camus, seek to clarify for himself and his contemporaries the little that he really knows, rather than give the impression, by mighty systems and many tomes, that he knows so very much? Is not the theological fragment more appropriate to our day than the system—a softer rather than a more strident tone to represent the broken-vision character of our Christian understanding? The author, then, is concerned with that limited, essential core of Christian understanding to which he believes the present-day Christian may assent with conviction. It is a *new* essence of Christianity in that it results from the Christian scholar's acceptance of responsibility for an attempt to say in and for his particular age—in its language and thought-forms— what can be said meaningfully of Christian truth and reality. As Dr. Hamilton unfolds his theme of Christian belief in the time of the death of God, his acknowledged dependence on the thought of Dietrich Bonhoeffer becomes increasingly clear. Indeed the book as a whole strikes one as the attempt of a contemporary Christian to respond to various sharp challenges to Christian thought and life found in Bonhoeffer's *Letters and Papers from Prison.*

The author makes it abundantly clear that it is not only the unbelieving secular man who has experience of the death of God today. Paradoxically enough the Christian too may have experience of that death. One of the difficulties that a reader of these books which use the language of the "death of God" will experience is that of knowing precisely what meaning the phrase is intended to convey. Dr. Hamilton interprets the fact and experience variously. At one time it means "the death in us of any power to affirm any of the traditional images of God." Traditional Christian language has lost its power to convict and convince. No doubt his meaning is somewhat similar when he further says: "It is the God described by the best and most sophisticated theologians of our time, who seems to many to have withdrawn from his world." Then again, as in Vahanian's book, the "death of God" is a synonym for the experience of "God's absence." Hamilton seems to sound again the note of longing struck by Baumer when he says that some Christians in the midst of their experience of God's absence find it possible to pray for his return. For them faith becomes hope. "To be a Christian today is to stand, somehow, as a man without God but with hope." *Apart* from Jesus the Christian experiences God as a wounding presence from which he would be free. This wounding presence is experienced also as an absence, so that God seems to be present to us only in ways we do not want him and absent in the ways we do want him. The attempt to say what God can mean to us today *with* Jesus leads us to seek to find in the language with which the New Testament sought to express his meaning the answers to our contemporary questions. Without indicating in any precise way how the answers discovered fit the questions asked, Dr. Hamilton finds the key to unlock the answers to his own questions, and apparently to "all the problems of belief in the time of the death of God," in themes which speak of our Lord in terms of lowliness, humiliation, suffering, and death, rather than in themes which speak of sovereignty, power, and authority in any ordinary sense of the terms. He frankly admits that he can find

little meaning in the Biblical witness to the exaltation and reign-
ing-in-glory of the risen Christ, though this language may represent something of final, eschatalogical significance and meaning. It is the Lord who is Lord only in his suffering and death
who is the One in whom the absent God meets us and in whom
the dead God lives. In him too we find the answer to the question about the Christian style of life, though the author does
not show how the characteristics of this style derive from life
in Christ. (On the contrary, he even states that some secular
men have described and lived by a similar style without confession of Christ's lordship.) Some of its characteristics are: a
wholesome sense of reserve in one's relations to others who are
friends; a combination of tolerance and anger towards the
enemy; the renunciation of every wish and hope to be more
than tolerated by others; the recovery of an unashamed commitment to goodness; the learning to live in the dialectical tension between rebellion and resignation in our relation to nature, man, and God.

In a footnote on page 12 Dr. Hamilton says: "My essay as a
whole is deeply indebted to Bonhoeffer and may be taken as a
theological response to the coming to age of the world as he
has analyzed it." Certainly the book is an answer to Bonhoeffer's challenge to every Christian to come out from behind
the shelter of the Church's believing and say what it is that he
really and truly believes. In his search for the "essence" of
Christianity the author does not attempt, as a hasty first reading of the book might suggest, any reductionist trimming of
the Biblical witness. Like Bonhoeffer, he would have us take
the whole Biblical witness seriously, always remaining open to
the possibility that any part of it might speak meaningfully to
us some day. But only that which does so speak at any time
should form part of a Christian's profession. The reviewer is
not so certain that the author has followed, or rightly interpreted, Bonhoeffer in answer to other crucial questions. Dr.
Hamilton's emphasis on experience would seem to call into
question Bonhoeffer's distinction between religion and faith;
what he has to say about the Church would seem to contradict
Bonhoeffer's view of the Church as Christ-existing-as-commu-
nity; and we are not sure that the meanings the author gives to

the phrase "the death of God" are precisely those of Bonhoeffer when the latter speaks of the God who died because men outgrew him in distinction from the God who is absent from the world because he died on the Cross. Above all, one could have wished that some mention had been made, because of its importance to the subject of the book, of Bonhoeffer's distinction in the *Letters* between what a man believes through self-persuasion and what he believes as gift of God. For even in a time of God's "absence" it is God himself who must speak his present Word.

JOHN S. DUNNE, c.s.c. / The Myth of God's Death

As NIETZSCHE told the story, it was a madman who came into the market place with the news "God is dead." After relating his news to a somewhat skeptical audience, the madman threw down the lantern he had been carrying and said, "I come too early; I am not yet at the right time." That was in the latter part of the nineteenth century, 1882 to be exact. Now, in the second half of the twentieth century, eighty-four years later, the news has been brought to the market place again, this time by a group of theologians. Outstanding among them are Thomas J. J. Altizer and William Hamilton, the authors of a collection of essays, *Radical Theology and the Death of God* (Bobbs-Merrill, 1966). The newsbringers have again seemed madmen to the skeptical audience they have met in the market place. Only now, I am afraid, they come too late; the right time is already past.

(165)

Sartre has said that the passion of man is the reverse of the passion of Christ. Christ's passion was the suffering of a divine being losing himself in order to become human; man's passion is the suffering of a human being losing himself in order to become divine. This reversal is the theme of the "death-of-God" theologies of Altizer and Hamilton. The double movement, according to them, has been progressing throughout human history. God has been steadily losing ground and man has been steadily gaining ground as man finds ways of solving more and more of his problems, of satisfying more and more of his needs, without appealing to God for help. The further back into the past we look, the more helpless man appears to have been in the face of life and the basic problems of life such as hunger, sickness, warfare and death. The further into the future we project this same line of development, the more we can expect man to have solved these problems and to have become capable of helping himself. From the vantage point of the present, where the line out of the past passes through into the future, God appears to be losing more and more of His functions, *i.e.*, to be losing Himself in order to become human, while man appears to be taking over more and more of the former prerogatives of God, *i.e.*, to be losing himself in order to become divine.

Hamilton thinks that the demise of God means the demise of all faith and hope, and that the only Christian attitude which is still possible is love. Altizer, on the other hand, speaks of "confessing the death of God" as one would speak of confessing faith and also, perhaps, as one would speak of confessing guilt. The faith would correspond to the original Christian faith in the kenosis, Christ's act of "emptying himself" by becoming a mortal man and dying. Only now Christ would be emptying himself of his divinity not merely through the life and death of Jesus of Nazareth but through all the history of the human race. The guilt would correspond to the guilt of deicide, the human responsibility for putting Christ to death. Only now the responsibility would be exercised not by contributing to the suffering and death of the historical Jesus so much as by man taking more and more responsibility for himself and depending less and less on God.

The death of god was one of the great themes of the old mythologies, so much so that it makes one wonder whether in the statement "God is dead" we do not have a piece of genuine mythology. If this is so, it will be a very interesting statement indeed, for it will represent a mythology which has had currency in modern times. Also this will mean that the "radical theology" of Hamilton and Altizer is theology in the original sense of the word *theologia* as it was coined by Plato, namely systematic mythology.

Neither Hamilton nor Altizer, I believe, would take very much offense at this suggestion. Altizer sees the beginning of theology in the theogonies of the ancient Greeks, and he sees the antecedents of his own thought in what he calls the "myth-making" of William Blake. The last essay in this book, in fact, is by Altizer and is entitled "William Blake and the Role of Myth in the Radical Christian Vision."

What do I mean, though, by suggesting that the sentence "God is dead" is a piece of mythology? To me this means that the death of God plays a role in our culture parallel to that of the "twilight of the gods" in the old Teutonic culture or to the death of the god Osiris in Egyptian culture or the death of the god Attis in Phrygian culture or the death of the god Adonis in Syrian culture. In almost every culture we know of we find the myth that the god is dead. What is more, the death of the god is usually the central event in the mythology.

The meaning of the myth seems always to be connected somehow with the mortality of man. It is as though the death of man is always seen as overshadowed by the death of the god. What the death of the god does is take the sting out of the death of man—it is unbearable to have to die if there is a being who enjoys immortality, but if everything without exception is doomed to die, even the god, then death can be accepted.

This appears to have been the role of the death of God in our own culture. It takes the sting out of death for us if there is no God exempt from death. The sentence "God himself is dead" appeared already in a seventeenth-century hymn, "O Grief! O Woe!" by Rist, and there it meant that God became man and died on a cross. It was quoted at the beginning of the nineteenth century by Hegel, only now the meaning that God died upon the cross became symbolic of a deeper meaning that there is no God. Actually the more prosaic statement "There is no God" serves the same purpose as the statement "God is dead." If there is no God, then there is no being exempt from death. "If there were gods," Nietzsche argued, "how could I bear not to be a god? Hence there are no gods." The trouble with saying "There is no God" or meaning "There is no God" when one says "God is dead" is that a new god emerges, death itself. If there is no being exempt from death, and if no being is God, then, as Hegel said, "death is the sovereign master of the world." Death holds sway over all beings. Nothingness is god.

Altizer and Hamilton are confident that the death of God outside of man means the emergence of God within man. If we take this to mean that the death of God will leave man the sovereign master of the world, their optimism seems rather shallow. For the sovereign master and the new god, as Hegel saw very well, will be death itself. This, in fact, is exactly what appears to have happened in the first half of the twentieth century with the advent of totalitarianism and total warfare. Death took God's place as the sovereign master. Man is never without his god, it seems, and always rules his world in the image of his god—either in the image of a creative power that gives life or else in the image of the destructive power of death. In the first half of the twentieth century it was in the image of death that man ruled his world. If there is any god that must die in the twentieth century, therefore, it is "death the sovereign master." This has been the feeling of some of the most acute observers of the contemporary situation like Albert Camus. It was before the advent of totalitarianism and total warfare that men like Hegel, Heine, and Nietzsche were saying "God is dead." After the emergence of the Moloch which took God's place in the first half of the twentieth century, men are "waiting for God" (Simone Weil) or, if they are in despair of His coming, "waiting for Godot" (Samuel Beckett). This expectancy, hopeful or hopeless as the case may be, is what characterizes the present situation, not an optimism founded upon the death of God.

The original message of Jesus, "Change your hearts, for the reign of God is at hand," if it were to be proclaimed now and

believed, would have a new significance. After the experience
of the first half of the twentieth century, the abiding threat of
a nuclear holocaust, and continual limited warfare in the latter
part of the century, it would mean something like this, "Take
heart, for the reign of terror is at an end." This message will
become credible, to be sure, only when man has found a practical way of ruling his world in the image of the creative power
rather than in the image of death. Until then we wait for God,
or if we are skeptical, we wait for Godot.

ROBERT McAFEE BROWN / What
Does the Slogan Mean?

AT THE HEIGHT of the "New Theology" controversy in
Great Britain in 1907, P. T. Forsyth remarked (rather uncharitably) that certain efforts at theological restatement seemed to
him "like a bad photograph: overexposed and underdevel-
oped." I am prompted (equally uncharitably) to apply the remark to certain of the writing connected with the contemporary "death of God" movement in Protestant theology.
(Those who take umbrage at this description are at liberty to
apply to my comments the retort that was directed to Forsyth,
that his own writings resembled "fireworks in a fog.")

I do not mean to imply that the question of the "death of
God" is an unimportant question upon which theologians can
simply turn their backs, but I do mean to imply and also to
state directly that the formulation of the issue in Thomas J. J.
Altizer's *The Gospel of Christian Atheism* (Philadelphia:

(170)

Westminster Press, 1966) seems to me so hastily constructed
and so obscurely presented as to remove it from the category
of writings that need to be taken seriously. If this sounds like a
harsh judgment, I can only respond that since Altizer harshly
writes off as irrelevant or wrong or both almost every other
Christian theologian who has ever lived, there can hardly be
objection if one theologian feels constrained to turn the com-
pliment back upon its originator.

For so long has Altizer's version of the "death of God" been
at the center of attention in the mass media that I, like many
others, have eagerly been awaiting a full and definitive treatment of exactly what he was trying to communicate. It was
therefore with more than a little eagerness that I turned to *The
Gospel of Christian Atheism*. Here, I was sure, would be the
definitive statement of the new position, the careful development of the argument, the contribution to the ongoing theological dialogue, that would give us something solid to which
to react. I approached the book with all the openness and receptivity I could muster, feeling sure that if there really *was*
something in the new movement, Altizer's book would tell me
so.

I was, to indulge in massive understatement, disappointed.
The book abounds in obscure terminology, loose use of language, sloganeering in place of argument, sweeping generali-
ties, and unsupported conclusions. Not only is the material unclear, but what *is* clear is far from having the self-evidential
quality that its author attributes to it. Under the circumstances, it would be preferable simply to ignore the book and
turn to the really significant attempts to discuss contemporary
theological issues (Cox, Robinson, Van Buren, Hamilton,
Hoekendijk, Cobb, Rahner, Schillebeeckx, and a host of others
spring to mind). But since the mass media have ordained Altizer as the high priest of a new "movement," it is impossible to
pretend that the book has not appeared. It must be examined
with some care, if only for the purpose of persuading others
that they need not accord it the same kind of attention. The
need to engage in this paradoxical stance of calling attention to
the lack of need to call attention is furthered by Altizer's recent suggestion (in *Radical Theology and the Death of God*, p.

170) that silence about his writings may be taken to imply assent to their content.

Whereof one cannot be silent, then, of that must one speak, and it will be clear already that the gravamen of my charge is that Altizer has not given us a statement with which we can really come to grips. It may be that he has got hold of something important, but if so the fact is not discoverable from his book. So the present essay, rather than being an attempt to initiate a dialogue with Altizer, is the recording of a feeling that no dialogue is called for, at least until he has made a more careful attempt to communicate his position.

My reactions, then, boil down to the following:

1. Either Altizer cannot write clearly; or
2. He can write clearly but does not care to take the trouble to do so; or
3. His subject matter is of such a sort that it is incommunicable in the prose style he has adopted; or
4. I am too dense to understand what he is writing about.

The conclusions to be drawn, respectively, from these reactions seem to me to be the following:

1. Altizer should stop writing books; or
2. He should take special pains in the future to try to communicate his position; or
3. He should turn to sheer evocative language and poetry, and stop trying to communicate through prose; or
4. I should stop writing reviews.

Those, if there be such, who do understand *The Gospel of Christian Atheism* will certainly opt for the fourth of these conclusions. For the moment, I incline to either (or both) the second or the third.

I

One of the main problems posed for the reader is that he is constantly confronted by words and slogans whose meanings are never clarified. This is particularly frustrating when Altizer is using traditional terms but with a special meaning of his own.

"Word" is a classic example. The term, with its upper-case "W," appears hundreds of times. By pages 17–18 we have been informed that "the Word is in process of renewing all things, not by recalling them to their pristine form in the Beginning, but rather by making them new so that they can pass into the End" (p. 18). Does this have something to do with the Incarnate Word or *Logos,* as might be expected in a book on Christian theology? Apparently not, for by the next page we have been told that "the principle of the Word can be and is indeed present, even though it is not possible to discern *any* traditional signs of its activity" (p. 19, italics added). What, then, are the criteria by means of which to discern signs of the presence of this Word, whatever it is? No more frustrating question can be asked of the book. We are urged to a "pneumatic or spiritual understanding of the Word" (p. 25), and we are urged to seek "a total union with the Word" (*ibid.*). But we never learn what this entails or how it is to be brought about.

"Epiphany" is another keyword, appearing interminably, but criteria for distinguishing proper epiphanies are noticeably lacking. "Sacrality," "primordial," "immanence," "every alien other," "Incarnation," are likewise key terms but it seldom becomes clear just what Altizer's special meaning for them is. When we do learn, the meaning is so novel as to make us wonder why the traditional terminology was retained. Incarnation, for example, is "the contradiction of life and the deification of nothingness" (p. 95).

I can only conclude that there is an "in" language by which members of the "death-of-God" school communicate with one another. But as long as they are going to write books for all of us, rather than letters to one another, I insist that they have the responsibility of giving the rest of us some help, not only in learning their terminology but in indicating on what levels they are using words. Rather than help of this sort, Altizer simply repeats and rearranges the key words and slogans on page after page. Here are two passages from the latter part of the book which are typical of the book as a whole, and my complaint is that we have no clearer understanding by the end of the book of the meaning of the key terms than we had at the beginning. We have simply heard them more often:

Insofar as an eschatological epiphany of Christ can occur only in conjunction with a realization in total experience of the kenotic process of self-negation, we should expect that epiphany to occur in the heart of darkness, for only the universal triumph of the Antichrist can provide an arena for the total manifestation of Christ (p. 120).

It is precisely because an epiphany of Antichrist abolishes the transcendent source of evil and nothingness by embodying a primordial chaos in the actuality of history that it is a redemptive epiphany, an epiphany unveiling the full reality of alienation and repression, thereby preparing the way for their ultimate reversal (pp. 121–122).

These are difficult enough, and one could quite properly take almost every phrase and ask the author to explain what he is trying to communicate to us. But it is even more bewildering to be told, again in a typical sentence, that "to know an alien and empty nothingness as the dead body of God is to be liberated from every uncanny and awesome sense of the mystery and power of chaos" (p. 96).

In the midst of paragraphs containing such sentences, the reader leaps with hope upon the announcement that he is to be told what is "the absolutely decisive and fundamental theological principle" of Altizer's position (p. 84). The answer is that "the God of faith so far from being unchanging and unmoving is a perpetual and forward-moving process of self-negation, pure negativity, or kenotic metamorphosis" (p. 84). From this, the reader is exhorted to be open to "truly new epiphanies whose very occurrence either effects or records a new actualization or movement of the divine process" (p. 84). But where are these epiphanies, and, more importantly, what are the criteria by which one is to discern them? The reader never learns.

At many points, "God is Jesus." On a few occasions, "the radical Christian confronts us with the liberating message that God is Satan" (p. 101; and cf. "this epiphany of God as Satan," p. 113). Repeatedly, of course, we are told that "God is dead," and that he "has actually died in Christ" (p. 103). Such statements leave one in utter confusion. If God is Jesus, and God is Satan, then presumably Jesus is Satan. If God is dead, and God is Satan, then presumably Satan is dead. If God has "actually died" in Christ, and God is Satan, then Satan "actually died" in

Christ. The last state of confusion is surely worse than the first.

Which brings us to the most confusing matter of all. What, indeed, does the slogan "God is dead" mean? We learn that God is Jesus, and that "God has truly died in Jesus" (p. 71)— and yet Jesus continues to be spoken of in the present tense, as "the Jesus who is actually and fully incarnate in every human hand and face" (p. 71).

> Truly to pronounce his name—and for the radical Christian the names of Jesus and God are ultimately one—is to participate in God's death in Jesus and thereby to know the God who *is* Jesus as the expanding or forward-moving process who is becoming "One Man" (p. 75).

So for the life of me I cannot see that God "is dead" at all. Perhaps on Altizer's terms he once was, but he surely is no more. Altizer goes on even more explicitly to talk about "a redemption issuing from the total presence of God in Christ, as God himself becomes the Word who is progressively incarnate in the actual processes of history" (p. 83).

Now if words have any meaning, the above quotations are saying *not* that "God is dead," but quite the opposite, namely that God is "progressively incarnate in the actual processes of history," and that God is "the expanding or forward-moving process who is becoming 'One Man.'" The phrase "God is dead" is thus dissolved into a misleading and inaccurate bit of sloganeering, that is disavowed in the very context of its proclamation. For Altizer, God appears to be very much alive. If this is so, Altizer should discard the slogan that has brought him so much attention. If it is not so, he should exegete the slogan in ways consistent with its proclamation.

Another type of linguistic difficulty is created by the exhortation that we should *will* the death of God (pp. 136, 146). What kind of use of language is this? Since Altizer so frequently asserts that God is already dead, the most we could possibly do, if Altizer is right, is to acknowledge the fact. What does it mean to "will" a past reality? All we can do is affirm it or deny it. When one considers the absolute finality with which the death of God is proclaimed by Altizer, as a sheerly unrepeatable and irrevocable event, one wonders how one could possibly add an iota to its irrevocability by "willing" it. If Altizer means that we should will to *affirm* the death of God, that would be another matter. But the distinction is never clarified.

Perhaps the greatest linguistic difficulty in the book is its diffuseness when presenting an alternative to traditional Christian faith. Altizer simply moves here to the language of ecstatic utterance: "All things will dance when we greet them with affirmation" (p. 154). If we wish to share in the vision, we get instructions such as the following:

> It is *precisely* by a radical movement of turning away from all previous forms of light that we can participate in a new totality of bliss, an absolutely immanent totality embodying in its immediacy all which once appeared and was real in the form of transcendence, and a totality which the Christian must name as the present and living body of Christ (p. 153, italics added).

There is an ecstasy here, but if the book is meant to share it with us, we need more direction than simply being told (precisely) to turn away "from all previous forms of light." Theology could, perhaps, be written as poetry (and Altizer's strong dependence on Blake and Nietzsche suggests that this is really the form in which he should write), but the reader needs more help if precision is to be defined in terms of the above typical quotation.

The trouble with ecstatic utterance is that in a prose context it too easily degenerates into sloganeering, which can be a very dangerous tool for a theologian. An image offered once can evoke a response; an image offered repeatedly begins to pall. Drawing from Blake, Altizer tells us, for example, that Jesus "is actually and fully incarnate in every human hand and face" (p. 71). The phrase is repeated at crucial points on subsequent pages (cf. pp. 83, 136), but we never learn what it really means. What does it mean to affirm that Jesus is "actually" incarnate in the hand pulling a trigger in Vietnam? Sometimes this presence in every hand and face is described as an epiphany (p. 83), sometimes as an incarnation (p. 136). Are epiphany and incarnation, therefore, identical?

II

Amid many things that are unclear in the book, one thing is absolutely clear. This is Altizer's total disavowal of the church —and, indeed, so it would appear, any form of community. He makes evident from the beginning that the Christian church is the real roadblock in the way of an understanding of "radical" Christian faith. "The churches are inadequately equipped to face such a challenge." Christian faith has gotten bogged down in "an increasingly archaic ecclesiastical tradition" (p. 9).

None of this, however, is a plea for the reform of the church; it is a plea for the rejection and disavowal of the church. The new theologian is not posing as a "reformer" (p. 26). The only truly contemporary theology will have to find itself "outside of the given and established form of the church" (pp. 9–10). The book is begun, continued, and ended in the same vein. "Theology must *never again* be enclosed within the classrooms and churches" (p. 12, italics added). There must be "a *total* negation of the human and historical world of Christendom" (p. 150, italics added).

I share a considerable amount of the exasperation Altizer feels about traditional church structures, but what surprises me in his total rejection of the community of faith is that I cannot discover him offering anything to take its place. The life of the radical Christian, if this book is any indication, is an utterly solitary one. Suppose I were persuaded of the truth of Altizer's gospel. Where would I go? With whom would I join? What kind of a community would there be through which to give expression to my new-found faith? I am left with the feeling that the only course of action open to me would be to go to Emory University and take courses under Altizer on the poetry of William Blake.

Altizer not only feels that the church is irrelevant and, since purveying a false gospel, misleading. He sees it as positively evil, in the fact that it finally becomes "the expression of the will to power," and to the degree that it claims to be the body of Christ it is already "set upon the imperialistic path of conquering the world" (p. 132). I would suggest that this picture of the church, though abundantly illustrated throughout Christian history, is particularly inappropriate as a description of what is happening in the life of the contemporary church. Rather than expressing "the will to power," the Second Vatican Council, for example, represents an exercise in the divesting of power. Rather than being "set upon the imperialistic path of conquering the world," Vatican II has represented a genuine and authentic attempt to refashion the image of the church as the servant of the world, and has declared a willingness to disengage itself from expressions of power that cloud the gospel. As Article 76 of "The Church in the World Today" puts it, the church "stands ready to renounce the exercise of certain legitimately acquired rights, if it becomes clear that their use raises doubt about the sincerity of her witness."

III

Altizer not only disavows the church, he also disavows the entire Christian past. A fully consistent Christianity "renounces *all* attachment to the past" (p. 50, italics added, cf. p. 77). Theology "must ever give itself to a negation of *every* past form of the Word" (p. 83, italics added). The Christian for whom Christ is to be truly present must adopt "the one principle" that "he can no longer be clearly or decisively manifest in *any* of his previous forms or images" (p. 137, italics added). We are even urged, in the concluding ecstatic portions of the book, to "speak against *every* previous epiphany of light" (p. 152, italics added). Altizer suggests that Christianity and Judaism are discontinuous, and goes on to argue that if there is a chasm between the Old Testament and the New Testament, there is no reason why there should not be a chasm between the New Testament and "a *whole* new form of faith" (p. 27, italics added).

I submit that this whole plea is nonsense (in the descriptive rather than pejorative meaning of the latter word), and that historical creatures cannot simply start *de novo* any time they feel like it. If we do this we are utterly at the mercy of whim and fancy with no criteria whatever by which to judge where the new epiphanies are. And the proof of the nonsense nature of the plea is that Altizer himself is unable to carry it through. For scarcely has he nailed down the total disavowal of the past than he appeals to the use of the past himself, and in a very crucial way: "The name of Jesus Christ is simply meaningless apart from its Old Testament background, for it is the God of the Old Testament who becomes fully actualized and historically real in Christ" (p. 87).

One simply cannot have it both ways here, particularly after having previously asserted that Judaism and Christianity are discontinuous, any more than one can say in one breath that we should "speak against every previous epiphany of light" (p. 152), and then on the same page insist that we get our marching orders from Second Isaiah—an epiphany of light if there ever was one.

If Altizer is to be consistent, it is hard to see how he can retain the name "Jesus" or the name "Christian." Christianity did not retain the name "Jew"; why should Altizer, offering a revelation to replace the Christian one, retain the name "Christian"? Altizer, far from being daring and far-out, is, simply in terms of his own presuppositions, much too timid. If we need, as he asserts again and again, a wholly new language, if we must disengage ourselves from all past forms and images of thought, then why retain archaic words like "God" and "Jesus" with the intolerable burden of outmoded freight they have to carry? I find this one of the most confusing points in Altizer's whole approach. In the midst of his impassioned and reiterated pleas for a break with the past, he draws back from asserting the full consequences of his own position.

IV

Not only does Altizer disavow the church and the past, but in doing so he often describes past Christian thought in ways that do a serious injustice to it. The "traditional" Christianity that he destroys so nimbly is usually a far cry from the real article. Illustration can be given from three areas.

(1) *The doctrine of Christ.* The crucial distinction between Altizer's position and the traditional position is stated by him in the following way: "The radical Christian reverses the orthodox confession, affirming that 'God is Jesus' [Blake's Laocoön engraving], rather than 'Jesus is God' " (p. 44).

I see no way in which one can responsibly assert that orthodox Christology is described by the statement "Jesus is God."
The most important battle in the early centuries was the mili-
tant unwillingness of Christian orthodoxy to settle for the confessional statement, "Jesus is God." The early struggle against
docetism was waged on these lines. The creedal controversies
of the third and fourth centuries were a similar attempt to
guard against this kind of one-sided emphasis. But Altizer, on
purely arbitrary grounds, will not allow the Christian heritage
to proclaim what it has, in fact, proclaimed. There may be a lot
of theological problems with the affirmation that Jesus was
"true God and true man," but *that* is the affirmation in terms of
which traditional Christianity must be challenged, not the
affirmation that "Jesus is God."

(2) *The doctrine of the Spirit.* For a writer who makes so
much use of the notion of the Spirit, Altizer is strangely unwilling to allow traditional Christianity to have any doctrine of
the Spirit. He insists that Christians, other than himself, are
confined to the past.

> Only a dead or dying theology could rest upon the principle
> that the Christian Word is fully or finally present in the past.
> . . . We must not betray that faith by falsely believing that
> faith is confined to either its primitive or its past historical ex-
> pressions (p. 18).

But who asserts that faith is "confined to either its primitive
or its past historical expressions"? The Christian orientation to
the past is to a past that becomes present, to events that, by the
power of the Holy Spirit, become contemporaneous. If there
were no doctrine of the Holy Spirit in Christian history, Altizer's case would be airtight. Unfortunately for his case, there
is a doctrine of the Holy Spirit. Whatever one thinks of that
doctrine, it has at least been a way of trying to affirm the *ongoing* activity of God, as against the notion of "confining" him
to the past. The same caricature is present when Altizer writes
about how wrong it is "to confine theological meaning to the
sacred history and scriptures of the past" (p. 82), as though,
once again, the past cannot become contemporary in the life of
the Spirit. Altizer's *bête noire* is "confinement," but only a
very jaundiced view of the history of theology need lead one

to the conclusion that proclaiming the death of God is the only way out of confinement. An appropriation of the doctrine of the Spirit is another.

(3) *The doctrine of God.* Altizer's characterization of traditional theology is indicated by the following: "Throughout its history Christian theology has been thwarted from reaching its intrinsic goal by its bondage to a transcendent, a sovereign, and an impassive God" (p. 42). As the theme develops, it is clear that terms like "impassive" are crucial to Altizer's designation. The God being described is Pascal's "god of the philosophers," the static deity of Greek metaphysics, a god who is "distant and non-redemptive," standing "wholly apart," a god who, following Aristotle, is pure actuality (p. 62). Christian theology is thus indited, "because it has *ever remained* bound to an idea of God as a wholly self-sufficient, self-enclosed, and absolutely autonomous Being" (p. 67, italics added). The only possible recovery will be by repudiating "all religious conceptions of the mystery of the Godhead, with their *inevitable* corollary that the sacred or ultimate Reality is impassive and silent . . ." (p. 85, italics added). What Altizer wants instead, is a God "who abandons or negates his original passivity and quiescence" (p. 86). It is thus insisted that the God of traditional Christian faith is: (a) originally passive and quiescent, and (b) that he does not abandon this passivity and quiescence.

One feels a sense of exasperation, let alone frustration, in trying to respond to this sort of argument. On what terms can one possibly deal with an assessment of Christian history which lumps the whole previous Christian tradition into the catchall of Greek metaphysics, defines God in those terms, substitutes the part for the whole, and then by dismissing the part creates the impression that it has invalidated the whole? Methodologically, that is what Altizer seems to have done, and it will not stand. One can legitimately object to the strain in Christian theology that Altizer here indites, but this by no means entitles one to insist that it is the normative, or the only, or even the crucial strain. To discredit the God of Aristotle, as Altizer wants to do, is by no means to have discredited the God of the Bible, who, if he is to be attacked, might more properly be attacked for overactivity rather than quiescence.

The same device is used to invalidate the relation of Word to Scripture: *"Of course*, a religious Christianity will dogmatically insist that the Word has been given its definitive and final expression in the Bible" (p. 49, italics added). This is far from being an "of course" statement. If a "religious Christianity" makes any kind of dogmatic insistence, it is surely that "the Word has been given its definitive and final expression in . . ." Christ, the Word Incarnate, the Word made flesh, and even this must be understood in the sense that that Christ continues to be active in the Spirit. It simply will not do to convict past Christian history of biblicism and then by discounting biblicism give the impression that one has thereby succeeded in discounting all past Christian history.

V

It is next to impossible to discover just what "radical Christianity" is, since the definitions become so arbitrary. For example, Nietzsche is cited as a Christian prophet. How can such an assertion be defended? Very simply. Define a "radical Christian" as one who realizes that "there is no way to true faith apart from an abolition or dissolution of God himself" (p. 25), and of course it follows that since Nietzsche believed in the abolition or dissolution of God, he was by very definition a radical Christian. Since "radical Christianity is inseparable from an attack on God," it follows that one who attacks God, particularly if he attacks him vehemently, is a radical Christian. Nietzsche eminently qualifies.

To me, this is playing with words in unhelpful, if not frivolous, fashion. One can prove anything this way, and I can just as persuasively argue that Billie James Hargis is the Pope of the Roman Catholic Church. How can such an assertion be defended? Very simply. I define the "pope" as one who sees that there can be no true papacy apart from an abolition or dissolution of the Roman Catholic Church. It follows that since Billie James Hargis believes in the abolition and dissolution of the Roman Catholic Church, he is by very definition Pope. Since the papacy is inseparable from an attack upon the Roman Catholic Church, it follows that one who attacks the Roman Catholic Church, particularly if he attacks it vehemently, is Pope. Billie James Hargis eminently qualifies. If the argument seems farfetched, I indicate only that in it I have merely paraphrased the argument of the preceding paragraph.

There is another dimension of the arbitrariness that I find confusing and inconsistent. Altizer insists that traditional Christianity has been wrong in asserting the finality of past events. By making something final out of incarnation, for example, traditional Christianity has thereby rendered itself unable to see subsequent epiphanies. Finality at all costs is to be avoided in favor of openness to new actions and epiphanies. It is therefore more than a little disconcerting to find Altizer proclaiming that with *his* position finality has at last burst upon the scene.

> The radical Christian is a revolutionary, he is given to a total transformation of Christianity, a rebirth of the Christian Word in a new and *final* form (p. 26, italics added).
> The radical Christian . . . maintains that we are now living in the third and *final* age of the Spirit (p. 27, italics added; cf. also pp. 64 and 76).
> The radical Christian proclaims that God has actually died in Christ, that this death is both an historical and a cosmic event, and, as such, it is a *final* and irrevocable event which *cannot* be reversed by a subsequent religious or cosmic movement (p. 103, italics added).
> The radical Christian affirms . . . that the death of God is a *final* and irrevocable event (p. 107, italics added).

What is sauce for the goose is sauce for the gander. If traditional Christianity is to be indited for claiming finality, Altizer's claims to finality stand under similar indictment.

VI

Altizer says that he finished *The Gospel of Christian Atheism* "while still riding the momentum of my initial enthusiasm" (p. 13). The fact is evident throughout. There may be enthusiasm, but there is no precision. There may be momentum, but there is no discipline. What should have been a clarifying statement becomes a confusing evocation. I can only conclude that if the "death-of-God" theology has a future, it will be in spite of this book rather than because of it. The book is not a gospel, for its self-styled good news is as diffuse as it is strident, and leaves the reader baffled rather than empowered. It is not Christian, for it demands an explicit repudiation of all that has previously claimed the name, and only by being inconsistent with its own premises can it claim the name. It is not atheism, for instead of no god it offers us a fresh god to take the dead god's place. The book, rather than demonstrating the death of God, succeeds only in demonstrating the death of this particular version of the death of God theology.

And yet, there is one saving grace toward the end. After all of the jaunty iconoclasm, there are a few paragraphs in which Altizer acknowledges the kind of risk to which he invites the reader:

> The contemporary Christian who bets that God is dead must do so with a full realization that he may very well be embracing a life-destroying nihilism. . . . No honest contemporary seeker can ever lose sight of the very real possibility that the willing of the death of God is the way to madness, dehumanization, and even to the most totalitarian form of society yet realized in history (p. 146).

While this scarcely carries the note of "gospel," it does convey a note of honest sobriety that one wishes had characterized the previous hundred and forty-five pages of sweeping denunciations and confident claims. It might even provide the way toward a fresh beginning.

Four Reactions

WARREN L. MOULTON

Apocalypse in a Casket?

THE ICONOCLASTIC CRACKING and breaking among the young Radical Theologians is exciting, and we must admire this latest attempt among theologians to discover personal credibility for all of us. These davids have slain goliath, god of the pious philistines—but getting the neck cut and the head raised on a spear is tough, messy business. Some of the davids wield two-edged swords and no doubt wear plastic aprons. And they are all determined to get in there and chop, since at this point the squad is small. In William Hamilton's "The Shape of a Radical Theology" (*Christian Century*, October 6) I thought for a moment that we saw the gory head of God go up on the spear. But these are beginnings, and what we saw was only dry-run papier-mâché. There will be dissenters, but the author's attempt to "see if there is anybody out there" will at the same time bring recruits.

However, there was something about the very character of Hamilton's article that revealed how insubstantial the death-of-God thesis is at this point. There seemed to be in the author a mood of cynical resignation, a the-whole-world-is-my-ash-tray attitude. So that some of us who have lately listened to the pallbearers around God's box wondered again: How much do you really care about any of it?

The Radical Theologians have been making noises like heroes, and some of us have cheered. We have read their literature, gathered our students to hear them speak, discussed them over coffee with our colleagues. And we have agreed that these are exciting minds. They suggest a new freedom with dignity, and this sounds good after the rigidity of neo-orthodoxy in the face of revolutions. We stand like beggars waiting further revelations. Then we receive another release, and its picture of the "shape of a radical theology" leaves us feeling like urbanites trying to read bird tracks. We are confused, and we have questions.

Those who tell us that God is dead must realize that for the most part theology is thus also extinguished. They have dissolved the center of reality. Since God is dead, what can we make of the rest of it? We cannot merely enjoy in Jesus only what is historically there (after editing, etc.): one great man with some good ideas and a lot of courage, like a few other people we know.

Furthermore, must we not concern ourselves about a new ethic? We have a good residue, and men are intelligent; there is very little to stop us from creating a modern, fast, urban great society. Besides, God has long since ceased to touch most people vitally. He has not even affected personal habits as he might have a few short puritan years ago: people quit smoking because of government reports, and no foul-minded little cleric is going to reduce religion to not smoking because of something about the body being the temple of God. Isaiah tells us that the temple was filled with smoke and the Lord appeared. Well, he waited too long. So we quit the tobacco *and* the Lord.

I

If it is true that what the Radical Theologian is saying is the
direction of things in our time, that this is truly all that is left,
perhaps we who are interested in their words might make a
few suggestions.

First, we would ask of these men humility rather than resignation, compassion rather than indulgence. Is the proud talk of
cult and journal put together in the name of the new Radical
Theologians necessary for dialogue at this time, or might it
wait? When some of us hear these death-of-God voices we
have a feeling that we are dealing with successful, highly pol-
ished young brains with a good grain, seated in a cosmic bridge
game with a young, cynical audience looking on. They play
with a grin, with perfect finesse. They may even put us off
with talk of being embarrassed because their shadow was showing on a TV god-game quiz, and of how this has given them a
psychic zipper-snag. We hear these cool, sophisticated, prophetic voices, and perhaps we long for a touch of the spirit of
priest and pastor.

Second, it would appear that without our faith in the reality
of God we can know little or nothing about the love which we
call *agape*. Jesus demonstrated love in a most definitive fashion
in his own life and death and in his commission of his disciples
—and the quality and nature of his love rested on his faith in a
living God. The Fourth Gospel suggests that love is what the
notion of God is all about. Paul said that love is all that finally
matters in man's communication with the realm of his reality.
Does not *agape* as discovered in Christ demand a living God?

One may frequently be in dialogue *about* this *agape*-God.
That is a fascinating theological game. But unless one believes
that God is alive in the world which we address and hear, unless one believes that other men are talking with and about this
same God, not only is reality shattered but God is removed
from our remembering, our imagining and our telling, is put
beyond all our seeking. Is not *agape*-love as discovered in
Christ fraudulent if we do not also believe in Christ's God?

This love is a love that does not stop; this is the love we use
to describe God. And this is the most significant thing we can

say about the love learned from Jesus: We have received through him a commandment from God not to quit loving, in order that our brother may escape the sickness that comes when one absolutely quits loving or concludes when and where his love stops. For a man to believe in a love that stretches forward without end to every brother in all conditions, he must trace it to its source in the infinity of man's reality which is God. Beyond any notion of the end of love is God. If God is not there my love becomes selective, tentative, budgeted, changes character to fit my mood. For most of us the word to love without ceasing must come from God, else our humanity rejects the word.

The work of living now can be attempted only if a man believes that there is a love at the heart of reality, and that despite the threat or fact of death the transcendent nature of things is love, that man as creature searching for the Creator of this love will survive. Are creature and Creator laughably one?

Evidence that God lives is there in the search for this never-ending love which we preach. I am alive only in my searching; when I quit, then I begin to die. If God is dead, will not man quit searching and loving? Perhaps instead of announcing the death of God I should simply register the death of myself and my brother. For if God is dead the search for *agape* stops, and man dies. Is Beckett right when he says, in *Waiting for Godot:* "God died in the nineteenth century and man disappeared in the twentieth"?

II

Third, since Hamilton calls for optimism he obviously does not think that man is dead. The "radical theology" does not have a central doctrine of sin; it sees a spirit of optimism as one of its important motifs. It may be only semantics, but optimism seems just a comic version of what has been called Christian joy. For the joy that was set before him Christ endured the cross. With the arrival of "optimism" and the departure of this particular joy, a central nerve is frayed. More than pure knowledge, dogma or mystical faith, the joy of which Paul wrote expresses the character of the Christian faith. We associate such joy with our Lord's overcoming the world (perhaps a coming-over to the world in a new and profound way?). It was his peace in Gethsemane. It was his poise before Pilate. It was the spirit of the early church. And it comes with a man's sense of the presence of God. Can it *be*, unless God *is?* Where God truly *is, there* is joy. Was God in Christ, reconciling the world joyously, even through the agony of incarnate dying?

Admittedly, there is little left on the human scene to make the human spirit sing. History is open-ended and every suggested finale is grim. We are hysterical at the thought of too many people and not enough food. The human kaleidoscope is changing; white is only a color for mixing. In every philosopher's nicely wrapped package we find the bomb. Our music is a dirge. Art depicts our pathos. A crucified Lord rots in the tomb, while the pep-rally revivals continue to call for the blood-bucket brigade. Our priests are content to throw dirt upon the dead.

What shall we say? It appears to be either the circus or prayers, hysterics or meditation, ravage or the cloister. But optimism sounds frivolous; joy sticks. Optimism appears to forget the news; joy will embrace the leper. Only this kind of joy can make it now. Without joy we are the candle snuffers and the lamp breakers of the world. Our Hallelujah Chorus is an organ grinder's tune unless we too can really come over to the world, expecting gritty pain, man's flight from God and his warm pool of pity—and come over in joy. Optimism begs; joy thrives in barrenness. Can we find this joy in the freedom of the determined barrenness of God's death?

III

Finally, with the demise of theology our Christology seems to deflate, to leave us with a depressingly sick Christ. If Christ presumed God, his motivation is now totally suspect, his words brittle as glass; and his crucifixion looks increasingly like something he really deserved. Is this where we must go?

Says Hamilton: "I am drawn, and I have given my allegiance. There may be powerful teachings elsewhere, more impressive and moving deaths. Yet I have chosen him and my choice is not arbitrary nor is it anxiously made to avert the atheist label. It is a free choice, freely made." This is good, but it seems to play to an ignoble dwarf in us that says, "I know it is silly, but this is the way I feel." Such an attitude can be as emotionally dependent as a billygraham convert, as irrational as a snake handler; it makes the existential leap little more than Elizabeth crossing the muddy street on Raleigh's coat.

Can we stick by Jesus just because we like the toys in his sandbox? Jesus is still the nicest guy we know, and we will not run away—but is this enough for a viable Christology? Obviously not. It has the ring of a final honesty, but it is more a jesus-jingle than a confession of discipleship. Yet we ask if any of us really offers any more of himself.

Is the good, solid humanism which Hamilton suggested not better, a more honorable discharge from the faith? If one is going, why not walk right past the bier and say, "It was great, Man, but that wavelength is full of static. See you around the god-quad, of course." In Hamilton's confession we are left with the feeling that the Jesus myth is poetically, mythically useful for a man finding his perspective—but let's sleep in on Sunday.

However, because of the element of truth I hear in Hamilton and others like him, I would suggest this: Jesus was proclaimed as the fulfillment of prophecy; the long imagined Messiah had come. The contemporary Christ is somehow the fulfillment of each theological man's prophecy regarding his saviour. The prophetic in each man is his cry of humanity. Gathering bits and pieces from his reality, the image of a saviour forms in his soul. The image of the Saviour Christ transcends the bread, wine and nails of his flesh, and the whole myth of man healed and God healing in Jesus remains as the Word of salvation to many and the promise to all. But the image of the Saviour Christ must also transcend each man's own trapped condition. Although he comes to me, I cannot limit him to my condition. He identifies with me and moves on to another who has also prophesied his coming. God in Christ invades humanity and each man; but he must be permitted to escape humanity and each man if he is to be alive and contemporary for every age. Jesus may be back there with the Caesars unless a new Christology fashions him in the prophetic vision of this day, unless he comes over to *this* world and saves us. And if men will not permit this of today's theologians, the churchman will continue to speak and not care, to hear and not believe.

J. ROBERT NELSON ⟩ Deicide, Theothanasia, or What Do You Mean?

THE USUALLY ASTUTE EDITORS of *Time* missed an opportunity to tie together two stories in their October 22 issue. Readers of the Religion section were first advised that the Vatican Council had exonerated the Jews of deicide. Then they were told that even if the Jews did not kill God, God was dead anyway. The Vatican's much-publicized statement would have conveyed enough confusion of thought to keep intelligent readers puzzled throughout the week, but the story on the God-is-dead thinkers provided double cause.

With its remarkable genius for garbling type the *New York Times* inadvertently defined "deicide" as "God-willing." But it is killing, not willing, of which the Jews have now been forgiven. With Catholicism's own brand of fundamentalists on their right side and the Arab states on their left, the Vatican councilmen have voted 7–1 for what they construe to be a

(192)

magnanimous statement. Left undefined is the inherent question of whether God himself was killed on the cross. This
smacks of the ancient idea of Patripassianism, a view which is
manifestly difficult to hold but which has never been satisfactorily shown to be heretical. The suggestion of such a thing is
in itself enough to cause a faithful Jew to cry blasphemy. But
then the Vatican fathers have compounded not only the confusion but also the sins of centuries of anti-Semitism by gratui-
tously excusing the Jews of a crime which the children of Israel have never acknowledged anyway.

The word "deicide" also suggests the current vogue of talking about the death of God. Perhaps "theothanasia" would be a
more accurate technical term, if such be needed. In any case,
the fat of esoteric speculation on the demise of the deity has
now been tossed into the fire of public criticism, and there will
be a lot of crackling and sputtering.

I

Every discussion of the perplexing idea seems to begin with
Friedrich W. Nietzsche. He, too, taught deicide. Speaking
through the madman of one of his vignettes (*The Gay Science*,
No. 125), he declared that the God of the Christians had been
killed not by Jews but by Christians, the church, and that curse
of history known as Christendom. Nietzsche really meant this.
"Verily, verily," he said unto us, "God is now dead." But most
Christians were unprepared to take him seriously. Indeed, the
preachers neatly pulled the fuse from his bomb by accepting in
a different sense the language of his accusation. Yes, sir, they
agreed: the intellectualism, the uncritical pietism, the rank superstition, the political Erastianism and the bourgeois respecta-
bility of the church had destroyed the false god, which for
centuries had displaced the true God of Jesus Christ. But no
one, said the preachers, should lament the death of *this* god, if
because of his death we can come closer to the true God. Thus
in recent years many Christians have been able to approve of
the late Paul Tillich's "God above the God of theism."

Nietzsche's bomb lay still and relatively harmless, apparently
a dud. But many years after a battle, on a beach or an aban-

doned field an ancient bomb explodes. Someone tampers with it, even tries to insert a new fuse. And—*bang!* So today the Nietzschean repercussions are being felt in the circles of younger ministers and theologians, in certain colleges and seminaries, in the student Christian movement. When did the explosion occur?

My own awareness of it dates from 1960, when an address was given at the national Interseminary Movement conference in Denver. The speaker was Prof. William Hamilton. Paraphrasing William Temple, he declared, "The great new fact of our time is the disappearance of God from the world. Our theology must be the theology of the death of God." (Already the characteristic imperative mood was in use.) He added that this was not the same as hearty, old-fashioned atheism which for generations has scandalized properly pious Christians. It is not the brash No given in reply to "does God exist?" It is neither atheism based on intellectual skepticism nor atheism stemming from agonizing experiences of evil and suffering. Nor is Hamilton's type of theothanasia just the same as old Nietzsche's proclamation of the euthanasia of God.

So far as human experience and history are concerned, Hamilton's concept of God's death seems almost a divine suicide. It is by what the insurance policies call an "act of God" that God has died. Or else he has just withdrawn himself from the human sphere of existence and knowledge more remotely than any of the neo-Reformation theologians have asserted. With little tone of regret Hamilton confesses (in the *Christian Scholar*, Spring 1965): ". . . we do not know, we do not adore, do not possess, do not believe in God. . . . We are not talking about the absence of the experience of God, but about the experience of the absence of God."

Recalling the pathetic and morose figure of the Swedish pastor in Ingmar Bergman's *Winter Light*, we can share the feeling of chill and void consequent on the shattering of that man's faith. Who would not be stunned and numbed by the brute realization that behind the symbols of divinity there is no longer any God? But Hamilton and his partners in this movement of thought are not Bergmanesque characters, weighted down by *Weltschmerz* and *Gottlosigkeit*. On the contrary,

Hamilton seems the very model of the modern man of the world, exulting in the wildness of little Beat poetry, big-beat music, pop art, civil rights demonstrations and all such ingredients of conformity to far-out nonconformity.

Yet all is not lighthearted gaiety with Hamilton, as though the death of the deity were an emancipation from the power of a grim despot. God's death is a signal to men and women to extract the full meaning, whether joyful or pathetic, from human society, culture and history. This has its sad aspects, as everyone knows. Jesus is introduced at this point, the humiliated Jesus who stands with and stands for his neighbor. Here Hamilton presents a clear and persuasive expression of Bonhoeffer's familiar theme: Jesus is the man for others, and we are called to suffer with him in a godless world.

II

If there is any reserve in Hamilton's exposition of the death-of-God idea, as in his affirmation of a partly recognizable Christology, there is none in the essays of Thomas J. J. Altizer. The Emory University professor has an evangelical passion for preaching what most Christians regard as a dysangelical message. He does it with a tone of assurance and a certainty, virtually a dogmatism, which some readers find very impressive, others very irritating.

Altizer is quite sure, to begin with, that the historical Jesus of the New Testament and of the church's teaching can no longer be a reality for us. Of "the church's image of Jesus," he says, "we can scarcely deny that it has disappeared from our history, and with it has disappeared every possibility of mediating the New Testament Jesus to our time and space." But that is not all. "The disappearance of the historical Jesus is but a particular expression of a far deeper reality, the death of God." Nor is this phrase intended to mean less than the words say. There seems to be nothing conditional or metaphorical to relieve the literal force of the assertion. "The theologian must be prepared to recognize that the death of God underlies every mode of our thought and experience," he continues. "Furthermore, we must not neglect to note that the very ground of

Christian theology calls upon the Christian theologian to recognize the death of God as an historical event. . . . God is not
simply hidden from view, nor is he lurking in the depths of our
unconscious or on the boundaries of our infinite space, nor will
he appear on the next turn of the historical wheel of fate."

In each recent article Altizer has proclaimed his message
with repetitious insistency. What startles the reader most is his
emphasis upon the historicity of God's death. It is an event, a
historical event, he keeps saying. Difficult as this may be to
accept as true, it is nevertheless a statement which can make
sense; i.e., it declares forthrightly that an event has taken place
in the context of human history.

My own father died in 1951; I record this as an event and
lament it. When Altizer states, as a self-evident basis of modern
theology, that God has also died a real death, we expect him to
tell us approximately when the event took place and under
what circumstances. But his silence about this is in inverse proportion to the stridency of his proclamation of it. Or are we to
infer that, after all, he is speaking in a merely metaphorical way
about man's apprehension of God? Or are his essays to be read
as poetry, so that they may mean to the reader whatever they
may mean? Having gained a measure of public attention, he is
under obligation to express his ideas with some precision and
definition.

Both Hamilton and Altizer confidently believe that their reflection on the death of God is really *theo*-logy, and furthermore that it is quite Christian. As though to vindicate this belief, Altizer plays a counterpoint to his theme of theothanasia.
It is the theme of the Word and the incarnation thereof. Certainly this distinguishes him from the ordinary atheists of
Feuerbach's lineage or from scientific humanists such as Julian
Huxley. But does his much talking of the Word (with capital
W) make his position a Christian one?

Most theologians would probably agree with Altizer when
he writes, "theology can preserve a Christian form only by
speaking an incarnate Word that fully confronts the concrete
time and space before it." At least we think we agree—until we
read further about this *Logos:* "Christian theology must proclaim the death of God if it is to witness to the Word of faith.

. . . A theological statement that proclaims the death of God must mean that God is not present in the Word of faith."

We keep asking: What is this Word of faith? But only this kind of reply comes back: "the Christian Word can neither be identified with an eternal God nor understood as the particular expression of an unchanging deity." Then comes the statement that approximates Christological clarity: "We Christians are called upon to be loyal only to Christ, only to the Incarnate Word who has appeared in our flesh, and therefore we should already have been prepared for the appearance of Christ without God."

Hamilton's appeal to the example of Jesus as the despised and rejected one makes sense, as do all sincere, humanistic commendations of the Good Man of Nazareth. But Altizer's Incarnate Word is, to me at least, a *Logos alogikos*, a wordless Word, an incarnation without flesh. Such allegations of meaninglessness perhaps do not disturb Altizer. Indeed, he makes a point of the need to see that faith is not only a moral scandal to the self-righteous but an ontological scandal to those who seek meaning in history. As Hamilton himself observes, Altizer's vision of things is "logically imprecise and calculated to make empiricists weep."

III

I have not observed that well-known empiricist Paul van Buren weeping over Altizer's vision. But very recently, restraining his tears, van Buren gave his estimate of Altizer's writing: he simply cannot understand it. This is an unexpected confession from one who is popularly reckoned to be the third man in the triumvirate of theothanatopsis. Moreover, he expressed astonishment at Hamilton's announcement that there would soon be an organization of death-of-God theologians, with a new journal, etc., etc. Apparently there is less communication within this trinity than is assumed.

Van Buren, moreover, has neither wept at God's funeral nor, like Altizer and the dancers at a Hindu procession to the burning ghat, leaped in corybantic exultation. He plays the role of the clinical diagnostician of linguistic maladies. He has calmly concluded that it is no longer possible to squeeze any juice of meaning from the three-letter word. And because the word "God" no longer conveys any meaning, it is questionable whether the alleged reality to which the word makes reference is meaningful. So God has not been "edged out of the world" nor has he suffered death as a historical event. He seems to be like Julian Huxley's depiction of the deity: "the last fading smile of a Cosmic Cheshire Cat." The Cosmic Cat is gone, the smile fades, the vacuum alone remains.

No, not just a vacuum. We must try to think and speak theologically without the word "God," writes van Buren, because, like the language of Barth, all God-language is of no "cash value" in the market place of contemporary intellectual exchange. (In van Buren's rejection of Barth's language about God, he might have said that it is as obsolete as a Confederate dollar. It is of interest that both Hamilton and van Buren have turned from their erstwhile mentors by an angle of approximately 180 degrees: Hamilton from Reinhold Niebuhr and Donald M. Baillie; van Buren from Karl Barth. But Altizer remains the devoted disciple of the great phenomenologist of religion, Mircea Eliade.)

So "God" is gone; but Jesus remains. Apparently van Buren also wishes to retain the Jesus of Bonhoeffer's prison letters, inasmuch as he prefaces *The Secular Meaning of the Gospel* with the wonderful poetic tribute to Bonhoeffer by W. H. Auden. Moreover, he endeavors to present Jesus in terms which are not at variance with the Christology of the Council of Chalcedon. But is it possible for us to discern the face of either the Jesus of Bonhoeffer or the Christ of Chalcedon in the setting of van Buren's secular ikon?

Demonstrating how serious disagreement in theology can make men turn upon their friends with impersonal vehemence, Langdon Gilkey wrote in the July 1964 *Journal of Religion* a mordant review of van Buren's book under the title "A New Linguistic Madness." Attacking at the very point of Christology, he observed: "If it was strange that the face of Harnack should stare back from the deep well of Jesus-Forschung, it is even stranger that the faces of Wittgenstein and Anthony Flew beam at us from the pages of Acts and Paul, and strangest of all when they keep popping out from behind the pillars in fifth-century Alexandria and Chalcedon." What Gilkey charges, of course, is that van Buren has tried to retain a semblance of the historic faith in Jesus Christ by turning the apostolic witness and its historic interpretation into a piece of Oxford-style empiricism. Thus we are told that the real meaning of the resurrection of Jesus can be found in the idea of a "discernment situation" in which the disciples caught the contagion of Jesus' sense of radical freedom. But this wonderful freedom (which he fails to define) is available to us also by contagion. Hence there is a secular gospel. But it carries no warranty from the source which used to be called "God."

So far as the persistent figure of Jesus Christ is concerned, it is not unfair to remind the "new theologians" whom we are considering that cake which has once been eaten can no longer be kept on the plate.

IV

What can those of us who have not caught by contagion the death-of-God conviction say about it and its protagonists?

First, we acknowledge the seriousness, vigor and daring of this new approach to some ancient issues. Certainly it cannot be rejected because of its novelty, any more than Christian faith can be proved to be true by its antiquity. Who of us doubts that we live in a literally new age of human experience and civilization? What Christian can be accounted faithful if he instinctively and then doggedly resists every reform and restatement of the gospel? The real question is whether the death-of-God theology is truly a theological *aggiornamento*, and a valid one at that.

Possibly there is an analogy here between art and theology. The innovation of calculated dissonance in orchestral music was greeted by most music lovers with expressions of disgust and horror. And the contemporary predominance of nonobjective painting and sculpture is still considered an aesthetic scandal by many who love their El Grecos, Cézannes, Rodins and even Rouaults. Has there now taken place in theology a sudden revolution, comparable to the revolutions in art? We should consider the possibility. In matters of artistic taste there are those who are disposed to love and conserve what is for them old but by no means obsolete. But when they are confronted by the radical innovators, they are not captured by the latter's insistence that the only true connoisseur of music or painting is the man who approves only and exclusively that which is avant-garde.

This is precisely what the death-of-God theologians seem to be saying by their categorical declarations. Van Buren speaks confidently of "the modern man," thus dividing all men into the categories of modern and not modern. Of course modern man cannot discern any meaning in the familiar theological language and concepts, he says—and this he assumes to be self-evident. But who is this modern man? He is typified, it seems, by the Oxford don, pontificating in his college's common room about the meaninglessness of words. Theologically he is beyond the fringe.

Altizer is just as sweeping in generalizing about what Christians *must* believe or not believe. He writes of "the contemporary theologian" or "the Christian theologian" or "the Christian" or "theology itself." And in every case his categoricals are made imperatives. These hapless people "must" or "ought" or "can only" think this way. A typical statement: The Christian theologian who is contemporary *knows* that the Biblical and traditional images of Christ are no longer meaningful. And then to impress the seal of higher dogmatism upon this dictum, he says that "we Christians are called upon" to think this way. But he does not identify the one who calls us.

Perhaps this generalization is merely a stylistic fault in such writing. But it may be more accurate to say that it is the prevailing mood. It leaves no room for those who wish to call themselves Christians, even theologians, but who beg to differ with the Colgate Rochester/Temple/Emory axis.

V

A second query concerns the legitimacy of the "new" theologians' use of the word "Christian." Everyone knows how loosely and irresponsibly this adjective has been employed, often to cover multitudes of sins. Nor ought we to be selfish and proprietary with respect to it. Nevertheless, the word has a definite reference and content. It speaks of the centrality of Jesus Christ, but not simply of the man Jesus, apart from his being the "anointed one" of God and thus the risen and living Lord.

We have seen that these three writers take care to express appreciation and esteem for Jesus. Hamilton finds in him the paradigm of ethical life in human relations; van Buren sees him as the carrier of the virus of human freedom; Altizer knows him as the rather ill-defined Incarnate Word. Will the real Jesus please step forward? But the three remain where they stand, because none is the real Jesus of Biblical witness and Christian faith. Apart from the living God whom Jesus called "Father" and whom he represents in person, word and deed, there is just no real Jesus Christ who can be known or addressed by a faith properly called Christian.

Hamilton would have us think that he is leading us into Bonhoeffer country; he has indeed done some excellent interpretative writing about Bonhoeffer. But it is highly questionable that "religionless Christianity" means "godless Christianity," even though some short texts from the prison letters point in that direction. I cannot see justification for isolating the later Bonhoeffer, or the late late Bonhoeffer, from the whole of his written testimony. I am persuaded to accept the judgment of some of Bonhoeffer's friends that the high Christology of his earlier writing remains the context for his final discourses on secularized Christianity. Nor can I believe that Bonhoeffer, were he now alive in this country, would join the death-of-God club.

A third comment grows out of the first two. The so-called new theologians have first planted their flag on the soil of Christian theology and claimed it all for themselves; next, despite protestations to the contrary, they have revealed by their writings that their peculiar theology can scarcely carry the name Christian. As a consequence, their implanted flagpole, intended to signify hegemony over the terrain of theology, has

been placed horizontally as a minus sign before the whole body
of Christian theology: Protestant, Catholic, liberal, conservative and all the rest.

The death of God is indeed a fascinating idea for the mind to
savor. For some it is exquisitely horrifying, for others exciting
and exhilarating. But it takes more than Altizer's reiterated
paean to the mystical "coincidence of opposites" to rescue
some of the central affirmations from the indictment of being
sheer absurdity and contradiction. The death-of-God concept
is to be rejected not only because it is offensive and perplexing
to many Christians, but because it contradicts and offends the
very rationality of those who profess this faith.

In conclusion, let it be agreed that there is a huge need today
for a reconceiving and recasting of Christian doctrine. But
there is no need, nor warrant, for destroying it. Opposition to
the death-of-God movement of thought does not entail any
diminution in our growing disposition to embrace the secular
sphere as the place created by God and in which the Word
became flesh. Profound insights such as those of Bonhoeffer
and the mounting data concerning the nature of man and the
universe constitute a healthy and immeasurable challenge to
Christians as they think of the reason and pattern of their living. We can gladly approve and support secularization today.
But never at the cost of accepting the grand delusion that the
living God of Jesus Christ is now dead.

DAVID MILLER / False Prophets in the Secular City

". . . From prophet to priest, every one deals falsely. They have healed the wound of my people lightly, saying, 'Peace, peace,' when there is no peace" (Jeremiah 6:14; 8:11). In his explanation of this jeremiad about the popularity of false prophets Martin Buber informs us that "vain confidence is the enemy of faith" because it leads to smug satisfaction with the secular situation. (See his *The Prophetic Faith*, Harper Torchbook, pp. 169–170.) One of the most embarrassing problems of the optimistic prophet has to do with verification: How does one who is optimistic about salvation authenticate his message when the majority of his hearers are confounded in their own search for religious meaning?

Of course Buber affirms that "the fulfillment or nonfulfillment of any prophecy" is not in itself a sufficiently sophisticated theological criterion for judging a prophet. Yet he

(203)

also affirms that "in days of false security a shaking and stirring word of disaster is befitting, the outstretched finger pointing to the historically approaching catastrophe, the hand beating upon hardened hearts" (p. 178). There is indeed a time for the optimism of Deutero-Isaiah, but every age must guard against premature forays into meaning which carefully sidestep Jeremiah. Or as a sign in a truck drivers' diner puts it: "If you can keep your head while everyone around you is going insane— you don't understand the situation."

Recent versions of optimism have appeared, surprisingly, from both the theological right and the theological left. The prophet to the left is William Hamilton (cf. his "The Shape of a Radical Theology" in the October 6 *Christian Century*, in which an American version of post-Bultmannian theology is apparent). The prophet to the right is Harvey Cox (cf. *The Secular City*, Macmillan, 1965, in which the real hero seems to be Barth). Hamilton has balanced his optimism in the past by emphasizing a radical death-of-God motif, but his step must now be watched lest he stumble into a post-neo-orthodox liberal victory which is pyrrhic. Cox has balanced his optimism about the faithfulness of urban secularity with an initial warning against mistaking secular*ism* for Biblical secular*ity*, but he must be watched lest his Biblical iconoclasm—a raillery against popular religious piety—be devoid of attention to the demonic aspects of mobility and anonymity.

I

One impression that *The Secular City* may leave with the reader is that modern urban society is in its every characteristic so like the heavenly society envisioned in the Scriptures that the "first heaven and the first earth" have indeed passed away; New York, or perhaps even Los Angeles, is now the new Jerusalem. The fault of this impression may be more the reader's than the author's, yet it leads the memory back to the warning from another and perhaps not less demonic prophet, Baudelaire: "The Devil's cleverest wile is to convince us that he does not exist." And Denis de Rougemont, in *The Devil's Share*, comments: "Let us grant that this trick has never been more successful than it is today."

It comes as no surprise therefore that Cox selects Albert Camus as the paradigm of one aspect of modern Biblical secularity. Hamilton also might have utilized Camus: his reading of the modern scene as turning toward optimism after a bout with postwar pessimism—á la "The Waste Land," *Lord of the Flies* and Niebuhr—is not too much unlike Camus' description of Sisyphus' ultimate discovery of the joy of his vocation after a preliminary frustration with his vocation's absurdity. Camus is expected as a reference not only because, as Nathan Scott has remarked, his work reflects a "modest optimism," but also because he places a positive evaluation on the demonic as a transforming factor. In *Les Justes* Camus speaks of "*meutriers délicats*," and in *The Rebel* of "calculated culpability." In the latter work, which Hazel Barnes calls "a philosophy of revolt," he wrote: "When the end is absolute—that is, historically speaking, when one believes it to be certain—then one can go as far as to sacrifice others. . . . Does the end justify the means? Possibly, yes." And in *The Fall* we read such passages as these: "who would have believed that crime consists less in making others die than in not dying oneself"; "those of Christ and those of the Antichrist . . . are the same anyway"; "don't lies eventually lead to the truth"; "falsehood . . . is a beautiful twilight that enhances every object"; "their [the atheists'] satanism is virtuous"; "I have accepted duplicity instead of being upset by it."

II

To translate this motif in Camus' writings into theological language is to say that Judas is the savior of man because if it had not been for his betrayal of Jesus the salvation-event would never have come to fulfillment. We recognize such reasoning to be a gnostic heresy of the Naasene and Ophitic variety. Traditionally, and in contrast to this heresy, the devil's work is saving only because God consecrates it to his own eschatological purpose (cf. Milton and Lessing). But in the optimism of

Cox and Hamilton, as in Camus, the distinction between de-
monism and beneficence is blurred in the name of transforming
energy; the distinction between secular and sacred is sloughed
to the end of potency. And this blurring is accomplished by
referring to modern man's experience of secularity—from
Ringo through split-level urbanity—as *not* being radically ambiguous. "Religionless Christianty" in Cox and the death-of-
God theology in Hamilton have led to death-of-the-devil theologizing.

But it is not enough to point to the faux pas. One must ask
what is the meaning of false prophecy in the post-Christian
age. Or to put it more constructively: What is the meaning of
the appearance of optimism in a concurring theological right
and left?

One explanation is to be arrived at by observing the evolution of religious consciousness from paleolithic times to the
present. During the late neolithic period and following through
to the seventh century A.D. there emerged a radically new religious expression. Prior to this seminal age in Western religious
thought, feminine and masculine, serpentine and aquiline,
chthonic and Olympian, lunar and solar, demonic and heroic
aspects of myths and theologies were undifferentiated. Salvation could come as well from feminine as from masculine
forces. Grace was as much a result of dark as of light. The
snake was honored for his (or her) dynamism, not abhorred
for lurid motivations. But all this, of course, changed. Judaism,
Christianity and Islam are part of a large movement, begun
prior to the age of Moses, that dissociates spiritual polarities
and, further, evaluates the masculine, aquiline, Olympian, solar
and heroic as "good." The rest are suspect, if not altogether
"evil." To place the Judaic-Christian heritage in this movement
is not to deny to it the uniqueness which recent Biblical and
systematic theologians have emphasized. It is rather to take a
somewhat larger view.

III

The larger view is needed if we are to understand what such
men as Cox and Hamilton are up to. They may unwittingly be

presenting from quite different sides a next step in the evolution of religious consciousness. And this new mode resembles a very old (paleolithic) type of spiritual meaning. I am not suggesting that Cox and Hamilton are presenting regressive or pathological theology. In *The Secular City* Cox insists strongly that he is opposed to pre-Biblical regressions in a post-religious age. I am rather suggesting that these men are continuing the Biblical, and the pre-Biblical, logic to a post-Biblical end. As a result they are offering a description of modern spirituality resembling preneolithic spiritualities in which orthodox Western distinctions between masculine and feminine, aquiline and serpentine, Olympian and chthonic, solar and lunar, heroic and demonic are confused.

But if the descriptions of Cox and Hamilton match our experience, there is yet one other dichotomy whose poles merge: the anachronistic distinction between "true" and "false" (cf. Nietzsche's "transvaluation of values"). If Cox and Hamilton have erred from a traditional point of view, perhaps their "pas" is not so "faux" when put in the light (dark?) of present reality. Perhaps it is only historically and academically, but not existentially, possible to make a traditional value judgment on these theological prophets. Perhaps, therefore, the existential meaning of the witness to optimism from both the theological right (Cox) and the theological left (Hamilton) is that we have here an announcement of the presence of a next step in "religion" as prophesied by Jesus of Nazareth: an age of the spirit (Paraclete) living in the world through man and his vision! A new Shamanism!

LARRY SHINER / Goodbye, Death-of-God!

NIETZSCHE KNEW only too well that everything we theologians touch is emptied of significance. The scoffing crowd stood agape when Nietzsche's madman proclaimed them the murderers of God, but when the theologians make the death of God their watchword the situation is merely comic. Of course, announcing that God is dead may be no more than a pose, one of a whole galley of poses assumed in an effort to arouse the attention of people who no longer find Christianity even worth despising. Indeed, the more we listen to panagyrics on the God-is-dead theme, the more it all seems like the old carnival shell game: no sooner have we watched the preacher touch God's corpse with his right hand than zip! God is back on the cross with Bonhoeffer, eternally waiting for our help.

But lately something wonderful has happened. A few death-of-God theologians have turned honest, or so it seems. Now

(208)

those "hard" radicals, Altizer (July 7) and Hamilton (October 6) assure us they mean it—God is *really* dead. But in the next breath they tell us this slogan is to be the basis of a theological program! It must be said that they are at least aware of the incongruity of calling their plan to drop God and keep Jesus a "Christian" theology. Hamilton candidly acknowledges that his "obedience to Jesus" motif presupposes our ability to know enough about the historical Jesus to make him a pattern for our lives—although of course we will not be able to obey Jesus completely, since he unfortunately lived too soon for the death of God. Altizer goes on to suggest that we have even lost the humanity of Jesus and can perhaps no longer name "Jesus" or the "Christ." Nevertheless he is confident that because God is finally and irrevocably dead we *can* speak of the "Incarnate Word" since "we speak of the Word when we say Yes to the moment before us." But the inconsistencies of such a program are far more serious than the ones Hamilton and Altizer have yet admitted, and "hard" radicals ought to face up to them.

For to get rid of God and keep a "Jesus ethic" of involvement with the present human situation is a species of absent-mindedness amazing to behold in a movement that takes its motto from Nietzsche. *He* at least knew better; he never tired of pointing out that Christianity is a whole and that one cannot give up faith in God and keep Christian morality. But most improbable of all, Altizer's form of death-of-God theology takes Nietzsche's great discovery of the Eternal Recurrence—the passionate Yes to life despite suffering and death—and christens it "Incarnate Word." Nietzsche always feared that someone would live to pronounce him holy. But to baptize the one whose whole vocation was to be the antichrist—that, as he would surely have said, shows a lack of taste.

No doubt there is much in Nietzsche's notion of yea-saying to this world that is really an unacknowledged echo of the Christian faith. But the yea-saying and the secularity of the Christian's existence derives from the desacralization of the cosmos which goes hand in hand with the understanding of God as Creator. If the Creator disappears, then the world and its powers may be on the way to becoming divinized again. Or at the least, as Nietzsche said, if we are to live as those who are capable of the murder of God we must ourselves become gods. (Altizer must be commended, on the other hand, for his exceptional capacity for irony in choosing "Incarnate Word" as his motto once the second person of the trinity has vanished.)

Perhaps the most wondrous incongruity of all in this new theology is its core concept—that God is *really* dead. Here an antimetaphysical, this-worldly theology has managed something most medieval Scholastics would never have dared: it has looked into the very dwelling of God—and found it empty. The only thing comparable to this feat is some utterances of the mystics. But one would certainly never find such metaphysical presumption in a Thomas Aquinas, who was only too conscious of the limits of natural theology and who knew that theology can only speak of the "living God" of the Bible, thanks to God's self-revelation. Apparently a new revelation has been vouchsafed to the death-of-God theologians, since they are not content to say that *for them* God is dead. No, God is irrecoverable; he will not come back! Others must be content with *analogia entis* or *analogia fidei;* the death-of-God theologians *know!*

Yet we must grant that by reducing the "death of God" to the absurdity of a theological program the "hard" radicals have made a great leap forward in the theological enterprise. For even before they have founded their journal they have shown us the next and final movement in the contemporary theological waltz. It is obvious that the only consistent step to take now is toward the position of the "granite" radicals. Even smaller in number than the "hard" radicals but infinitely more optimistic, they will be the true yea-sayers to the present moment—to automation, sex and civil rights. For they will not let themselves be trammeled by "obedience to Jesus" or gnostic mythology like "Incarnate Word." It's goodbye to Sartre and Kafka, to Heidegger and Beckett and all the rest who think the death of God makes this world a night of emptiness or even a sort of hell. Yes, it's even goodbye to the death of God, for the "granite" radicals will quietly bury him, leaving only a tasteful little marker that will not disturb the symmetry of the cultural landscape. These hardest of all radicals will, of course, be tough minded but superconfident, passionate but calculating, etc. But one thing they will not be: they will *not* be Christians. Nor will they worry about it. Least of all will they try to make Christians out of Nietzsche—or Herzog!

W. RICHARD COMSTOCK

Theology After the "Death of God"

A Survey of Recent Trends in Religious Thought

RECENTLY a number of American theologians have written books and articles in which reference to the "death of God" plays a prominent part. One of them asserts that "we must live the death of God if we are to exist in our world, for the confession of the death of God is now the price of the Christian's contemporaneity." Another examines "the difficulty of finding any meaningful way to speak of God." A third declares that "the death of God is a public event in our history."

Such language is startling. It is true that in poetry and novels the theme of "God's death" has been expressed for some time. Tolstoy describes the anguish of the dying Ivan Ilyitch over the absence of God. E. E. Cummings notes that with "Jehovah buried," "Eternity is now a Five Year Plan." Kafka writes a haunting parable on the death of the "Imperial Emperor" who has sent his courier forth with a message—a message that is meaningless because of the sender's demise. Ingmar Bergman broods on the "silence of God" in many of his films.

Yet it is easier for a poet than a theologian to make such references. Paul van Buren makes the interesting point that astronomy has excised the alien elements of astrology from its concern and chemistry has done the same with alchemy. He suggests that theology embark on a similar program in regard to its traditional references to God. Yet a glaring difference is obvious. Astronomy and chemistry have freed themselves from entanglement with matters foreign to their own fields. But could astronomy eliminate all reference to astral bodies and chemistry all reference to chemicals without destroying the integrity of their respective areas of investigation? Similarly, is a theology possible without reference to theos, the divine, God?

Etymology, however, should not be allowed to decide the issue. Creative exploration in religion has almost always been expressed in the form of radical negations that contained underlying affirmations. Thus the Taoist attacked the Confucian emphasis on the cultivation of moral integrity by affirming that "when the Great Tao ceased to observe, benevolence and righteousness came into vogue." Gautama Buddha explored the possibility of attaining the Hindu goal of deliverance by means of a rejection of the two fundamental categories of Hindu thought—Brahman and Atman. Many passages in the writings of the Hebrew prophets seem a violent attack on a priestly religion with whose orientation they have important affinities. The early Christians were called atheists by their contemporaries. Similarly, the present use of extreme negations may actually be evidence of a creative ferment that is taking place in contemporary religious thought.

If so, the negations are the one factor that brings together in dialogue otherwise very different theological approaches. At the moment, no set of common presuppositions are the basis of a distinctive "death of God" school. Only T. J. J. Altizer and William Hamilton use the phrase with continued enthusiasm, and very different outlooks seem to be emerging from their respective applications of it to current problems. In addition, many of these writers are profoundly influenced by the prison letters of Dietrich Bonhoeffer and his references to a "religion-less Christianity." Thus they are really more concerned with the "death" of religion as a world view than with the "death of God."

Furthermore, the methods of these new thinkers are dissimi-lar. Van Buren uses the techniques of linguistic analysis to dis-cover the rules by which a religious-Christian language may operate without the use of the referent "God." Altizer, on the other hand, thinks in terms of a phenomenological history of religion, seeing man's consciousness developing from an ar-chaic sacred form to a modern secular one. Gabriel Vahanian is a cultural critic of the modern post-Christian age. Harvey Cox is a social analyst of the secular form and style of urban life. It is likely that a situation similar to that which occurred in the thirties will repeat itself. At that time, it was common to iden-tify the thought of Karl Barth, Rudolf Bultmann, Paul Tillich, and Reinhold Niebuhr as "neo-orthodox." Further develop-ments disclosed that differences more significant than their sim-ilarities made the title, considered as the designation of a single school, misleading. In analogous fashion it is probable that the further work of these younger theologians will sharply diverge into contrasting positions, since the seeds of such differences are already present in their most recent discussions.

In the present essay, I offer a survey of the major themes present in the discussion of these new thinkers concerned with the death of God or of religion. However, their observations are part of a broader pattern of thought that includes many famous twentieth century theologians, philosophers, and mys-tics. To discern the main features of this pattern, the phrase "death of God" is suggestive and useful as an "element" whereby the basic aspects can be discerned in "solution." Con-sequently, an examination of the catalytic function of this striking image in the thought of Friedrich Nietzsche is one helpful method in distinguishing the shape of current issues; for although he did not first invent the phrase, he is clearly responsible for its widespread use in the twentieth century. A survey of its meaning in his philosophy will enable us to con-sider more profitably its implications for the contemporary stage of theological exploration.

Nietzsche's Challenge

In 1882 Nietzsche published *The Gay Science*, in which he included a striking parable about a "madman" who on a bright morning lights a lantern and runs to the market-place where he calls out unceasingly: "I seek God! I seek God!" In response to the mockery of his audience, the madman declares, "Where is God gone? . . . I mean to tell you! *We have killed him.* . . . The holiest and the mightiest that the world has hitherto possessed, has bled to death under our knife. . . . There never was a greater event,—and on account of it, all who are born after us belong to higher history than any history hitherto!" [1] In the works that follow *The Gay Science*, Nietzsche undertakes the task of formulating a new kind of thought that has appropriated the full implications of this radical declaration.

At first glance the importance of Nietzsche's effort may elude us. Atheism is not his personal discovery, nor does he offer a cogent intellectual attack on traditional theism that displays the technical brilliance of a Hume or Kant. Thus it cannot be said that Nietzsche's works are in any sense a determining "cause" of the rising tide of theistic unbelief in Europe. As Camus observes: "Nietzsche did not form a project to kill God. He found him dead in the souls of his contemporaries." Twentieth-century poets and thinkers did not become concerned about the "death of God" only because of what Nietzsche wrote. Rather, already acquainted with the experience of radical theistic doubt, they found in Nietszche's parable a vehicle for the distinctive expression and recognition of their own feelings and thoughts.

Nietzsche's contribution coincides with the task of both poet and philosopher. His imagination reveals synthetic powers of unification whereby divergent themes are fused through concrete imagery. Ambiguous, complex, multi-significant meanings are merged into single compelling aphorisms, striking parables, and overwhelming visions. Thus the "God" whose death Nietzsche proclaims is a symbolic vehicle through which the dissolution and destruction of a number of related viewpoints that have been important in the history of Western man is proclaimed.

First, this "God" is essentially related to an "other world," whether considered as a metaphysical world above the physical one, or a supernatural one above the natural one. "I beseech you, my brothers, *remain faithful to the earth*, and do not believe those who speak to you of other-worldly hopes! . . . Once the sin against God was the greatest sin; but God died. . . . To sin against the earth is now the most dreadful thing. . . ."

Second, he is a moral God who has a will by which good and evil are determined and the ultimate meaning of existence is discovered. "To look upon nature as if it were a proof of the goodness and care of a God; to interpret history in honor of a divine reason, as a constant testimony to a moral order in the world and a moral final purpose . . . as if everything were a dispensation, an intimation of Providence, something planned and sent on behalf of the salvation of the goal: all that is now past. . . ."

Third, he is fixed in a static eternity without change. "Evil I call it and misanthropic . . . all this teaching of the One and the Plenum and the Unmoved and the Permanent. All the permanent . . . that is only a parable. And the poets lie too much. It is of time and becoming that the best parables should speak. Let them be a praise and a justification of all impermanence."

Fourth, this God destroys human creativity. The static perfection of this omniscient omni-observer freezes the free becoming of the future into a determined dead fate. Man is solidified into an ugly object that "is" what this God has seen. Man's creativity and capacity for dynamic growth is thus destroyed by the fixed gaze of this eternal "look." "I feel only my will's joy in begetting and becoming . . . away from God and gods this will has lured me. What could one create if gods existed? . . . The God who saw everything, *even man*—this God had to die. Man cannot bear it that such a witness should live. . . ."

Fifth, the Christian God is a God of "pity"; but pity encourages slackness of energy, weakness, a diminution of the power to affirm existence. "Most recently I heard this: God is dead; God died of his pity for man."

Finally, this God claims the prerogative of "mystery." He is not available to the scrutiny of human reason. "God is a conjecture; but I desire that your conjectures should be limited by what is thinkable. Could you *think* a God?" [2]

Where did this image of the divine originate? Clearly, three sources have contributed to its formation in western culture. First is the Lord proclaimed in the Bible, the One with the creative power to bring the world into being, a deity with a Holy Will for Israel and all mankind, a living God with purposes and plans. Second is the metaphysical schema of the Greeks, whereby the world is seen as an hierarchial cosmos centered around a single overarching principle called the Good (Plato), or the eternal, immutable Substance that is the object of aspiration of all beings (Aristotle). A third source is even more important. Scholars like Durkheim and Eliade find in the primitive distinctions made in all cultures between the sacred and profane, between the holy and the secular, between numinous reality and mundane phenomena the very heart of religion. Otto described the experience of the holy as containing a sense of power and being (*tremendum*) that is mysterious, uncanny (*mysterium*), and possessing overwhelming value (*fascinans*). Eliade argues that it is through the fundamental experience of the sacred that primitive man understood his world to be a cosmos rather than a chaos. Its appearance provided man with "the fixed point, the central axis for all future orientation"; around this holy center one could organize the heterogeneous experiences of his existence into a meaningful whole possessing order, integrity, coherence. [3]

Thus the God of Western Christendom has been the moral, metaphysical, and sacred point of unity, whereby man's cosmos revealed its meaning, importance, and ultimate value. The "death" of this God means not only the end of belief in a certain anthropomorphic deity, but, more important, the death of all the functions that he performed for Western man. With Him goes the sense of a transcendent and ultimate norm for the value of this world, of a final purpose and a single meaning which could serve as a focus for human aspiration. With Him goes the religious aspect, the metaphysical structure, the sacred dimension of existence.

If it is Nietzsche's purpose to announce mankind's freedom from religion, metaphysics, and the sacred, [4] an intriguing question may be raised about his choice of a mythic form in which to state his meaning. Nietzsche does not argue that the God hypothesis is logically untenable and without experimental ver- ification. He refers to the murder of God under the knife of man. This is the archaic language of ancient poetry, religion, ritual; the language of dramatic event and concrete happening that occurs within a grand context of numinous emotion. Such myths have in the past been a primary vehicle for religious expression. They are intimately connected with the sense of the holy and have been used to describe "the various and some- times dramatic irruptions of the sacred into the world." [5] Why should an image fraught with such overtones and memories be used in the present context?

In *The Birth of Tragedy*, Nietzsche expresses his sense of the importance of myth, without which "every culture loses its healthy creative natural power." He calls myth the "concen- trated picture of the world," and declares that it "gives mean- ing" to man's "life and struggles." [6] However, this is an early work and Jaspers observes that "in his youth, Nietzsche as a classical philologist often spoke of myths, but in his later life he seldom so much as used the word." [7] Although he continues to make use of a kind of mythic thinking in his references to Zar- athustra and Dionysius, the fact remains that the basic catego- ries of his mature thought are formed with the intent of free- ing man from bondage to the dogmatic perspectives usually connected with myth.

Why then is atheism here proclaimed in the mythic form of dramatic event? It must indicate that Nietzsche is experiencing in his own consciousness a transition from a religious-sacred sensibility to a secular-profane one that he considers represent- ative of a movement in mankind as a whole. Nietzsche knows that ancient man has been religious man who has organized his world view around the distinction between the sacred and the profane. If modern and post-modern man as the heirs of this *weltanschauung* are to be truly free of it, the liberation must be decisive and definite. Simply to ignore the sacred by using lan- guages of logic and science which are oblivious to it is not suffi- cient. The "power" must be truly "broken" and this requires that the modern sensibility enter one last time into the domain of the sacred through mythic language, there to commit one final act of violence. The existence of the sacred God will not be coldly denied by a calculation of logic. Rather, man as culture-hero must "murder" the deity and thus exorcise his numinous power. "The holiest and the mightiest that the world has hitherto seen" must bleed to death under man's knife within the context of a religious emotion that is uncanny, fearful, full of awe. The earth seems to be "loosened" from the sun and man plunges into an "infinite nothingness" where the night comes on "continually darker and darker." Thus atheism uses myth to destroy myth. The culture-hero has performed his supreme act: the murder of God that brings to man a frightful gift, unlimited freedom and unbounded creativity.

The price paid for this last use of myth is an ambiguity of meaning pervading the pronouncement. Can the "death of God" refer to an ontic event? Does it mean that once there existed in the realm of beings an entity Who was Supremely Powerful, but who has at some point in the present time ceased to exist? Is man consequently bereft and "abandoned"? Such an interpretation is "fantastic," yet great myths are able to infuse their images with the sense of ontic reality that is difficult to resist while under their spell.

Yet since the time when Greek philosophy broke free of the power of myth through the use of logos (reason), the acceptance of myth in such a literal and primitive manner has not been possible for large numbers of people. Just as Rudolf Bultmann recommends a program for the demythologization of Christian myths, so Nietzsche suggests the manner in which his own myth may be demythologized. This is done by considering the "death of God" as an event taking place in the realms of man's linguistic activity and of his corresponding states of consciousness. On this view "God" is a symbol. The event of God's death refers to the fact that for modern man the symbol "God" has lost its vitality and functionality in the storehouse of his semantic tools. It has ceased to convey religious power and denotative significance. The sign has become meaningless; the symbol is dead.

Even closer to Nietzsche's central meaning is the shifting of the focus from either an ontic reality or a symbol that has "died" to the human consciousness in which the death takes place. In this third interpretation, the "death" refers to the death of belief, to an emerging state of human awareness in which reference to a transcendent realm of value and meaning is excluded. Once man saw his world as irradiated by a divine presence that was the center of power, purpose, ultimate concern. Now he sees his world as a profane landscape that at no point discloses the irruption of the sacred into its secular existence. Such an emphasis is the dominant one in Nietzsche's mind. The "death of God," he makes clear, means that "the Christian God has become unworthy of belief." The "event" is the "decay of belief in the Christian God, the victory of scientific atheism." Formerly, "all events were of a different lustre, for a God shone forth in them." [8] Now man turns to an earth in perpetual process without design, purpose, or sacred axis.

Susanne Langer observes that the ultimate end of a good myth is "not wishful distortion of the world, but serious envisagement of its fundamental truths; moral orientation, not escape." [9] To Nietzsche, the symbol "God" stands for a certain kind of broad orientation toward the world, a symbolic form of consciousness. The "death" of God points to a fundamental change in perspective, the occurrence of a radical event. Something has happened, is happening, if not to the Divine Life, then in the history of human consciousness. The basic presupposition of this myth is that man is not a static being whose nature and forms of apprehension are immutably fixed by either God or Nature. He is an historical consciousness, ever in process, who is presently undergoing a transformation from religious man into secular man. On this point the varying historical accounts of Hegel, Cassirer, Eliade, and Heidegger concerning transformations in human consciousness are all pertinent.

Furthermore, the hysterical and melodramatic violence implicit in the phrase "death of God" should not cause the religious heart and the theistic mind to miss the profound respect for the symbol "God" that is communicated in Nietzsche's attack on it. He observes: "attacking is to me a proof of goodwill and, in certain respects, of gratitude. By means of it, I honor a thing, I distinguish a thing." [10] To Nietzsche, "God" is "the holiest and mightiest that the world has hitherto pos-

sessed." A transformation in consciousness that eliminates this
sacred focus of concern is thus a tremendously significant phenomenological event that requires the most serious consideration. His myth reveals an appreciation of the importance of
the religious stance far different from the careless neglect of
thinkers incapable of his extreme imagery and expression.

Of course, many of the features of his description and the
implications he draws from it can be challenged. Myth has no
claim to infallibility. It functions as a creative focus to our attention; it cannot determine that what is finally seen by others
shall be identical with the vision of the original myth-maker.
Myth should be used, not as inerrant revelation, but as a heuris-
tic tool for exploration. Thus two suggestions implicit in
Nietzsche's myth must be resisted. One is a deterministic view
of the inevitability of this or any historical process. The appearance and apparent direction of a movement of consciousness does not mean that its final shape has already been decided.
Second is an over-confidence in our ability as phenomenological
observers to comprehend immediately every aspect and nuance
of the event in process. The shape, extent, and ultimate import
of the emerging secularism are not yet completely clear. Two
questions remain: Is Nietzsche's myth really a description? Or
is it rather a prescription of what he thinks could happen and
ought to happen? Nietzsche's madman decides that "prodigious
event is still on its way" for "the light of the stars needs time,
even after they are done, to be seen and heard." And Nietzsche
observes that "God is dead: but as the human race is constituted . . . for milleniums yet . . . people will show his
shadow.— And we—we have still to overcome his shadow!" [11]

It would seem that both descriptive and prescriptive elements are present in Nietzsche's symbol. The event of an
emergent, dominant secularity has not yet occurred in mankind as a whole; but it has taken place in the minds of many
philosophers, poets, and cultural leaders, as well as large portions of the general populace. Many contemporary theologians
have discovered its presence within their own sensibilities, although not in the radical shape described by Nietzsche. For
these reasons the phenomenon that he announces requires attention, exploration, interpretation. In the remainder of this

essay, some of the theological and anti-theological positions that the catalytic potentialities of this myth have released are considered.

The Death of Religion

To Nietzsche the death of God means the elimination of far more than a particular anthropomorphic deity. To him, "God" is the dramatic symbol for a world view that is oriented toward an "other world" in which resides a static perfection that, already complete, deprives the becoming process of this world of its importance and creativity. The emerging consciousness of contemporary man is one that has a predominantly "this worldly" focus. The existence of an "other world" is either directly denied or, at least, the priority of emphasis is placed on the problems and needs of this world as the locus of proper concern.

The excitement aroused by John Robinson's *Honest to God* has centered on his forceful recognition of the presence in modern theology of this shift in perspective. Hence much criticism of this widely read tract has been beside the point. It has been accused of a lack of originality, but Robinson's purpose is simply to describe an existing congruence of "this-worldly" orientation that has appeared both in technical theology and in popular religious attitudes. Furthermore, the criticism that he tries to synthesize the positions of very heterogeneous thinkers misses the mark, since his point is not that they reveal an identity in the details of their analyses, but that they agree on this central matter. The three theologians whom he chooses as examples—Rudolf Bultmann, Paul Tillich, and Dietrich Bonhoeffer—clearly substantiate his thesis. Bultmann has urged that Biblical theologians undertake the task of "demythologizing" the mythic world view found in the New Testament, with its three-storied structures comprising the earth at the center, heaven above, and an underworld below. He argues that the gospel message (kerygma) of the New Testament must be separated from such spatial models of divine transcendence. Tillich acknowledges his affinities with a naturalism that has abandoned ontological dualisms between nature and super-nature. He rejects the notion of a metaphysics that deals with "transempirical realities, with a world behind the world, existing only in speculative imagination," [12] and attempts to construct a theological interpretation of the one world of human experience.

In his famous prison letters, Bonhoeffer explores this theme in a manner that has been suggestive and extremely influential on the most recent stages of the discussion. Although the phrase "death of God" is not prominent in his work, so many of his points approximate Nietzsche's vision that we are not surprised to learn that Bonhoeffer was an enthusiastic reader of Nietzsche in his youth.[13] Bonhoeffer prefers to speak of the demise of metaphysics and of religion in a world that is now understood without the necessity of reference to an "other-worldly" God. The world has clearly "come of age" and, in reaching its "adulthood," has become secular and "this worldly." Bonhoeffer's purpose, then, is to consider the possibility of exploring a "religionless" Christianity.[14]

What does Bonhoeffer mean by the demise of "religion"? Although exactness of definition cannot be found in the tentative suggestions of his letters, several basic characteristics of what he means by religion do emerge. First, religion shares with metaphysics the orientation toward an "other world." Second, it cultivates an inward or individualistic search for a salvation from this world and a retreat into an "other worldly" religious realm. Third, religion posits a special sphere of holy ritual, private prayers, and monastic retirement within the world that is somehow considered to be more important than the mundane tasks of everyday life.

Fourth, religion uses the God of this other world as a *deus ex machina;* as an illicit problem-solver. Bonhoeffer points to the secularizing process that has occurred in all the sciences whereby God is no longer used as a hypothesis to explain any of the facts of physics or biology. He suggests that theology has made one final effort to find a use for God in the realm of psychology and existential analysis. There it is argued that man in his anxiety and guilt still needs the transcendent God to assist him. But Bonhoeffer suggests that even here the process of secularization is taking place, and that profane man is finding "this worldly" resources with which to cope with fear and death. Related to this fourth point is a final observation: that religion holds to the "premise" that there is some kind of *a priori* need in man by which he hungers after the divine reality. On this view, man is *homo religiosus* and finds in the structure of his nature some point of contact with God, at least in the form of a feeling of aspiration toward Him. But if such man ever existed, it now appears that he was a transitory historical phenomenon; modern man has become profane man who is religionless—*i.e.*, devoid of this *a priori* premise.[15]

There are important points of congruent emphasis between Nietzsche's "death of God" and Bonhoeffer's "religionless Christianity." Both proclaim the importance of the phenomenon of secularism for modern thought and both identify this phenomenon with the abandonment of metaphysics and religion. Nietzsche's anti-metaphysical stance is a strident articulation of an attitude held by many modern philosophers and secular thinkers.[16] Bonhoeffer's formulation, in turn, describes an attempt among Biblical theologians to extricate an authentic Biblical view from the "other worldly" forms of thought that have been so widely rejected and thus to show the continued relevance of Biblical faith to the modern mind. Here we might accuse such theologians of a certain lack of gallantry. In seeking to elude Nietzsche's hostile knife, they are willing to allow it to plunge into the heart of the metaphysical enterprise without regret. They somehow hope that if theology can be separated from a fatally wounded metaphysics and religion, it will be invulnerable to the death blow aimed at them all.

In the present survey the substantive issues raised by Nietzsche and Bonhoeffer are accepted as important, but the restricted connotation given to "metaphysics" and "religion" is not adopted, because it generates more confusion than clarity. In the twentieth century, it has become clear that although some metaphysical and religious systems have been connected with an "other worldly" perspective, metaphysics and religion are not thereby essentially and inevitably associated with radical dualisms. Nietzsche's dictum that it is "of time and becoming that the best parables should speak" has actually become the key insight of contemporary ontology and metaphysics.

There are three reasons why the secular suspicion of metaphysics is without foundation. First, major examples of twentieth-century ontology have demonstrated an orientation toward this world. Phenomenology and existentialism have converged on the attempt to disclose the basic structures of our present human existence. American thinkers like James, Santayana, and Dewey, while rejecting an "other-worldly" metaphysics, produced naturalistic ontologies of their own, and Alfred North Whitehead has developed a "speculative philosophy" that is a "system of general ideas in terms of which every element of our experience can be interpreted." [17]

Second, these "systems" are not fixed and static schemes that are oblivious to history, process, and creative advance. On the contrary, they provide general categories in which the sense of pluralistic diversity and openness to future growth can be conceptually expressed. Third, these general concepts are not "non-empirical" but, on the contrary, are directed toward the description of "every element of our experience" (Whitehead).

Neither can "religion" be simply identified with radical dualisms and with the attempt to "use" a Holy Reality to solve mundane problems. The latter could as well be called "magic" as "religion"; the former has been prevalent in many religious systems, but so has an alternative emphasis upon "this world" as the locus of concern. To be sure, Bonhoeffer has a right to his own definition of "religion," but such a restricted understanding of the term does violence to the historical usage which has been broader and included both supernatural and non-supernatural forms of belief. If "religion" is restricted to world views with radical dualisms, then some other term is still needed to indicate all those life orientations, whether dualistic or not, that have a point of ultimate and absolute focus for their devotional and ethical strivings in which inheres the sense of holy and sacred value. We will employ the term "religion" in this broader sense, unless the context indicates the more narrow usage adhered to by Bonhoeffer and his followers.

To sharpen the substantive issue behind these semantic differences, it is helpful to consider some distinctions among the three basic terms—mundane, secular, profane. All three first appear on the historical scene in a religious context where they are used to express a fundamental contrast between this world (mundane) and another world; this time (secular) and a time of holy consummation; or ordinary reality (profane) and the sacred reality of absolute majesty and value. Thus the adjective *mundane* conveys a spatial and substantial connotation. Its present use expresses the conviction of modern man that there is only one world of space and time, with no second world either spatially "above" or metaphysically "beyond" it (Robinson). Since the adjective *secular* has a predominantly temporal connotation (this age), it may be used to articulate the conviction that if no final meaning to this world can be found in an other world, neither can it be found in some other time. The "worldly" present flows into a "worldly" future with no holy consummation to give meaning to the process as a whole. Thus, finally, world and time alike are *profane*. Within the units of mundane space and the moments of secular time appears no point of sacred orientation and ultimate focus to the aspirations of human existence.

This last point is the crucial one. The importance of an "other world" or a time of consummation resides in the sacred aura that is attached to it. Deprived of holy value, a world of metaphysical forms, of substantial spirits, or even of an omnipotent deity, becomes simply an extension of the one world of all mundane and profane phenomena. The emphasis upon "this world" (mundane) and "this time" (secular) is a way of expressing the conviction that all terms of discourse must now exhibit basic continuities with each other and with the fundamental locus of human experience where meanings are determined and verified. The "event" of modern secularity is basically a decision to relate all thought, discourse, and action in a radical manner to this common "world" of man's mundane experience.

The question that remains is whether the entities of mundane space and the moments of secular time comprise a totally profane nexus without the presence of any ultimate focus to give a sacred significance to the course of human life. To answer this question a further interpretation of mundane secularism is required. One possibility advanced by Nietzsche might be called a "secular interpretation of secularism." Here is developed a view of a mundane world that is totally profanized in every respect. In contrast, we may also note a "religious interpretation of secularism" in which a holy center is still recognized in the "depth" of secular phenomena. Such is the position of Paul Tillich. By insisting on the "death" of religion, Bonhoeffer takes issue with Tillich; his alternative can still be characterized as a "religious interpretation," however, if the broad sense of that term we have already indicated is accepted.

Bonhoeffer's intention becomes clearer when we accept his reversal of the terms. He is concerned more with the secular interpretation of religion (or, as he would say, of "Christianity") than with the religious interpretation of secularism. Acutely aware of the event of modern secularity, he feels that the religious (or Christian) stance itself must be understood in a new way. In a religious *weltanschauung*, the category of the holy receives a priority of emphasis in the polar distinction between sacred and profane. It is the central phenomenon through which the mundane world is understood. In a secular *weltanschauung*, the situation is reversed. The profane becomes the focus of interpretation through which all other phenomena, including the holy, if it is recognized at all, are interpreted.

To Nietzsche this radical profanity involves the total abandonment of God, metaphysics, religion. Bonhoeffer agrees and yet continues to cultivate a Christian faith that is expressed in and through this secular form of consciousness. Such a stance is paradoxical and ambiguous. One point, however, should be noted. The purpose of Bonhoeffer and many of his disciples is to provide faith with a "secular interpretation" that does not necessarily make it acceptable to the modern mind, but acceptable to itself within the new situation. As Van Buren astutely observes, a "secular interpretation of the Gospel" is required because the modern Christian discovers the seeds of profanity within himself, and not only in others to whom he wishes to communicate.

In the light of these varying possibilities, three tasks are considered in the following sections: (1) the secular interpretation of secularism; (2) the religious interpretation of secularism; (3) the secular interpretation of religion.

Secular Interpretations of Secularism

Nietzsche's final philosophy represents a radical attempt to express and thereby bring into the light of total consciousness the full implications of the "death of God." As he puts it, he wants to exorcise not only God, but all of his "shadows" from the realm of human purview. These shadows appear in many guises, even in a philosophical thought that believes it has abandoned religious categories. Design, moral order, divine or natural law, teleology, Reality, Truth, Reason are some of the names which continue to operate as a focus whereby an ultimate meaning or absolute point of orientation is imposed upon the world. Nietzsche asks: "When will all these shadows of God cease to obscure us? When shall we have nature entirely undeified? When shall we be permitted to naturalize ourselves . . . ?" [18]

Nietzsche calls upon man to accept a total profanization of his consciousness. This necessitates an initiation into an overwhelming nihilism, where no fixed meaning or ultimate value is recognized, either in an other-worldly heaven or this-worldly moral order of things. The world is "to all eternity chaos"; "everything is there, but no purposes"; only the flow of happenings without plan or design. The death of God means primarily the death of any moral interpretation of the world.

Jean-Paul Sartre attempts to continue this Herculean task of expurgating all traces of sacred value from his atheistic existentialism. He knows that "atheism is a cruel and long-term affair" and the alertness and ruthless determination with which he uncovers and annihilates vestiges of a sacred orientation remaining in his consciousness are remarkable for the tenacity of purpose they reveal. For example, after obvious forms of a religious sensibility have been destroyed, he still discovers in himself a sense of artistic "calling" that sustained him in earlier years and which he now rejects as one more atavistic symptom of bad faith. [19]

Both Nietzsche and Sartre consider the world to be "meaningless" and "valueless." By this they do not mean that the world is something negative and evil, but simply that terms of positive or negative value cannot be applied to it as a whole. [20]

References to the purpose, inherent direction, ultimate significance of the world are unintelligible. Yet Nietzsche and Sartre
do not thereby encourage nihilism and futility. Rather they
call upon man to live with the awareness that he himself in his
concrete existence is the creative source of his own meanings
and values. If the world is a moral chaos, without direction or
goal, this is all the more reason for man to accept responsibility
for the establishment of purposes which he has freely formed
and not merely discovered in nature, heaven, or the will of
God. Thus Nietzsche affirms: "Creation—that is the great redemption from suffering and life's growing light." He asks:
"Can you give yourself your own evil and your own good and
hang your own will over yourself as a law? Can you be your
own judge and avenger of your law?" [21] And Sartre declares
that "Life is nothing until it is lived; but it is yours to make
sense of, and the value of it is nothing else but the sense you
chose." [22]

This emphasis on human freedom, responsibility, and creativity coincides with Bonhoeffer's influential references to a
world "come of age" and reaching "adulthood." In this new
state of secular consciousness, man has a sense of his autonomous powers; his reason is capable of understanding his mundane world and his technological skills are able to control and
transform its movements according to his own purposes and
plans. Furthermore, even the values and goals that he pursues
can be created out of his own resources without the assistance
of some divine law or immutable religious guide. Maturity is
the abandonment of a state of helpless dependency. One no
longer requires a God to perform functions he can now do
himself. Neither does he foist on the divine the responsibility
for the accomplishment of tasks that are clearly his own autonomous concern. The echo of the enlightenment can be heard in
these assertions. Kant had already observed that "Enlightenment is man's leaving his immaturity . . . self caused . . . by
lack of determination and courage to use one's intelligence
without being guided by another. . . . Have the courage to
use your own intelligence!" Added to this theme is a new confidence engendered by recent technological advance with its
many successes and awe-inspiring accomplishments.

It is in response to this mood that Bonhoeffer announces the death of religion as dependence on a transcendent *deus ex machina*. Secular man does not need a divine problem-solver. Bonhoeffer observes that "there is no longer any need for God as a working hypothesis whether in morals, politics or science." He wishes to abandon the resistance of many religionists to this development and observes that "the attack by Christian apologetic upon the adulthood of the world . . . is . . . in the first place pointless, in the second place ignoble, and in the third un-Christian." It seemed to Bonhoeffer that such attacks are "like an attempt to put a grown-up man back into adolescence; *i.e.*, to make him dependent on things on which he is not in fact dependent any more." Bonhoeffer wants to devise a new theology of strength rather than weakness, maturity rather than childish dependency, confidence rather than despair.[23]

However, Nietzsche maintains that this maturity requires a costly initiation: acceptance of the death of God as the conscious abandonment of all transcendent supports and guidance beyond the confines of the autonomous self. On this point Bonhoeffer and many of his American admirers who advocate the death of religion introduce a variation into this description. According to them, man enters into his adulthood without the dramatic and violent decision in favor of a strident atheism. Thus Bonhoeffer prefers to speak of modern man as living in the world "as if there were no God." It is a world "without God" rather than a world in which God has "died." The difference in phrasing points to a description of secular man who has discovered that he does not "need" God to solve his scientific, philosophical, or psychological problems, and is content to bypass the whole issue of theism or atheism as irrelevant to his concerns. Thus Van Buren notes: "Today, we cannot even understand the Nietzschean cry that 'God is dead!' for if it were so, how could we know? No, the problem is that the *word* 'God' is dead." [24]

In *The Secular City*, Cox develops this approach in a most suggestive way. Like Bonhoeffer, he rejects an existentialism concerned with anxiety and doubt, especially when it involves an underlying religious concern. Cox writes:

As for "the anxiety of doubt" about the God of theism, the closest today's man gets to such a state is a mild curiosity or at most a kind of wistfulness. Urban-secular man came to town after the funeral was already over. He feels no sense of deprivation and has no interest in mourning.

Both philosophical existentialism and Paul Tillich's theology are expressions of the mourning period which began with the death of the God of metaphysical theism and Western Christian civilization, but the wake is now over. That is why existentialist theologies and philosophies do not partake of the spirit of the emerging age but symbolize rather the passing of the old.[25]

This passage is intriguing but it finally misses the mark, because it does not fully face the point of the atheism advocated by Nietzsche and Sartre. As we have seen, the "death of God" is not promulgated by them as a counsel to despair, but as the necessary prerequisite to the full autonomy and confidence desired by secular man. Nietzsche wants to cultivate a "joyous wisdom" and Sartre a "stern optimism." As Nietzsche observes, the event of the "death of God" leads to "the reverse of what was to be expected—not at all sad and depressing, but rather like a new and undescribable variety of light, happiness, relief, enlivenment, encouragement, and dawning day . . . our hearts overflow with gratitude, astonishment, presentiment and expectation . . . our ships can put out to sea in face of every danger . . . perhaps never before did such an open sea exist." [26]

The positions of Bonhoeffer and Cox raise a question they do not adequately answer. If secular maturity is considered to be the fruition of a process and development taking place in the history of culture, it may be asked whether its *terminus ad quem* is better described by Nietzsche or by Bonhoeffer and Cox. Whereas Cox suggests that a strident atheism is a sign of cultural adolescence, Nietzsche's myth challenges us with an alternative possibility. Perhaps it is a secularism that has not faced directly and clearly the question of atheism that has not yet fully come of age. At any rate, it is a sign of uncertainty that Cox, after having dismissed philosophical existentialism in the manner just indicated, later acknowledges his own involvement in the question raised by one eloquent existentialist—Miguel Unamuno—who asks: "Is man alone in the universe or not?" In this context Cox confesses that to him "whether God exists or not is a desperately serious issue." [27]

But if so, it may be wondered if the kind of secular man who does not "ask religious questions" can be taken, as Cox urges, simply "as he is." It would seem that the "depth" secularism articulated by Nietzsche must be distinguished from a "surface" kind that avoids serious issues and accepts the comforts of urban life with a superficial and thoughtless complacency. We must ask whether the secular mind, unable even to understand Nietzsche's myth, has achieved a vital maturity, or has not rather refused the pain and sacrifice involved in radical decisions that alone can lead to an authentic adulthood. It is surely significant that in Nietzsche's original parable, the madman proclaims the "death of God" to people very much like those whom Van Buren and Cox describe. They "already do not believe in God" and do not find any importance, and certainly not any terror, in what the madman is proclaiming.

What kind of people are these? They do not seem mature in any profound sense. Are they not those whom technocracy is protecting from pain and frustration? Their confidence is not in autonomous powers put to the test, but in the techniques of an industrial civilization that functions like Dostoevsky's "grand inquisitor" to keep them in a state of contented dependency. They inhabit Huxley's "Brave New World" and are those whom Tillich calls the "blessed animals." Nietzsche calls them the "last men" who have "invented happiness" and have become "one herd" with no shepherd. "Everybody wants the same, everybody is the same: whoever feels different goes voluntarily into a madhouse." [28]

It is this kind of secularity that evoked Santayana's dismay when he overheard a conversation between a modern father and daughter at a railway station. When the child asked if God had made the railroad tracks, she was told, "God didn't make it. It was made by the hands of man." Santayana, himself a materialist and an atheist, found himself agreeing with the literal sense of the answer but disagreeing entirely with its tone and underlying connotations. It seemed to Santayana to express a mood of "impatience, conceit, low-minded ambition, mechanical inflation, and the worship of material comforts." It was "puerile human vanity trying to justify itself by a lie." [29]

Bonhoeffer was aware of this kind of surface secularism and in one passage distinguishes the kind of "worldliness" that he advocates from the "shallow this worldliness of the enlightened, of the busy, the comfortable, or the lascivious." Both Nietzsche and Bonhoeffer are thus united in their rejection of secular banality, but the profundity that each of them seeks in opposition to it is found in different directions. One cultivates the secular depth of a radical and total profanization of consciousness; the other encounters the religious depth of a "beyond" in the midst of life.

Religious Interpretations of Secularism

Using the terminology of William James, we can say that the depth secularism of Nietzsche is a "tough-minded" or "hard" interpretation of the "death of God" myth. However, several recent attempts have been made to provide a more "tender-minded" or "soft" interpretation, whereby secularism is still understood from a religious point of view.

A. The Holy Depth. The most important of these is Tillich's formulation of a theology of secular culture in which it is argued that "religion as ultimate concern is the meaning-giving substance of culture and culture is the totality of forms in which the basic concern of religion expresses itself. In abbreviation: religion is the substance of culture; culture is the form of religion." [30]

Tillich attempts to overcome the tension between an autonomy and a heteronomy through an understanding of the possibility of theonomy. Secular autonomy holds that man, as the bearer of reason, is the source of his own meanings and values. Heteronomy, on the other hand, presents the norms and rules of life as some alien and external authority to which he must relinquish his freedom and blindly submit. In a theonomous situation, man discovers that the meaning of his life is appropriated as a holy ground or depth to his existence that is the essence of his own being at the same time that it transcends it.

Tillich urges contemporary man to seek for the establishment of a "theonomous culture" that will express "in its creations an ultimate concern and a transcending meaning not as something strange but as its own spiritual ground." [31]

Tillich thus views secularism from both a positive and negative point of view. If secularism is the recognition of the fact that no finite being is in itself worthy of an unconditional concern, it is an expression of the "Protestant principle" that "protests against any absolute claim made for a relative reality." [32] On the other hand, if secularism is an orientation toward the "surface" of reality that denies its relation to its own unconditional ground, then it has become a distorted form that, having lost its theonomous roots, will oscillate between claims to a shallow autonomy and a frenzied subservience to heteronomous authoritarianism.

Tillich's counsel is to develop the autonomous forms of culture to their full powers of expression without hesitation. Yet in the concern for truth, justice, beauty, power, and community man will still experience a seriousness of orientation that manifests a sacred ultimacy inherent in all his endeavors. Granted that there is no single meaning or purpose to the world that can be detected through a mundane analysis. Nevertheless, the relation of human existence to a "creative ground of being and meaning" is encountered in the experience of anxity, courage and love, and in ecstatic moments of religious participation in the "telos" of human creativity and aspiration. The "meaning" that cannot be stated in discursive prose may yet be expressed in religious symbols that become the creative focus of a culture's deepest aspirations.

It is in the light of this analysis that Tillich can view the "death of God" in a positive way. If the God of theism is merely a highest being, then the recognition of his incapacity to be the focus of an unconditional concern is a positive religious gain. However, even in a state of radical doubt, in which all gods, all absolutes, all foci of sacred orientation disappear,

> something remains, namely, the seriousness of that doubt in which meaning within meaninglessness is affirmed. The source of this affirmation of meaning within meaninglessness, of certitude within doubt, is not the God of traditional theism but the

"God above God," the power of being, which works through those who have no name for it, not even the name God.[33]

B. *The Secular Mandate.* Such a position is representative of many contemporary religious interpretations of secularism that Larry Shiner calls "dialectical" because they assert the continuing presence of vital relationship between sacred and secular, even in a predominantly profane orientation.[34] These positions can be contrasted with the views of many of the younger secular theologians who have followed Bonhoeffer's lead and found Tillich's formulation inadequate.

Bonhoeffer accuses Tillich of attempting to interpret the secular transformation of man in a religious sense "against its will." He "sought to understand the world better than it understood itself, but it felt entirely *mis*understood." Cox, as we have seen, affirms that secular man is simply "puzzled by Tillich's fascination with 'meaninglessness'"; he feels no "anxiety of doubt," but at most only "a kind of wistfulness" about the question of God.[35] On this interpretation, modern secularity is a phenomenon that has completely abandoned the sacred, and does not feel the need for its reinstatement in any form. Thus the emphasis is on profanization as a "historical" process that is freeing itself of the holy rather than maintaining a "dialectical" relation to it.

But in that case, what kind of religious or theological interpretation of secularism is still possible? Is there any other alternative besides the holy secularism of Tillich and the radical secularism of Nietzsche? Cox encourages an approach that seeks to "nourish the secularization process, to prevent it from hardening into a rigid world view, and to clarify as often as necessary its roots in the Bible." [36] In Cox's discussion, three main aspects of the secularization process assume especial importance: the elimination of the sacred from all areas of mundane life, the development of man's autonomous creativity, and the abandonment of any concern for an ultimate meaning to existence. To Cox, acceptance of these three features requires the death of "religion" and "metaphysics," but not of a continuing relationship with the major themes of "Biblical faith."

Concerning the first feature, Cox uses the thesis of many historians, that the Hebraic insistence on the holiness of the transcendent Lord has helped to disenchant the "gods" of nature, to desacralize the "gods" of politics, and to deconsecrate the "gods" of human values. If only the Creator is sacred, this world becomes a profane landscape that man can examine and attempt to use for his own purposes without fear.[37]

Concerning the second feature, Cox argues that "an authentically Biblical doctrine of God not only survives the view that man himself is the source of cultural meanings, but actually supports and encourages such a view." [38] Cox suggests that the creation account in Genesis 2:4–24 contains a divine mandate whereby man is given the task of "naming" the features of creation and of subduing and directing them according to human goals. Properly understood, this is a call to secular maturity, to the autonomy of adulthood, and to creative acts of a humanity "come of age." Thus the modern sense of freedom, power, and autonomous creativity proceeding from man himself is no Promethean defiance of the laws of a jealous God; on the contrary, it is a mature acceptance of the divine mandate to accept responsibility for a continuation of the creative process by forming the conditions for human life in a human world.

> Here is a truly exalted view of man. God does not simply insert man into a world filled with creatures which are already named, in relationships and meaning patterns already established by decree. Man must fashion them himself. He doesn't simply discover meaning; he originates it.[39]

Concerning the third point, Cox argues, as we have already noted, that urban-secular man "does not feel this compulsion to find some inclusive and overarching meaning." But Cox points out that the Biblical God does not offer Himself for "use" in this way "as the kingpin in an ontological system" which "is not much different from wheedling Him into watering my corn." Rather the Hidden God meets man in the events of historical and political change where specific tasks of making the human world truly human are given him. Thus a truly secular theology adopts "the living lexicon of the urban-secular man," and discovers that politics has replaced metaphysics as its expressive form.[40]

In spite of many intriguing features in this analysis, it is difficult to see how it provides a distinctive alternative to the positions represented by Nietzsche and Tillich. Cox's analysis
seems to encourage either a further movement of the "irrevers-
ible" process of secularization toward Nietzsche's profane autonomy or else the acceptance in some form of Tillich's view
of a dialectical and continuing vital relation between the secular and sacred aspects of existence. At critical points in their
discussion, Cox and Bonhoeffer finally opt for this latter possibility.

For example, although Cox urges us to accept a world that is
radically desacralized, it remains a world in which the Hidden
God is present at the junctures of historical change. But such a
world in which the Holy One is still relevant in mysterious
ways beyond the control of man has not been profanized to the
extent demanded by Nietzsche, who rather argues that even if
the Biblical view once assisted in initiating the process of secularization, it allowed, at best, for the emergence of cultural adolescence. To Nietzsche's profane man, adulthood means the
death of all the gods, including the Hidden God of the Bible,
who, after liberating man from bondage to nature and politics,
is now felt to be an oppressive check to the full development of
man's autonomy. Modern man will not settle to be a junior
partner in the firm. He must put his former employer in total
bankruptcy and take over the full management of the company
himself. Thus Eliade writes:

> Modern non-religious man assumes a new existential situation;
> he regards himself solely as the subject and agent of history,
> and he refuses all appeal to transcendence. In other words, he
> accepts no model for humanity outside the human condition as
> it can be seen in the various historical situations. *Man makes
> himself*, and he only makes himself completely as he desacral-
> izes himself and the world. The sacred is the prime obstacle to
> his freedom. He will become himself only when he is totally de-
> mysticized. He will not be truly free until he has killed the last
> god.[41]

Cox considers such a view to be "secularism," of which he
disapproves and contrasts with "secularization" as a process by
which all absolutes, including atheism, are desacralized. But the

distinction works best in the area of political secularization. Secularism as an ideology must be willing to be one force among many in the contemporary scene, and not assume the status of an established secular faith demanding the subjugation of all other powers to it. But the pressing question that still demands an answer is not whether the ideology of secularism will accept a relativized position within the social order, but whether, within the consciousness of the individual himself, secularity will or will not assume an absolute or total form. Nietzsche's "death of God" myth is a challenge to accept just such a task of profane totalization of the self in all its feelings, aspirations, and forms of thought. By retaining his orientation to the Hidden God, Cox, with Tillich, obviously has refused to accept the full force of this challenge without important qualifications.

Concerning the issue of autonomous creativity, Cox observes that when "the tyrant God of both atheism and theism disappears, . . . the partnership of God and man comes into focus." He concludes: "Given the fact that man in dialogue fashions the meanings by which history proceeds . . . one utterly crucial question remains: Is this responsibility something which man himself has conjured, or is it *given* to him?" He decides: "Man in order to be free and responsible, which means to be *man*, must answer to that which is not man." [42] But such a position is very different from the kind of autonomy advocated by Nietzsche and Sartre, and is very close to those of religious existentialists like Tillich and religious metaphysicians like Whitehead, whom Cox has supposedly rejected. Tillich emphasizes the participation of human existence in the creative power of the divine ground of being and meaning. Whitehead refers to the "particular relevance (of God) to each creative act as it arises from its own conditioned standpoint in the world." [43] In more ecstatic language Buber writes:

> Creation happens to us, burns itself into us, recasts us in burning—we tremble and are faint, we submit. We take part in creation, meet the Creator, reach out to him, helpers and companions.[44]

Cox uses language formed by Biblical personalism to affirm that man "works as God's partner in ordering the chaos." The

terms differ, but the underlying intentions converge. To all of
these thinkers, including Cox, secular and sacred movements
within the process of life meet and interact with one another.

Similarly, Bonhoeffer and Cox do not differ with Tillich on
the question of "ultimate meaning" as much as some of their
statements suggest. Tillich nowhere claims to have stated in
metaphysical terms a meaning that is the rational key to a system of thought. He does argue that man's personal existence
reveals a concern for the ultimate significance of his life, which
is the heart of what we call religion, in the broad sense of the
term. Cox seems to be in basic agreement with this view of man
when he insists that modern secular man still experiences the
transcendent "as those aspects of our experience which can
never be transmuted into extensions of ourselves."

It is difficult to detect any difference from Tillich in Cox's
assertion that

> the difference between men of Biblical faith and serious non-
> theists is not that we do not encounter the same reality. The
> difference is that we give that reality a different *name*, and in
> naming it differently, we differ seriously in the way we re-
> spond.[45]

And Bonhoeffer also searches for God at the "center of life"
and declares that through the man Jesus Christ "life has a meaning for us." [46] Evidently the search for ultimate meaning, and a
point of sacred focus in the midst of the secular phenomenon,
has not really been abandoned by Bonhoeffer's progeny, any
more than it has by Tillich. It would seem that the "historical"
interpretation of secularism must retain some form of the "dialectical" interpretation if it is to keep any kind of religious or
theological orientation at all.

C. The Profane Burden. Another aspect of the preceding
analysis that requires further consideration is the emphasis on
optimism and the positive affirmation of secularity. On this
point Bonhoeffer's thought is more complex than has so far
been indicated. Having explored the need for a theology of
strength and joy, his further remarks make clear that this is
only one strain in the "polyphony" of life.[47] Strength and joy
provide a ground base that is a counterpoint of pain and sacri-

fice. To Bonhoeffer, worldliness is a polar category containing both secular and Christological themes:

> I don't mean the shallow this-worldliness of the enlightened, of the busy, the comfortable or the lascivious. It's something much more profound than that, something in which the knowledge of death and resurrection is ever present. . . . This is what I mean by worldliness—taking life in one's stride, with all its duties and problems, its successes and failures, its experiences and helplessness. It is in such a life that we throw ourselves utterly into the arms of God and participate in his sufferings in the world and watch with Christ in Gethsemane.[48]

In Bonhoeffer's letters there is the suggestion that the secular consciousness is accepted by the Christian as a strange form of redemptive suffering.

> The God who makes us live in this world without using him as a working hypothesis is the God before whom we are ever standing. Before God and with him we live without God. God allows himself to be edged out of the world and on to the cross. . . . Man is challenged to participate in the sufferings of God at the hands of a godless world.[49]

This thought is also expressed in the writings of Altizer, though the elements of his position owe more to Eliade than to Bonhoeffer. Altizer's position is a difficult fusion of Biblical theology, a phenomenology of the sacred, mystical patterns of negation, and a Hegelian sense of the movement and transformation of consciousness through historical dialectic.

He sees the two views of reality—the sacred and profane—in radical opposition. To the fully developed secular consciousness, Holy Reality is meaningless, is nothing. But in similar fashion affirmation of the Holy Reality means the eschatological "end"; the annihilation of an independent, profane mode of being. The present moment in history is one in which the secular consciousness is emerging as supreme. God has died; the sacred is eliminated; only profane being exists. Altizer differs from many of his colleagues in the specific attitude he takes toward this phenomenon. To Cox, the profane consciousness is fulfilling the mandate of the creator God of Genesis. Thus, "we must learn to love it in its unremitting secularity." Hamilton finds that he is not "particularly cast down or perplexed" by the acceptance of God's death. Altizer's writings, on the contrary, reflect a religious sensibility that enters the profane world with pain and terror. He observes that the Christian cannot isolate himself from "the emptiness, the meaninglessness, and the sheer horror of the world." Since the secular mode of consciousness is now the present form of being human, the Christian religious man cannot refuse this form without refusing his humanity. He "lives *this* life, sharing all its fullness and emptiness, its joy and its horror, knowing that his destiny is to live *here* and *now*, allowing his life to be the metal which God's fire will transform into his Kingdom." [50]

The radical aspect of Altizer's position is that he has rejected the possibility that modern man can adhere to the sacred view of Eliade's primitive shaman. Nor does he accept the attempt of Tillich to show that secular man still retains the sacred in the form of the ultimate concern that emerges in the midst of his profane pursuits. Altizer believes that a historical faith must move in and through the present moment of radical and total profanity to a "new" reality beyond. Thus the acceptance in radical form of the "death of God" means that what is hoped for is not just a repetition of past forms of religious consciousness. Something truly "new" is longed for. Thus, "The Christian World moves only by negating its own past expressions." It is seeking an "eschatological end that transcends a primordial beginning." [51]

Altizer thus shares with Tillich the concern for a new theonomy in which the emptiness of the profane is again open to the fullness of the sacred. Yet Altizer attempts to combine the dialectical and historical elements in this interpretation in a more radical manner than Tillich does. Tillich suggests that perhaps the theonomy will emerge within a culture structured by Christian symbols properly chastened and purged. Altizer rather suggests that the Christian symbols themselves must undergo a more radical negation and "death" as the price to be paid before the present profane reality is transformed into a sacred theophony once again.[52]

Secular Interpretations of "God"

The myth of the "death of God" focuses attention on the various understandings of the ensuing secular consciousness that are possible. However, an opposite task also presents itself: to consider how the new form of secularism in turn may affect the understanding and interpretation of religion. But a secular interpretation of Western religion becomes fundamentally a secular interpretation of "God," which has been the central symbolic focus of Western religious aspiration.

This powerful symbol has a rich texture and complexity of meaning that can not be summarized in a single definition. The dramatic myths and stories of the Bible have caused many to interpret it in anthropomorphic terms, but the Bible also contains an emphasis on God's mystery and incomprehensibility; no images of Him are to be made, and his mysterious Name is to be treated with a sacred circumspection. As we have seen, Nietzsche associates the symbol with a variety of themes: the other world, ultimate purpose, immutable perfection, moral will, Holy Love, Sacred Mystery. God's "death" announces a new consciousness in which all of these points of orientation are absent.

However, contemporary attempts to refer in a secular fashion to "God" as the focus of at least some of these themes continue to be made. These efforts represent a variety of philosophical and religious backgrounds. One characteristic that almost all of them hold in common is a sense of reticence about direct reference to "God" either in language or in action. All direct characterization of "God," whether as a Holy and Personal Will, the fulfillment of existence, the meaning of life, the ultimate focus of concern, the ground of being, the lure of feeling, etc., are felt to be ambiguous, inadequate, inappropriate.

This situation is caused by the fact that, in a secular world, language is itself mundane and its meanings are all formulated by empirical references to aspects of worldly experience. A religious use of this language must consequently be indirect, elusive, and oblique. This reticence is not considered to be a forthright denial of the actuality of "God," but a recognition of the inappropriateness of any direct and immediate form of orientation toward it. In some manner, the divine presence is still recognized, yet a tension and agony is experienced in any attempt to articulate it by the use of mundane vehicles of expression.

In a striking manner that reflects the contemporary dominance of the profane consciousness, the agony of theistic speech can be recognized in both particular Christian theologies and in more general philosophies of religion.

A. Secular Christology. For example, there is a tendency in recent Protestant thought that in its most radical form (Hamilton and van Buren) has culminated in a "Christological atheism." This puzzling attempt to retain a religious orientation toward Christ "without God" is more understandable when interpreted as the climax to a style of theological reticence already present in the more conservative positions of Barth and Bonhoeffer.

Although Barth is often considered to be a dogmatic, almost reactionary thinker, the fact is that his traditional theology is founded on a very profane analysis of the human situation. Barth accepts the contemporary rejection of natural theology and of any attempt to find a point of contact between the human and the divine. He maintains that no mundane evidence, argument or experience can reveal the presence of God within the world. Yet Barth is not a profane secularist, but rather a profane theologian experiencing the agony of theistic speech. In an early essay, he makes three paradigmatic assertions: "We ought to speak of God; we are human, however, and so cannot speak of God; we ought therefore to recognize both that we should speak of God and yet cannot, and by that very recognition give God the glory." [53]

Barth then uses this very tension as the basis for a "High Christology." In the miracle of his revelation in Christ, God is declared to have established his own ground of reference and meaning. He who cannot be meaningfully spoken about or manipulated within a mundane context is now proclaimed through that "worldly" act in Christ where he makes himself known. Barth here follows in the tradition of those Christian thinkers who have discovered in the Bible the Hidden God

(Pascal), the *deus absconditus* (Luther), the Divine Incognito
(Kierkegaard), who can be the proper object of neither sense
perception, human feeling, or rational conceptualization. Furthermore, Barth's position enables him to accept the death of
religion or of God with equanimity. The Mysterious Reality
of the Hidden God is distinguished from all mundane "gods,"
including the "God" of Western Christendom. The latter is
considered by many Barthians to be a fusion of improperly
understood Biblical insights, with philosophical notions of an
immutable substance and the cultural projections of ultimate
human ideals formulated by European civilization. It is argued
that all such human "gods" are born in the womb of consciousness and eventually die. Perhaps we are now at the end of an
era and are witnessing the demise of the God of Christendom.
Faith in the Living God is not threatened by such an event.
Thus the early Barth can note:

> What men this side of resurrection name "God" is most char-
> acteristically not God . . . he is, in fact, "no-God." The cry of
> revolt against such a god is nearer the truth than is the sophis-
> try with which men attempt to justify him.

Indeed, "The revolt of Prometheus is wholly justified when
once Zeus—the 'no-God'—has been exalted to the throne of
God." [54]

Some of the new secular theologians are obviously continuing this emphasis, with refinements. Vahanian describes the
emergence of a post-Christian era in which "the death of God
means the death of those pagan deities that had somehow survived in the Christian cultural conception of God." However,
he entertains the hope that this event may "yet enable Christianity to clarify the Biblical concept of God as the Wholly
Other, because he is the Creator and not a natural force." [55]
Altizer also refers to the death of God who is an "idea," even if
it is called "absolute, infinite, unconditional, true Being." Cox
contemplates the possibility that "our English word *God* will
have to die, corroborating in some measure Nietzsche's apocalyptic judgment that God is dead!" But Cox contrasts the subject of this death with "the One we met both in the life of

Jesus and in our present history as the liberator and the hidden one." [56]

However, the secular theologians who are influenced by Bonhoeffer are dissatisfied with Barth's position even while being strongly influenced by it. Bonhoeffer rejects Barth's "positivistic doctrine of revelation" that is given to man on a "take it or leave it basis," and suggests that the dogmatic form of his later expositions has obscured the essentially "worldly" character of the gospel.[57] Evidently the resistance to Barth from this quarter is caused by the ease with which Barth is finally able to talk about the nature of God and his attributes once the fact of revelation is accepted. Bonhoeffer is concerned to formulate a mundane Christology in which such direct references to God will be more radically subordinated to a focus on the secular Jesus.

The seeds of an approach Bonhoeffer did not live to formulate in detail are found in the following note:

> What do we mean by "God"? Not in the first place an abstract belief in his omnipotence, etc. That is not a genuine experience of God, but a partial extension of the world. Encounter with Jesus Christ, implying a complete orientation of human being in the experience of Jesus as one whose only concern is for others. This concern of Jesus for others the experience of transcendence. This freedom from self, maintained to the point of death, the sole ground of his omnipotence, omniscience and ubiquity. Faith is the participation in this Being of Jesus (incarnation, cross and resurrection). Our relation to God not a religious relationship to a Supreme Being, absolute in power and goodness, which is a spurious conception of transcendence, but a new life for others, through participation in the Being of God. The transcendence consists not in tasks beyond our scope and power, but in the nearest thing to hand.[58]

The crucial sentence here is: "Our relation to God [is] not a religious relation to a Supreme Being . . . but a new life for others." As Bonhoeffer meant it, God is not thereby denied; nevertheless, the personal orientation of Christian man turns from God to the neighbor. Jesus has given to man the freedom to be concerned, not with the divine, but with the "other" in his needs and problems. Cox is very close to Bonhoeffer's intent when he observes that modern man is turning from the compulsive interest in "finding" and "experiencing" God to the Christological task of being "for others" in the midst of social and political change. "God wants man to be interested not in Him but in his fellow man." [59]

On such a view God is "dead," "absent"; not only because of the difficulty of theistic speech, but because of the improper diversion reference to God can create for religious action. God must be considered as a reality only obliquely and indirectly known, because Christian man is not called to aspire for a direct awareness of him, but to orient himself toward the worldly being of the other person in his need. In Bonhoeffer's thought, this theme is also associated with the assumption of the profane burden that is encountered in Jesus. "The God who is with us is the God who forsakes us"—just as Jesus cried "My God, My God, why hast thou forsaken me?"

Two other recent thinkers have offered a more radical interpretation. Whereas Cox still holds that in Jesus the Hidden One acts in ways not available for human inspection and manipulation, Hamilton finds that even this God has "died." But the "time" of his death is "also the time of obedience to Jesus. . . . The Christian is defined . . . as the man bound to Jesus, obedient to him and obedient as he was obedient." [60]

Van Buren attempts to justify Bonhoeffer's hope that a non-religious interpretation of Christianity is possible by means of a method that "never occurred to Bonhoeffer." Van Buren makes use of a verification principle developed by certain linguistic philosophers to argue that "statements of faith are to be interpreted . . . as statements which express, describe or commend a particular way of seeing the world, other men, and oneself, and the way of life appropriate to such a perspective." Following Bonhoeffer's lead, the Christian is described as one who has adopted the perspective of a new freedom for others revealed in the life of Jesus. In this secular interpretation, all reference to a transcendent God is eliminated as redundant and meaningless. If, in a momentary lapse, theistic language is used, the secular theologian would ask if the life of Jesus has not shown that God "wants men to stop trying to peer into the clouds and to obey God's will by thinking out their existence in terms of man—specifically the man in whom God has said all that he has to say to men?" [61]

The positions of Hamilton and Van Buren can be interpreted as a radical but logical development of a trend within Protestant theology which, even in its more orthodox phase, has excised all attempts to relate a "general" knowledge of God in the human mind and heart with the "particular" revelation in Christ. Theology becomes identical with—Christology. A Christomonism expels any other meaningful reference to the divine. Finally, we reach the position of an "atheistic Christology," which, once its historical antecedents are understood, is a curious, but no longer paradoxical, phenomenon.

What is paradoxical about this position is its ambiguous relation to a radical secularism. Its advocates sometimes imply that their stance is an attempt to help the "secular Christian" understand his own orientation within the emergence of the profane world-view. But in other moods they imply that they are addressing "secular man" in a radical manner. However, in a world in which all absolutes have "died," it is far from clear how an absolute commitment to the man from Nazareth is any more attractive or meaningful than the commitment to "God" which has been rejected. From a radically secular viewpoint, varying evaluations of Jesus' teaching and his "perspective" are possible. As a purely profane achievement, his life may still warrant respect, but hardly the absoluteness of commitment that Hamilton and Van Buren advocate and which will surely seem, granted their presuppositions, increasingly to be a last atavistic survival from a "religious" age in a "profane" age where it does not belong.

All these positions, from Barth on the "right" to Van Buren on the "left," exemplify the same reticence about theistic language connected to a Christological focus with varying degrees of emphasis. To Barth, it is in and through Christ that the "Hidden God" is truly "known." With Bonhoeffer and Cox, his mysterious actuality is still encountered, but more indirectly and obliquely through the confrontation with "the Man for others." With Hamilton and Van Buren, the presence has receded even further from the locus of awareness, so that only Jesus remains as the point of meaningful religious reference. In

one important sense none of these positions exhibits a radical
secularism; they are all fundamentally addressed to "Christian
man" who wants to understand the secular form of his faith.
They do not confront "secular man" with any reason why he
should retain the one absolute of obedience to Jesus, if this is
really a world in which all absolutes have "died."

B. *Secular Existentialism.* The same reticence about theistic
language expressed by the thinkers just considered has been retained by others within the categories of an existential personalism or humanism. Bultmann, who shares much of the perspective just considered, argues that a general analysis of
human existence through concepts is possible, but that it only
provides knowledge of the world as a system of "objects."
However, within the moments of our concrete living existence, another kind of "non-objective" knowledge is possible.
For example, love can be analyzed in a general, objective manner, but the actual existential love between two persons is only
"known" within the encounter itself. So the reality of God is
not known through general analysis but through faith as the
existential response of obedience to the One who is met in
Christ, though never comprehended apart from the encounter
itself.

Buber argues in a similar manner, though without the Christological orientation. He refers to the I-it relationship where a
person achieves only an abstract, partial contact with the other,
and treats him as an abstract object to be manipulated and used.
The I-thou meeting, on the other hand, achieves mutuality,
wholeness and concreteness. Finally, through the vistas of these
finite I-thou relationships, man becomes aware of the Eternal
Thou, that absolute relationship in which the Eternal Other
can only be "Thou," never "it." "The extended lines of relation meet in the eternal thou." This analysis has a profound
"this-worldly" emphasis. Buber asserts that the meeting with
the Eternal Thou is the establishment of the meaning to life
which "is not that of another life, but that of this life of ours,
not one of a world yonder, but that of this world of ours, and
it desires its confirmation in this life and in relation to this
world." [62]

Both Bultmann and Buber insist on the indirect, elliptical

character of this existential knowledge of the divine. As Buber puts it, God is addressed, not expressed, for every attempt to conceptualize his reality as "thou" transforms him into an idolatrous "it." Thus Buber, in a manner similar to Bonhoeffer, warns against a false orientation toward "God" instead of the world in which authentic relation occurs:

> Meeting with God does not come to man in order that he may concern himself with God, but in order that he may confirm that there is meaning in the world. All revelation is summons and sending . . . the man who seeks God . . . instead of allowing the gift to work itself out reflects about the Giver—and misses both.[63]

C. Secular Mysticism. The linguistic reticence concerning references to God is expressed in an even more extreme form by a number of writers who develop what might be called a secular mysticism. Mysticism does not here mean the attempt to find release from the problems of this world through entrance into some higher realm of being, but rather a radical experience of the agony of using mundane language to express what cannot be said in its secular categories. A speechless awareness remains of that which cannot be directly indicated in words.

Surprisingly, some results of recent linguistic analysis have supported this mood. A rigorous account of verification, reference, and meaning shows the difficulty or impossibility of denoting "God" according to the norms of the ordinary usage of words. It is true that some analysts following the "later" Wittgenstein attempt to show contexts in which the word "God" can still be meaningfully "used." But if one adheres to the more restricted sense of meaning enunciated by the "early" Wittgenstein, the presence of the mystical remains. The early Wittgenstein declares that the "world is the totality of facts" and that "God does not reveal himself *in* the world." However, he notes: "There is indeed the inexpressible. This *shows* itself; it is the mystical."

The concluding sentence of the *Tractatus* has lent itself to a most suggestive ambiguity. Wittgenstein writes: "Whereof one cannot speak, thereof one must be silent." Most logical positivists have interpreted this to be a denial of the significance of mysticism, but in the light of the other sentence cited, an opposite understanding is also possible. Perhaps it expresses an appreciation of that which the silence expresses in a manner that speech cannot approximate.[64]

Does the "death of God" mean the death of religious word and sign? Has "God" as formulated symbol vanished so that his presence may be known in a way that is both more direct and more indirect at the same time? Is the "death of God" the call to mysticism rather than atheism? Or has the myth rather announced again the strange affinity that often appears between them?

One modern mystic—Simone Weil—calls at least some forms of atheism "a purification of the notion of God." Thus: "A method of purification: to pray to God, not only in secret so far as men are concerned, but with the thought that God does not exist." Or again: "God and the supernatural are hidden and formless in the universe. It is well that they should be hidden and nameless in the soul. Otherwise there would be a risk of having something imaginary under the name of God. . . . Christianity (Catholic and Protestant) speaks too much about holy things." A less paradoxical statement is: "I am quite sure that there is a God in the sense that I am quite sure my love is not illusory. I am quite sure that there is not a God in the sense that I am quite sure nothing real can be anything like what I am able to conceive when I pronounce this word. But that which I cannot conceive is not an illusion." [65]

Mysticism so understood has significant affinities with prophetic iconoclasm and what Tillich calls the "Protestant principle." Symbols that were originally offered as vehicles of sacred expression are now seen as idols that have substituted a finite form for the inexpressible reality. The "death of God" is the recognition that a once numinous Image exerting a powerful influence on Western civilization is itself only an "Image" and not, as Buber puts it, the One "who shines through all forms and is Himself formless," the One who is "the deep abyss out of which images arise." [66] Mysticism, atheism, and prophetic iconoclasm participate in a common task: the purgation of images, the purification of symbols, and the destruction of idols.

Frequently this radical purgation leaves the residue of one negative image or anti-image—the absence of God or the Sacred Void. Language becomes extremely paradoxical as mystical negations reveal underlying affirmations and all affirmations are subjected to purifying negations. Thus the very absence of God from the profane world becomes an allusive testimony to the reality of his presence.

Such language offends common sense and the norms of a rigorous logic. Yet many existentialists have argued that a negation can be the subject of a positive experience. For example, Sartre has an intriguing analysis about the experience of a room in which Pierre used to be encountered, but from which he is now absent. Sartre argues that Pierre's former companion now experiences not only the positive features of the room that remain, but the absence of Pierre from it.[67] Whether or not this analysis is valid from a phenomenological or linguistic point of view, it can be used as a model for a kind of mystical language used about the presence of God's absence in the world.

Such language is used in some interesting and surprising contexts. For example, in Huxley's *Brave New World* the director of the technological utopia is asked:

> "Then you think there is no God?"
> "No. I think there quite probably is one. But he manifests himself in different ways to different men. In pre-modern times he manifested himself as the being described in these books. Now . . . he manifests himself as an absence; as though he weren't there at all." [68]

From a variety of authors, similar reference is made to the Eclipse (Buber); "the nothing as the hither side of God" (Altizer); the void (Weil). Hamilton, in a curious manner, expresses himself in the same vein, even while attempting to maintain a "tough-minded" denial of God's existence. He writes: "God is dead. We are not talking about the absence of the experience of God, but about the experience of the absence of God." [69] His effort to achieve a definite clarity in his denial fails, because the latter reference to an "experience of the absence" has even more mystical overtones than the former reference to an "absence of the experience."

But if the negative awareness of the divine remains, why

should it take such a paradoxical and elusive form? Here the traditional approaches of Biblical religion, mysticism, spiritual piety, and existential personalism coalesce and converge. In the personal terms of Biblical theism, shall we speak of the absence as a deliberate withdrawal? Is it a sign of the holy displeasure over the sin of man? Or is it rather a sign of the sacred mercy and creative love? Is it true, as Simone Weil puts it, that "God could create only by hiding himself. Otherwise there would be nothing but himself"? Is the absence, then, a necessary aspect of the secular mandate? God allows himself to be edged out of the world, so that man may have room to develop his autonomous powers. Is the absence of God his gift to the necessary coming of age of his world? Or, in the language of piety and mysticism, shall we interpret the void as that "dark night of the soul," the period of thirst and testing that precedes the beatific moment of union with the divine? Or shall we, with Buber, rather say that our dehumanized relations with man and nature have created the monster of an "I-it" that, "gigantically swollen," steps in "and shuts off from us the light of heaven"?

One cause of the sense of the "absence" of God leads secular man to Nietzsche's preferred image of God's "death." It is not only the agony of language to express the inexpressible that is experienced by the contemporary mind; it is also the agony of human suffering. As Nietzsche insists, the moral God of benevolent purposes is "dead" in a world in which the pain of children and the misery of countless persons is an oppressive reality.

But in the secular mysticism we are considering, the nihilism of a futile emptiness is countered by the nihilism of a meaningful void. If God is known as an Emptiness that cannot be expressed and who, in the presence of evil, is absent, two religious responses remain for secular man. The first is the sense of secular time as the moment of waiting for the emptiness to be filled. Buber, Weil, Altizer, Hamilton, Vahanian—all, in different ways, approach the mood of T. S. Eliot's *Four Quartets:*

> I said to my soul, be still, and wait without hope
> For hope would be hope for the wrong thing; wait without love
> For love would be love of the wrong thing; there is yet faith

But the faith and the love and the hope are all in the waiting
Wait without thought, for you are not ready for thought:
So the darkness shall be the light, and the stillness the dancing.[70]

Developing this approach further in a mystical direction, Simone Weil speaks not only of "waiting," but of "fidelity *in the void.*" In the presence of evil, pain, and suffering, I am aware of the absence of God, of meaning, of fulfillment. Yet by accepting this lack and emptiness, I participate in a mystical movement of life as well as thought, whereby "The void is the supreme fullness, but man is not permitted to know it." Thus, "By redemptive suffering, God is present in extreme evil. For the absence of God is the mode of divine presence which corresponds to evil—absence which is felt. He who has not God within himself cannot feel his absence." [71]

At times the emphasis on suffering love causes the mystical sense of absence to be transformed into positive reference to a "suffering God." At this point, writers from metaphysical, mystical, and Biblical traditions converge on a common attempt to reconstruct a divine image that is a radical alternative to the "God" whom Nietzsche has declared "dead."

Nietzsche declares that the omniscient and omnipotent Creator destroys man's freedom and creativity and is incompatible with the chaotic world of suffering. In a number of twentieth-century minds has emerged a new image of the power of God that is expressed in the "weakness" of suffering love rather than the energy of dynamic force. Thus Whitehead, like Nietzsche, rejects the image of the Oriental Potentate creating and ruling the world through his overwhelming might. Whitehead finds in parts of Plato and the Galilean Jesus the strands of another theme that does not "emphasize the Ruling Caesar, or the ruthless moralist, or the unmoved mover. It dwells upon the tender elements in the world, which slowly and in quietness operate by love." God uses "persuasion," not force; he attracts rather than impels. "The power of God is the worship He inspires." Nor is this love unrelated to the tragedies and pains of life. God's life is involved in man's life, and the tragedies of lost value belong to the divine as well as the human dimension of existence. "God is the great companion—the fellow-sufferer who understands." [72]

Buber rejects, with Nietzsche, the image of the God who freezes man into an object with his "look"; this is the pseudo-divine object who appears in the I-it relationship. But in the religious I-Thou meeting, God is the Other who confirms the rich concrete selfhood of man's own being. God has enough "power" to let man be himself without absorbing him into his own identity, or destroying man's creativity by making him into the dead object of divine scrutiny.

A more ecstatic mysticism is advanced by Weil. She notes the opinion of Thucydides that every being must, by a necessity of nature, exercise all the power of which it is capable. But the "power" of God is discovered in his capacity to deny his strength; to let the world be, and to suffer with it. Weil refers to the "crucified God" and asserts that "in our being, God is torn. We are the crucifixion of God. . . . The mutual love of God and man is suffering." [73] Berdyaev writes: "We can only reconcile ourselves to the tragedy of the world because God suffers in it too." Tillich affirms: "The power of God is that he overcomes estrangement, not that he prevents it; this is the meaning of the age-old symbol of the god participating in creaturely suffering. . . ." Finally, as we have noted, Bonhoeffer, having celebrated the power and strength of the world, expresses his awareness of a corresponding "powerlessness and suffering of God." He declares: "Only a suffering God can help."

The sensitivity of Nietzsche's mind to the nuances of the contemporary outlook is revealed in his anticipation of this very theme of the "suffering God." A concern with "power," of course, dominates Nietzsche's explorations, but in Christian compassion he can find only a temptation to indulge in human weakness and mediocrity. Thus his myth combines irony with insight by suggesting that God has died of his "pity" for mankind. God and his followers experience a heightened ability to feel the pain of the world that is not overcome by a corresponding will to power. The God who must die, and the human sensibility that must die with it, is one that is driven by the agony of "pity" into the search for escape into religious heavens, metaphysical realms, "other worlds" that, because they are not this world, are "nothing."

The issues here are complex and not yet finally settled. Twentieth-century religious thought is clearly attempting to devise a theology of love that combines the truth about strength with the truth about compassion. Nietzsche offered an impressive warning about the distortions of pity alienated from strength. Perhaps he failed to recognize the distortions of power alienated from sympathy as the capacity to "suffer with." Nietzsche's myth is thus subject to two alternative interpretations: either it is the God or pity who has died to make room for autonomous man; or it is the God of worldly power who has died to make room for the strength of holy suffering.

Conclusion: The Unification of Life

Nietzsche's proclamation of the death of an "other-worldly God" has announced the dissolution of radical dualisms. The converse of this is the affirmation of a unification of life and human existence. If we agree to accept the unification of the "other world" and "this world," can this feat include a synthesis of the historic dichotomy between the sacred and the profane?

One impressive attempt to accomplish the task through a secular metaphysics has been offered by Whitehead. He demonstrates the ability of contemporary metaphysics to survive Nietzsche's knife by providing a general analysis of time, creativity, and change. Rather than the last gasp of a dying worldview that is other-worldly and static, Whitehead represents a new movement toward metaphysical thought that is this-worldly and "open" to the process of dynamic change. As far as theology is concerned, the most radical feature of Whitehead's position is his willingness to apply mundane categories directly to God. In an intriguing manner, he uses the very objection raised by Bonhoeffer and Cox against metaphysical religion as its basic justification. Bonhoeffer and Cox object to the "use" of "God" as a *deus ex machina* hypothesis that solves problems within an ontological system; Whitehead argues that the mistake of past theology has rather been to view God as "an exception to all metaphysical principles, invoked to save their collapse." He urges us instead to consider "God" as "their chief exemplification." [74]

In this manner, he seeks to show how theology can be mundane and secular and at the same time include the sacred focus of life in a general, unified perspective. Thus he points to the mutual relation of God and nature by means of their common participation in the "formative character of the actual temporal world." A major characteristic of this world is creativity or "temporal passage to novelty." Men live in "a common world of mutual adjustment, of intelligible relations, of valuations, of zest after purposes." The process of change is directed toward an increase in value that reveals the presence and power of God as a factor in that growth. "The power by which God sustains the world is the power of himself as the ideal. He adds himself to the actual ground from which every creative act takes its use. The world lives by its incarnation of God in itself." Yet God also "transcends the temporal world, because . . . He is the actual fact from which the other formative elements cannot be torn apart." [75]

Such an attempt at unification differs sharply from Nietzsche's. His radical secularism seems to imply that the unification takes place through elimination of God and of any ideal focus. If the sense of sacred orientation and ultimate meaning is excised from life, then a single profane reality remains. However, it can be argued that what Nietzsche actually accomplishes is the sacralization of the profane reality itself in its totality.

In spite of Nietzsche's rage at the thought that some day he will be pronounced "holy," the fact remains that, as Erich Heller observes,

> He is, by the very texture of his soul and mind, one of the most radically religious natures that the 19th century brought forth, but endowed with an intellect which guards, with the aggressive jealousy of a watch-dog, all the approaches to the temple.[76]

Nietzsche records, for example, the observation of the "Old Pope" to Zarathustra that "you are more pious than you believe. . . . Is it not your piety itself that no longer lets you believe in a god?" [77] But what kind of piety is possible after the "death of God"? And Nietzsche rejects the idea—which he considers Christian—that suffering is "the path to a sacred existence," by which he means an "other world." But he contrasts this rejected view with the judgment that "*existence is considered sacred enough* to justify even a tremendous amount of suffering. The tragic man affirms even the harshest suffering: he is sufficiently strong, rich, and deifying for this." [78]

It might seem that Nietzsche's goal of the "overman" contradicts his affirmation of love for the meaningless process itself. Indeed, Nietzsche argues that man seeks the "epoch" of the "condition of maximum power," and even allows for the use of the symbol "God" as the "culminating moment; life is an eternal process of deifying and undeifying." [79] This positive use of "God" in these late notes substantiates an observation made in *Zarathustra* that "in the case of the gods, *death* is always a mere prejudice." [80]

Nietzsche insists, however, that nature as an evolutionary movement does not itself have any "purpose," though man may himself choose the goal of "maximum power." *Amor fati* remains as the response to the meaningless and chaotic alternation of "deifying" and "undeifying" moments that characterize the eternal (*i.e.*, unending) succession of time. In Tillich's terminology we might say that Nietzsche has attempted to uncover a "secular depth" within the profane meaninglessness by revealing the sacredness of the meaningless itself. Tillich attempts, rather, to uncover a "depth" which reveals the meaning that informs the meaninglessness of the mundane and transforms it.

Both Buber and Tillich are concerned with the possibility of "unification" of the sacred and profane aspects of life. Buber is influenced by the Hasidic attempt to "hallow" everyday existence. He declares that "man was created for the purpose of unifying the two worlds" of the sacred and the profane.[81] Tillich considers the existence of "religion" as a special sphere among others to be evidence of a "tragic estrangement of man's spiritual life from its own ground and depth." He is impressed by the vision in the Book of Revelation where it is declared that there is "no temple in the heavenly Jerusalem," hence no special distinction between sacred and secular realms.[82]

How does this unification take place? The younger theologians advocating the death of religion are afraid of any tendency to "thwart and reverse the liberating irritant of secularization" (Cox). They do not want a sacralization that will mean an atavistic return to a religious world in which "powers" of nature or politics are deified and given an absolute authority over human life. Such a situation would be the result of a kind of sacralization, accomplished through the direct identification of the mundane phenomenon with the sacred, which, in prophetic categories, is idolatry.

But perhaps it is possible to consider a "unification" that is accomplished, not by idolatrous "identification," but by "sacramental participation." In this view, all aspects of existence are profane and yet capable of being "hallowed" without thereby becoming idols. Secularization is a necessary process whereby the relative and finite character of any particular worldly phenomenon is recognized. But sacralization is the integral complement of the same process whereby its participation in an orientation toward the sacred significance of existence is made possible.

It can be argued that this kind of dialectical sacralization is a firmer support to the positive features of secularization than is the attempt to eliminate the sacred completely. If the sacred is a necessary constituent of human life, its radical exclusion will not be possible, and the unwitting deification of some mundane phenomenon—the nation, an economic movement, etc.—will take place in spite of all strictures against it. A proper recognition of the inescapable function of the sacred in human life is the only adequate protection against the havoc caused by its fierce distortions. Consequently, Tillich counsels a "waiting" for "salvation"—i.e., the healing of the separation and the organic union (not identification) of the ultimate depth-focus of life with its surface emptiness.

The present situation is not the moment of healing, but the time in which the texture and meaning of one element—the profane—is being explored with greater fervor and energy than ever before in history. As we have seen, many of the secular theologians ask us to see this movement as the necessary development of human maturity. The partial secularization and the partial sacralization of the world that was prominent in the past may now be viewed as a transitory stage of development that can be left without regret. Yet the younger theologians must make clearer whether they differ from Tillich as radically as they sometimes suggest. Do they really envisage with religious equanimity the total profanization of the world without its corresponding sacralization as an alternate strain in the polyphony of full adulthood? Is it not true that the secular mandate must also be a profane burden to the religious heart that still aspires toward the holy center of existence?

The coming of age of mankind may be a time in which his secular maturity is a precondition for a new religious adulthood whose final shape we now can only dimly see. In all cultures, the entrance into maturity has required an "initiation" that involved suffering, pain, and courage. Perhaps the serious encounter with Nietzsche's myth is one element in this process for Western man. Thus Tillich observes that "the sacred depth in things" cannot be "approached in ordinary ways." He suggests that perhaps our initiation into this reality will be accomplished

> by accepting the void which is the destiny of our period, by accepting it as a "sacred void" which may qualify and transform thinking and action. I have not tried to present a well-balanced synthesis between religion and secular culture. I have tried to show their one theonomous root and the void which necessarily has followed their separation, and perhaps something of a longing for a new theonomy, for an ultimate concern in all our concerns.[83]

Postscript

By definition it is obvious that religious thought in transition does not stand still. An article attempting to pin down contemporary nuances in process is already behind "the times" as soon as written and hopelessly dated by the time it gets into print. Yet I hope that the issues I have noted are at least still recognizable. If I were writing the article now, the following corrections or additions of emphasis would be made.

First, I have learned that Harvey Cox does not hold to the extreme rejection of "metaphysics" and "religion" that seemed to be suggested by some of his passages in *The Secular City*. I understand that a revised edition will qualify the rejection and make clear at least some senses in which secular metaphysics and religion are compatible with the secular city.

Second, I now wish I had included some reference to the creative function that the "death of God" motif may play in the emerging dialogue between Eastern and Western religious traditions. To note only one example, the Buddhist cultivation of sunyatta or "emptiness" suggests intriguing affinities with Weil's "fidelity to the void." Altizer, of course, has been alert to this possibility and his discussions of the relation between Christian eschatology and Buddhism are one of the most interesting parts of his thought.

Third, I wish I had brought out more sharply that the resistance to "religion" by some of the younger theologians is directed against a dualism somewhat different from the two metaphysical "worlds" that I have considered. Rather the attack is against "religion" as the espousal of two life spheres within the one cultural world. One of the major concerns of thinkers like Robinson, Hamilton, and Cox is to reject the religious judgment that the secular world of technical achievement is alien to or in opposition to a sacred sphere of ultimate importance. These thinkers are calling us to a new "religious" or "Christian" style of life that is as much at ease with racing cars, television sets, and the Beatles as it is with majestic mountains, gothic cathedrals, and the music of Bach. On a deeper level, it is the question of the new style of the technical "expert" trained to solve specific problems requiring a definite "know-how" that is contrasted with the more traditional style of the theological synthesist and his general "know-why."

Still accepting metaphysics as an "o.k." form of intellectual endeavor, I have been most interested in "world-views," while these thinkers have been more concerned with "life styles" than my essay has indicated. I would still argue that the two are intimately related, but would now admit that the latter deserves more attention than I have given it. (See Cox, *The Secular City*, and William Hamilton, *The New Essence of*

Christianity, New York: Association Press, 1966). Finitude makes certain that we cannot do and say everything.

Finally, I am convinced that a part of the intellectual task involved in dealing with the "event" of secularism is the achievement of greater semantic clarity in the use of terms. In the section on the "death of religion" I make some tentative suggestions on this point. Since then I have been impressed with some recent discussions among sociologists and anthropologists which I think are very helpful. (See Charles Y. Glock and Rodney Stark, *Religion and Society*, Chicago: Rand McNally & Co., 1965, especially Chapter I; Milford E. Spiro, "Religion: Problems of Definition and Explanation," in Michael Banton, *Anthropological Approaches to Religion*, New York: Frederick A. Praeger, 1966, pp. 85–126.) Whereas my analysis suggests that the polar distinctions of sacred-profane, religious-secular, holy-mundane are almost synonyms, sharper separation between the sacred-profane pole and the religious-secular might be more useful. According to this latter approach, religion refers to an orientation toward some kind of supernatural realm containing the Gods or a Higher Reality (*e.g.*, Brahman). A secular society is one that has rejected such a supernatural orientation in any form. However, such a society is not, by definition, necessarily a profane one. It might, as when the political or national life assumes the status of an ultimate concern, exhibit the characteristics of a sacred society even while also being a predominantly secular one. As I see it, the task demanded of any further exploration of these issues is a more exact clarification of these obscure but important terms.

Notes

1. Friedrich Nietzsche, *Joyful Wisdom*, trans. Thomas Common (New York: Frederick Ungar, 1960), pp. 167–8.

2. Reference to the first and third through sixth aspects of Nietzsche's God are found in *Thus Spake Zarathustra* in *The Portable Nietzsche*, trans. Walter Kaufmann (New York: Vik-

ing, 1945), pp. 125, 198, 199, 202, 397. The second aspect is found in *Joyful Wisdom*, p. 308.

3. Mircia Eliade, *The Sacred and the Profane*, trans. Willard Trask (New York: Harcourt, Brace, 1957), p. 3.

4. George A. Morgan, *What Nietzsche Means* (New York: Harper Torchbooks, 1965), p. 50.

5. Eliade, *op. cit.*, p. 97.

6. Friedrich Nietzsche, *The Birth of Tragedy* in *The Philosophy of Nietzsche* (New York: Modern Library, n.d.), pp. 326–327.

7. Karl Jaspers, *Nietzsche*, trans. C. Wallraff and F. Schmitz (Tucson: The University of Arizona Press, 1965), p. 371.

8. *Joyful Wisdom*, pp. 307, 185.

9. Susanne Langer *Philosophy in a New Key* (New York: Signet), p. 153.

10. *Ecce Homo* in *The Philosophy of Nietzsche*, p. 18.

11. *Joyful Wisdom*, pp. 105, 151.

12. Paul Tillich, *Biblical Religion and the Search for Ultimate Reality* (London: James Nisbet, 1955).

13. Eberhard Bethge, "The Challenge of Dietrich Bonhoeffer's life and Theology," *The Chicago Theological Seminary Register*, LI (1961), 2, p. 32.

14. Dietrich Bonhoeffer, *Letters and Papers from Prison* (London: SCM Press, 1953), letters dated April 30, 1944, June 8, 1944 (hereinafter *Letters*).

15. *Letters*, pp. 91, 92, 94, 108, 116, 121.

16. Nietzsche does distinguish between an "other-worldly" metaphysics which he rejects and a more acceptable metaphysics of the temporal process itself. See Rose Pfeffer, "Eternal Recurrence in Nietzsche's Philosophy," *The Review of Metaphysics*, XIX (1965), 74, p. 282.

17. Alfred North Whitehead, *Process and Reality* (New York: Macmillan, 1929), p. 4.

18. *Joyful Wisdom*, p. 153.

19. Jean-Paul Sartre, *Words* (New York: Fawcett, 1960), pp. 156–160.

20. *Joyful Wisdom*, p. 152.

21. *Thus Spake Zarathustra*, pp. 199, 175.

22. Jean-Paul Sartre, "Existentialism Is a Humanism," *Existentialism from Dostoevsky to Sartre*, ed. Walter Kaufmann (New York: Meridian, 1957), p. 309.

23. *Letters*, pp. 93, 108, 121.

24. Paul M. van Buren, *The Secular Meaning of the Gospel* (New York: Macmillan, 1963), p. 103.

25. Harvey Cox, *The Secular City* (New York: Macmillan, 1965), p. 80.

26. *Joyful Wisdom*, p. 276.

27. *Secular City*, p. 242.

28. *Thus Spake Zarathustra*, p. 130.

29. George Santayana, *My Host the World* (New York: Scribner's, 1953), p. 29.

30. Paul Tillich, *Theology of Culture*, ed. R. Kimball (New York: Oxford University Press, 1959), p. 42.

31. Paul Tillich, "Religion and Secular Culture," *The Protestant Era*, trans. James L. Adams (Chicago: The University of Chicago Press, 1948), p. 57.

32. *Ibid.*, p. 163.

33. Paul Tillich, *Systematic Theology* (Chicago: The University of Chicago Press, 1957), II, p. 12.

34. Larry Shiner, "Toward a Theology of Secularization," *The Journal of Religion*, XLV (October 1965), 4, p. 279.

35. *Letters*, p. 109; *Secular City*, p. 80; cf. p. 20.

36. *Secular City*, p. 36.

37. *Ibid.*, Ch. I.

38. *Ibid.*, p. 73.

39. *Ibid.*, p. 74.

40. *Ibid.*, pp. 253, 258, 260–261.

41. *The Sacred and the Profane*, p. 203.

42. *Secular City*, pp. 77, 259.

43. *Process and Reality*, p. 522.

44. Martin Buber, *I and Thou*, trans. R. G. Smith (New York: Scribner's, 1958), p. 82.

45. *Secular City*, p. 260.

46. *Letters*, p. 130.

47. *Ibid.*, pp. 79–100.

48. *Ibid.*, p. 124–125.

49. *Ibid.*, p. 122.

50. *Secular City*, p. 4; William Hamilton, "The Death-of-God Theology," *The Christian Scholar*, XLVIII (Spring 1965), I, p. 48;

Thomas J. J. Altizer, *Oriental Mysticism and Biblical Eschatology* (Philadelphia: Westminster, 1961), *passim;* "Nirvana and the Kingdom of God," *New Theology,* 1, M. Marty and D. Peerman, eds. (New York: Macmillan, 1964), pp. 164, 166.

51. Thomas J. J. Altizer, "Creative Negation in Theology," *Christian Century* (July 7, 1965), p. 867.

52. Thomas J. J. Altizer, "A Theonomy in Our Time?" *The Christian Scholar,* XLVI (1963), 4, pp. 356–62.

53. Karl Barth, "The Word of God and the Task of the Ministry," *The Word of God and the Word of Man,* trans. Douglas Horton (London: Hodder and Stoughton, 1935), pp. 183–217.

54. Karl Barth, *The Epistle to the Romans,* trans. E. Hoskyns (London: Oxford University Press, 1933), pp. 40, 48.

55. Gabriel Vahanian, *Wait Without Idols* (New York: George Braziller, 1964), p. 246.

56. *Secular City,* p. 265.

57. *Letters,* p. 109.

58. *Letters,* pp. 164–165.

59. *Secular City,* p. 265.

60. William Hamilton, "The Shape of a Radical Theology," *The Christian Century* (October 6, 1965), p. 1221.

61. Van Buren, *The Secular Meaning of the Gospel,* pp. 156, 171, 198.

62. Buber, *I and Thou,* p. 75.

63. *Ibid.,* pp. 115–116.

64. Ludwig Wittgenstein, *Tractatus Logico-Philosophicus,* trans. C.K.D. (London: Routledge and Kegan Paul, 1922), 1, 6.432, 6.522, 7. See F. S. C. Northrop, *Man, Nature and God* (New York: Pocket Books, 1962), pp. 238–246 for discussion of Wittgenstein's "mysticism."

65. Simone Weil, *Gravity and Grace,* trans. A. Wells (New York: Putnam's, 1952), pp. 66, 104–105, 167.

66. Martin Buber, *The Eclipse of God* (New York: Harper Torchbooks, 1952), p. 45.

67. Jean-Paul Sartre, *Being and Nothingness,* trans. Hazel Barnes (New York: Philosophical Library, 1956), pp. 9–11.

68. Aldous Huxley, *Brave New World* (New York: Harper, 1946).

69. Hamilton, "The Death of God Theology," p. 31.

70. T. S. Eliot, "East Coker," from *The Four Quartets.*

71. Weil, *Gravity and Grace,* pp. 68, 70, 72.

72. Whitehead, *Process and Reality*, pp. 520, 532. Cf. his *Science and the Modern World* (Cambridge: at the University Press, 1929), pp. 238–239.

73. Weil, *Gravity and Grace*, pp. 55, 141.

74. Whitehead, *Process and Reality*, p. 521.

75. Alfred North Whitehead, *Religion in the Making* (New York: Macmillan, 1957), pp. 89–90, 119, 156.

76. Erich Heller, "The Importance of Nietzsche," *Encounter*, XXII (1965), 4, p. 64.

77. *Thus Spake Zarathustra*, p. 374.

78. *The Portable Nietzsche*, p. 459.

79. Friedrich Nietzsche *The Will to Power*, trans. A. Ludivici (New York: Frederick Publications, 1960), pp. 122, 181.

80. *Thus Spake Zarathustra*, p. 426.

81. Martin Buber, "The Way of Man According to the Teachings of Hasidim," *Religion from Tolstoy to Camus*, ed. W. Kaufman (New York: Harper Torchbooks, 1964), pp. 440–441.

82. Paul Tillich, *Theology of Culture*, ed. R. Kimball (New York: Oxford University Press, 1959), p. 8.

83. Tillich, "Religion and Secular Culture," p. 65.

ABOUT THE EDITOR

BERNARD MURCHLAND teaches philosophy at the
State University of New York at Buffalo. He recently
edited *Two Views of Man* and is the translator of *The
Drama of Vatican II,* by Henri Fesquet, to be published
by Random House, spring, 1967. Mr. Murchland has
translated Lepp's *The Authentic Morality* and other
books, and has written for *Commonweal, Worldview*
and other journals of opinion.

ABOUT THE CONTRIBUTORS

ROBERT ADOLFS, Prior of the Augustinian priory Mar-
ienhage in Eindhoven, The Netherlands, is the author of
The Church IS Different.

EUGENE B. BOROWITZ is Professor of Education and
Jewish Religious Thought at the Hebrew Union College-
Jewish Institute of Religion in New York City.

ROBERT McAFEE BROWN is head of the Department
of Religion at Stanford University.

JOHN B. COBB, JR., is Professor of Theology at the Southern California School of Theology in Claremont.

W. RICHARD COMSTOCK is Assistant Professor in the Department of Religious Studies at the University of California, Santa Barbara.

JOHN DUNNE, a member of the Congregation of the Holy Cross, teaches theology at the University of Notre Dame.

WILLIAM O. FENNELL, an Associate Editor of *The Canadian Journal of Theology*, teaches at Emmanuel College in Toronto.

ROGER HAZELTON is on the faculty of The Andover-Newton Theological School.

WARREN L. MOULTON is Associate Professor of Parish Ministry and Field Education at the Central Baptist Theological Seminary in Kansas City, Kansas.

DAVID MILLER is Assistant Professor of Religion at Drew University, Madison, New Jersey.

JOHN WARWICK MONTGOMERY is a Professor at Trinity Evangelical Divinity School, Deerfield, Illinois.

J. ROBERT NELSON is Professor of Systematic Theology at the Boston University School of Theology.

MICHAEL NOVAK is an Assistant Professor in the Special Program in Humanities at Stanford University.

EMERSON W. SHIDELER is Professor of Philosophy at Iowa State University.

LARRY SHINER is an Assistant Professor of Religion at Cornell College, Mount Vernon, Iowa.

F. THOMAS TROTTER is Dean and Associate Professor of Religion and the Arts at the Southern California School of Theology.

GABRIEL VAHANIAN is Professor of Religion at Syracuse University.